Crime and detection

On the 8th August, 1963, the Glasgow to Euston mail train was robbed of about two and
a half million pounds.

Substantial rewards will be paid to persons giving such information as will lead to the
apprehension and conviction of the persons responsible.

The assistance of the public is sought to trace the whereabouts of the after described persons.

...N BARTHELEMY, aged 25 years, height
...in. Last seen 16th April, 1964, wearing
... jumper with high neck and long sleeves,
...blue skirt, brown overcoat with black
...er collar and black leather calf high boots.

RONALD EDWARDS alias RONLD
CHRISTOPHER EDWARDS, also known as
"BUSTER", aged 32, florist club owner, 5ft. 6in.,
stocky build, complexion fresh, hair dark brown,
eyes brown, London accent, scar left of nose and
right forearm.

JUNE ROSE EDWARDS, née OTHERY,
aged 30, 5ft. 3in., hair black. May be accompanied
by daughter NICOLETTE, aged about 3 years.

DALY,
Ross.
...pregnant
daughter oth.
PATRICIA, aged   brown
right-of foot.

...ET O'HARA, alias BRIDIE MOORE,
...years, height 5ft. 2in. Last seen 11th
..., 1964, wearing loose-fitting grey tweed
...with herringbone pattern, three buttons,
...to coat was a scarf of the same material
...black fringe, black skirt, fawn cardigan,
...black mottled pattern blouse, either black
...underclothes.

BRUCE RICHARD REYNOLDS, alias
RAYMOND ETTRIDGE and GEORGE RACHEL,
aged 31, born London, motor and antique dealer,
...ft. 1in., complexion fresh, hair light brown,
...es grey (may be wearing horn-rimmed or rimless
spectacles), slight cleft in chin, scar left eyelid,
...eek and right forearm.

FRANCES REYNOLDS, aged about 24, 5ft. 4in.,
slim build, ...

...slim
...ight brown, eyes ...
...Driver.

£1,000 REWARD

STOLEN

ON THE 28th APRIL, 1966
FROM A HOUSE IN MELINA PLACE,
St. JOHNS WOOD, N.W.8.

SHEREE WHITE, aged 30 to 35, 5ft. 6in.,
complexion light coffee-coloured, hair dark brown.
May have 6 months old baby and be accompanied
by white miniature poodle dog called "GIGI".

Telephone WHItehall 1212 or the nearest Police Station.

...tropolitan ...est, New Scotland Yard, S.W.1.

...8th Century Diamond Spray Brooch:

...Row Graduated Pearl Necklace:

...by and Diamond Bow Brooch set

... Black Pearls:

...tique Diamond Leaf Spray B...

Crime and detection

an illustrated history from 1840

by Julian Symons | Studio Vista

Designed by Arthur Lockwood

© Julian Symons 1966

Published in 1966 by Studio Vista Limited
Blue Star House, Highgate Hill, London N19
Set and printed in 10 on 11 pt Baskerville

Distributed in Canada by General Publishing Co. Ltd
30 Lesmill Road, Don Mills, Toronto, Ontario

Made and printed in Holland by
NV Drukkerij Koch en Knuttel
Gouda, Holland

Contents

Up to 1900

IN THE BEGINNING WAS ORGANISATION

DOES CRIMINAL MAN EXIST?

20th century first half

INTO THE FINGERPRINT AGE

MURDER, SCANDAL AND CORRUPTION

THE GANGS AND THE F.B.I.

In our time

Introduction

This book tries to trace the story of crime and its detection from the beginnings of organized police work in 1829, when Sir Robert Peel's Police Act was passed, up to the present time. It is primarily a picture book in the sense that it is based upon interesting pictures, but it is not simply a picture book with captions, for every development and every interesting case is discussed in nearly 80,000 words of text.

The first problem for the compiler of such a book is to draw lines of demarcation showing what he is going to include and leave out. I have confined myself to the kind of crime that is investigated by the police. This means that espionage cases are excluded, because they are usually the province of some form of secret police. Political offences and demonstrations are omitted unless they involve crime that comes within ordinary police jurisdiction, like the cases of Sacco and Vanzetti and the Scottsboro Boys. I have not stuck rigidly to these rules. A book of this kind would be incomplete without reference to the assassinations of the Archduke Franz Ferdinand and of President Kennedy, but it would seem to me absurd to try to record every important assassination attempt in the nineteenth and twentieth centuries. I have been ruthless in some other respects, particularly in dealing with famous legal figures and famous detectives. To discuss in detail the law's connection with crime and the different legal systems in various countries would have involved too many technicalities for a picture book like this one, and it is a sad truth that nothing fades more quickly than the fame of great detectives. It would have been easy to produce a picture gallery of such detectives, but few modern readers would know their names or remember their cases. To those who remark the book's other omissions, I should like to point out that it is not an encyclopaedia, and I take comfort in the fact that nobody has yet produced a genuine encyclopaedia of crime or of detection.

Let me move from what has been left out to what is included. You will find here an account of the principal developments in criminal investigation from the year of Peel's Act to the present time, and fascinating they are, or so I have found them. I had not fully realized before compiling this book how greatly any police force depends for success upon efficient organization. The great detective in modern times has justified the adjective by his knowledge of crooks and gangs, his intuitive sense of a suspect's truthfulness or dishonesty, and half a dozen other qualities, but (this is something most detectives will admit) it is the administrative and scientific organization behind him that brings quick success in solving crimes. That is why this book is concerned with Bertillon's anthropometric system, the uses of photography, the discovery that fingerprints are unique and that bullets may have unique characteristics too, the immense improvement in police record systems and the latest equipment for analysing blood, fibres and hair, rather than with individual feats of detection. There can be no doubt at all that police forces in almost every country have become more effective during this century, and this is primarily because they have come to terms with science and are prepared to use it. Organization plus modern equipment plus able, honest men are what make a good police force, and the first two of these are as important as the third.

Police organization has improved, but in almost every country crime increases. This is partly because in the West we live in a permissive society which accepts crime and tries to understand rather than to outlaw it, partly because criminals have kept pace with the police in their awareness of modern techniques. Or perhaps they haven't quite kept pace. It is a cliché that all crooks wear gloves nowadays because they know about fingerprints, but as the Great Train Robbery shows this assumption is not always true even of professional crooks. Society's best defence against professional criminals is their incapacity to organize themselves. The experience of Chicago in Prohibition years shows what can happen when a city has a partially corrupt administration and police force and is confronted by criminals with even the modest talent for organization shown by Johnny Torrio and Al Capone. Criminals to-day make use of many modern tools, but society has one great advantage over them. They do not trust each other.

I have tried to avoid turning the criminal side of the book into an anthology of famous cases, and to show several aspects of criminal activity – robbery, fraud, forgery, counterfeiting – but I have had to face the fact that most crime is dull and most criminals are stupid. A fraud carried out on the scale of a Philip Musica, the crook who as F. Donald Coster became the head of a famous drug firm, is fascinating, and so is a badger game like that practised on 'Mr A', the nephew of an Indian Prince. Both Philip Musica and 'Mr A' find a place here. But the ordinary badger game practitioner or con man is a half-smart petty crook of little interest to anybody, not even to himself.

The exception to this rule is the crime of murder. Does murder interest us so much because it is the final act, a barrier between 'civilized' and 'primitive' man that we feel must never be crossed? And is it for this reason that murderers are often treated so much more harshly than criminals whose acts may exceed those of murderers in their atrocity? The amount of space given to murder in this book is a mark of my own interest in the crime, its origins and its consequences. There are cases here that everybody will know. 'Brides in the Bath' Smith, Ruth Snyder and Judd Gray and Dr Crippen may stand for many more. There is a selection of the mass murders and killing of children by psychopaths that raise a cry for the carrying out of the death penalty or the use of flogging. There are *cause célèbres*, like Oscar Slater, Caryl Chessman, the Rosenbergs – who are included because of the international interest in their story, and because it posed so sharply the question of capital punishment. There are bizarre cases famous in their own countries but not outside them, like the story of Robert James the 'Rattlesnake Murderer'. And still many famous cases, in Britain, the United States and France particularly, have been left out either because there was little interesting pictorial material to illustrate them or because they were too complicated to describe in the space at my disposal. It is my consolation that some of the pictures, and some of the cases, may come freshly even to connoisseurs of crime.

Julian Symons

Acknowledgments

The contents of this book reflect to a certain extent the generous help given to me by police authorities in some countries and cities, the unwillingness to co-operate shown by others. In the United States I owe a debt to the New York Police Department, who provided a number of pictures from their archives and also allowed photographs to be taken of some rare items in the New York Police Museum. The Police Departments of Chicago, San Francisco and Los Angeles readily responded to my requests for pictures and information, and the Federal Bureau of Investigation sent a large collection of prints illustrating their activities. The staff of the New York Public Library were patient and helpful in looking out material.

In Canada I must thank especially Staff Superintendent Charles W. Wood of the Ontario Police and Mr H. J. Funk of their Attorney-General's Laboratory, who showed much interest in the book and gave me a great deal of material, some of which unfortunately arrived too late for inclusion. The New Zea-land police authorities at Wellington gave me a history of the force and also supplied me with photographs. Mr Hugh J. Murphy of the News and Information Bureau at Australia House in London made helpful suggestions, and so did the Mitchell Library in Sydney. The Indian and Pakistan High Commissioners' Offices both obtained material for me.

All of the news agencies I approached were helpful, but some need particular mention. In New York Mr Maurice Davey and Mr Nat Andriadis of U.P.I. were unwearying in searching out material from the recent and distant past. Few requests baffled them (although, like other agencies, they were unable to provide me with prints from Communist countries) and none ruffled their patience. In London Miss Figgis of Express Features, Mr A. Adams of Mirrorpic and Mr H. E. Bray of the London Electrotype Agency were especially helpful.

And so to individuals. I must mention first Mr and Mrs Thomas M. McDade, who not only gave me hospitality but also let me loose on the great mass of criminal material accumulated in, appropriately enough, the cellar of their house. Thomas McDade has turned from the pursuit of criminals as an F.B.I. agent to the bibliographical study of their activities, and he is probably America's foremost collector in this field of books and pamphlets relating to the nineteenth century. Several of the most interesting early prints here come from his collection. Mr Roger Butterfield made helpful suggestions, in particular about possible sources of information. Mr D. Graham, Superintendent Radiographer of the Victoria Infirmary, Glasgow, kindly gave me details of the remarkable experimental work he and Mr Gray have carried out on fingerprints. Mr Terry Mead, of the *Sunday Times,* made many helpful suggestions about possible picture sources.

A key to the abbreviations used for some picture sources is set out below. Other sources are listed without abbreviation.

ACL	A.C.L. Bruxelles
AP	Associated Press
BM	British Museum
CP	Culver Pictures
FBI	Federal Bureau of Investigation
ILN	Illustrated London News
LEA	London Electrotype Agency
NYCMPB	New York City Missing Persons Bureau
NYPD	New York Police Department
NYPL	New York Public Library
NYPM	New York Police Museum
NZPD	New Zealand Police Department
RTHPL	Radio Times Hulton Picture Library
SFPD	San Francisco Police Department
UPI	United Press International

Up to 1900

IN THE BEGINNING WAS ORGANIZATION

The Peelers

An organized police force began to take shape in England when Sir Robert Peel's Police Bill received the Royal Assent in June 1829. Before then, law enforcement had been in the hands of magistrates and watchmen, and its operation had been haphazard. Some magistrates were efficient and honest public servants, like Sir John Fielding at Bow Street, who established the Bow-Street Runners. Other magistrates were both corrupt and lazy. In any case, since watchmen often received only eight pence a night, and other thief-takers were paid by results, there were obvious temptations, as Sir John himself put it, 'to prostitute the useful employment of a thief-taker to the procuring of both public and private rewards, at the shameful and shocking price of innocent blood'.

The Peelers or Bobbies (both slang phrases derived from Peel's name) were designed to change all that, and to check the immense increase of crime in London. They were a purely metropolitan force, and they were the first English policemen to be employed full time at a regular wage, from £50 a year for a constable to £200 for a Superintendent. They were given a uniform of blue cloth, with black chimney-pot hat. A high collar, with a stock fastened by a buckle, made it almost impossible for the Peeler to turn his head. He carried a rattle to call for help (replaced in 1880 by a whistle) and a baton marked 'Police Officer', and he was also equipped with a striped armlet to wear as an indication that he was on duty. Education was not considered necessary, and about a third of the original force of 3000 men were unskilled labourers. Among the rest, previous occupations ranged from bakers to blacksmiths. Many proved totally unsuitable to act as policemen, and the turnover of men was rapid. In the first eight years 5000 men were dismissed and another 6000 resigned.

From the beginning, the force which Peel's courage and vision had created was a success. It was housed first at Whitehall Place adjoining Great Scotland Yard, or as it soon became known simply Scotland Yard, and then in the eighteen-eighties it moved to a new building at the Parliament end of Whitehall which was confusingly known as New Scotland Yard – confusingly because a street called 'Great Scotland Yard' still exists in Whitehall, now quite unconnected with police work. For twenty-one years the force had two joint Commissioners, Richard Mayne and Colonel Charles Rowan, and it was thanks largely to their disciplinarianism that the Metropolitan Police Force took a distinct and decent shape. The Peelers were not detectives, and a separate Detective Office was not established until the eighteen-forties. Their primary duty, as laid down by Peel himself, was the prevention of crime. 'To this great end every effort of the police is to be directed. The security of person and property, the preservation of public tranquillity and all the other objects of a Police Establishment will thus be better effected than by the detection and punishment of the offender after he has committed the crime.'

Pious words: but they checked the great spate of drunkards and prostitutes brought in at first by triumphant Peelers under the impression that arrests were the only important thing. Within a year or two the vigilance of the Peelers had driven many criminals out of London. They went to the provinces, to such places as Hull, where 39 officers looked after the welfare of 36,000 inhabitants on the old principle of 'no prisoner, no pay', or to Liverpool, where 240,000 townspeople had no police body at all except a few elderly night watchmen. Slowly the English counties and boroughs abandoned their systems of parish constables and night watchmen and began, often reluctantly, to organize their own police forces. They insisted on retaining much local power, a fact which led to confusion and inefficiency. By the end of the nineteenth century the whole of the British Isles was covered by a network of local police forces who referred back in some matters, but not by any means all, to the Metropolitan Police Force at New Scotland Yard.

Charles Pierce. In 1850 he was the last survivor of the original 'Peelers'
RTHPL

Sir Robert Peel   *RTHPL*

Tom Smith, a well-known London policeman of the 1850s
RTHPL

Boys in the Snow, by John Leech, about 1860. 'I spy blue, I spy black, I spy a peeler in a shiny hat'   *RTHPL*

13

The public don't love them

Peel's courageous action as Home Secretary was a slap in the face for English dislike of authority, especially authority wearing a uniform. The police were given uncomplimentary names, like 'blue devils' and 'raw lobsters'. They were called 'crushers' and 'coppers' because of their alleged beating of suspects. The elementary drill they were given led to the suspicion that they would be used as a para-military force to subdue the people, and it was even said that they were the backbone of an army designed to put the Duke of Wellington on the throne. Cruickshank's cartoon shows the common feeling that the police would interfere with individual liberty, and soldiers for their part resented the fact that civilians were allowed to arrest men in Army uniform. Peel himself was subjected to much personal abuse.

Anger against the police force ranged from the Tory swells of St James's, some of whom were summoned for their refusal to pay the Police Rate, to the complaints made by several varieties of Radicals. One complaint, made in the eighteen-thirties, was against the wearing of plain clothes (or as they were then called coloured clothes) by a Sergeant arresting three thieves. The Radicals said that this was un-English, and when the Reform Bill was under discussion a handbill appeared saying that men should come armed to meetings because 'we assure you from ocular evidence that 6000 cutlasses have been removed from the Tower, for the use of Peel's bloody gang' The feeling of the people about the police at this time

– I confess, it is my nature's plague to spy into abuses; and oft, my jealousy shapes faults that are not *Othello*

The Common Informer

is shown by the fact that when P.C. Culley was stabbed to death while helping to disperse the crowd at a political meeting, the jury brought in a verdict of 'justifiable homicide'. They were escorted home by torchlight, and later given medals. A decade later there were bitter complaints about police interference with Chartist meetings, although generally this was no more than was necessary to keep the peace.

The strength of this feeling was slowly dissipated, but it never disappeared. Many radicals in Britain

'Do you know your street door is open?' by George Cruickshank
RTHPL

'Distwessing – Vewy' *Punch*
X. 42. 'Did you call the police; sir?' *Swell (who would perish rather than disturb his shirt collar.)* 'Ya-as, a-i've had the misfortune to dwop my umbrellaw, and there isn't a boy within a mile to pick it up – a – will you have the goodness?'

Police wear beards *RTHPL*

today dislike certain aspects of police authority, including the way in which they sit in judgement on complaints involving police officers – whereas, for instance, New York has recently appointed civilians to a Review Board. They dislike also the close linking of policeman and paid informer, which is common throughout Europe. It seems likely that the British police are still among the most honest and least violent in the world, yet there are constant stories about police brutality and corruption. The

citizen's attitude to the police reflects the nature of his society. Hated and feared in the violent days of their birth, the organized police force had become regarded by the eighteen-eighties as a bulwark to defend the life and property of respectable Victorians against the criminal and lawless lower classes. In our time, when all social values are questioned, the integrity of the police as a body and their possible use as an arm of the state (in the case of a nuclear war, for instance) is under discussion again.

Police at a Chartist meeting in the 1840s

New Scotland Yard in the 1880s:
The Commissioner's Office
View from the River

15

France, Russia and the great Vidocq

The development of police forces elsewhere in Europe was largely ordered by their identification with the state. In France a Lieutenant of Police was given office in 1667, and although of course it was his function to suppress crime, he was also a political figure of considerable importance, charged with caring for state prisoners. Fouché, Napoleon's chief of police, set up an organization of spies and informers, both in France and elsewhere, unexampled both in its thoroughness and in the care with which it was administered. But a police minister like Fouché can exist only under an authoritarian regime. The powers he exerts, like those of a Himmler or a Beria, are intolerable to any democratic government.

In 1817 a former convict named Eugène Vidocq, who had been working for some time as a police spy, was given the job of forming a small Brigade de Sûreté. These detectives were mostly former criminals like Vidocq himself, and their number increased from four to an eventual twenty-eight. They were paid by results, and the results were spectacular. They effected more than 750 arrests within a year of their establishment. It was sometimes suggested that Vidocq and his agents committed the crimes for which they afterwards discovered culprits, but this was never proved. By his own account Vidocq was a master of disguise, was never worsted in a fight and rarely refused by a woman. He always went heavily armed, and had no hesitation in wounding or even killing a criminal. After ten lucrative years he resigned, and became a very successful private detective.

Such was the first chief of the Sûreté. He was succeeded by an ex-housebreaker named Coco-Latour, who also made a large number of successful arrests, but from the eighteen-thirties onwards the Sûreté was in respectable hands. The Sûreté Nationale, as it became, moved in the last quarter of the nineteenth century to the Quai des Orfèvres, where it is still housed. French nineteenth-century detectives had the reputation of possessing great perseverance and ingenuity, although they were regarded as less methodical than their English counterparts. Like London, Paris had and retains its own police force, the Prefecture of Police.

Elsewhere in Europe police forces were limited by national development – thus, even after Germany had become a unified country individual police forces operated in the various states, and in fact continue to do so. Undoubtedly the most famous force outside Britain and France at this time was that of Russia. Infamous would perhaps be a better word than famous. George Augustus Sala, who was robbed four times within a month in St Petersburg during the eighteen fifties, wrote that:

> As grandmasters of the art and mystery of villainy, as proficients in lying, stealing, cruelty, rapacity, and impudence, I will back the Russian police against the whole world of knavery

Semi-apocryphal stories about their corruption were legion. A typical one tells of a nobleman who lost some silver and plate, saw his property in a pawnbroker's shop, submitted his plate-chest with the rest of his silver in it to the police to prove his claim, and never saw it again. Certainly the Russian police were brutish and ignorant beyond the ordinary. General Baranoff, head of the police in 1881, found to his dismay that many of his men could not sign their own names. The force was divided into the regular police, operating chiefly in the provinces, who were armed, mounted and reasonably paid, and the far more important Third Section, which was charged with the suppression of all political opposition – a task in which it was far from successful, in spite of the almost absolute authority it enjoyed under a succession of absolute monarchs. Even the local policeman was often savagely authoritarian. Vera Zassulich tells in her Memoirs of a visit made by a village policeman to a seamstress's hut, in the company of the tax collector. The seamstress was told that her tax payments were in arrears, and then the policeman and the tax-collector wrecked the hut, smashing up the stove, breaking the crockery and taking off the woman's horse and cow to be sold.

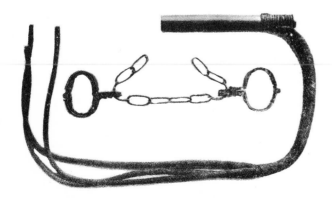

Whip and manacles used in Russian prisons

Prefecture of Police, St Petersburg, late 19th century

Paris Police vans, late 19th century

Entrance to Paris prison of La Grande Roquette

Vidocq

Paris Morgue, about 1850

17

America: a little police history

The beginnings of police forces in the United States are linked with big cities, and they are both varied and confused. The great distances between places, the constantly changing flux of the population, and an unwillingness to give more power to the police than had been possessed by night watchmen, combined to make growth uneven.

In New York Jacob Hays was appointed High Constable in 1802, and gathered round him a group of tough law enforcers who were hardly police as we understand the word. The Leatherheads, so called from their hats, appeared in 1827, carrying great 33-inch clubs to deal with rowdies. In New York, as in most of the country, the police system consisted of a night watch, with a separate watch for day service. This extraordinary arrangement caused a great deal of friction, and in 1844 the city of New York sensibly consolidated the two. In the following year the first chief of police, George Washington Matsell, was appointed, and the Star Police, who wore an eight-pointed copper badge, came into being. The name 'copper' or 'cop' has become permanent. A few years later Brooklyn and New York were co-ordinated under the same police authority, and other cities, including Boston, New Orleans and Baltimore followed suit in extending police boundaries,

George Washington Matsell, first chief of police in New York *NYHS*

New York police, an early photograph   *NYPL*

although within a few years some of them moved back towards a purely municipal force.

In Chicago a police department was established in 1855, and three years later they were given an official uniform consisting of a short blue frock coat, a gold-banded blue cap and a brass star. Chicago's first detective force was created in 1861. New York had had what may by courtesy be called a detective squad a quarter of a century earlier, although their prime function was to keep order. A Detective Bureau was created in 1882.

Elsewhere the growth of police forces followed the growth of cities. In San Francisco a City Marshal was appointed in 1849, but his force of twelve men was quite unable to contain such gangs as the Hounds, who met in a tent which they called Tammany Hall. In 1851 a Vigilance Committee was formed, and an organized police force eventually sprang from this body – one of their leaders was the city's first chief of police. In the eighteen-sixties a system of military drill was introduced, and the police began to wear uniforms. In Los Angeles, which grew more slowly, a six-man paid city police department came into being in 1869. Eight years later uniforms were commissioned.

These and other American police forces did not ignore technical innovations. The New York force used telegraphy from its beginnings in 1845; the San Francisco Police Department was the first in the

The shooting of crusading editor James King in San Francisco by James P. Casey, a member of the city's Board of Supervisors in 1856. The shooting led to the formation of a Vigilance Committee which practically took over the function of keeping order in the city *SFPD*

country, and one of the first in the world, to use photography; patrol wagons and telephone communication systems were instituted in many cities during the eighteen-eighties. But American police forces were bedevilled from the start by the power and influence of dishonest politicians. Whereas in Britain police forces were kept almost completely clear of national and local politics, in the United States the Mayor often disposed unscrupulously of an enormous amount of patronage.

Telegraph instrument used for communication between police headquarters and station houses from 1847 to 1893 *NYPD*

Patrol wagon of the 1880s *NYPL*

Native policeman, Cape Town

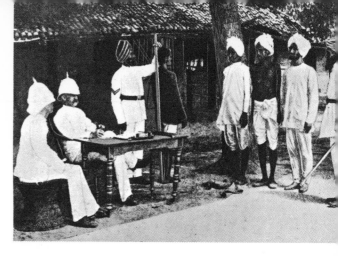

Measuring a recruit for the Indian Police

In all sorts of uniforms

In British colonies the police systems were generally under the jurisdiction of British officers, but they retained many local features. In Australia a body of mounted police was formed in 1825 on the direction of Governor Brisbane of New South Wales. They were smartly dressed in semi-military fashion, and carried sabre, carbine and horse pistols. They were supposed to maintain order and to capture bushrangers, and not until 1862 was a central police organization set up in Sydney. The black native trackers, who were capable of distinguishing the foot tracks of wallaby and wombat, achieved apparent miracles as they led the white police in pursuit of criminals. The trackers were often able not merely to follow the wanted men, but to give an amazingly precise account of their actions on the trail. In Canada the North-West Mounted Police, established in 1873 and charged with keeping order over

thousands of square miles, soon became a romantic legend. Their equipment issue was military, from scarlet serge tunic and forage cap to button stick, and they would have been surprised to be called policemen. They were armed with revolvers and Winchester repeating carbines.

One great distinction between British and American police on one hand, and almost all other police systems on the other, was that elsewhere most of the policemen were ex-soldiers. An American writer put it succinctly: 'In England the police are civil employees whose primary duty is the preservation of public security. On the Continent, on the other hand, the police force is the right arm of the ruling classes.' The Turkish policemen shown here bayoneted and beat to death in the courtyard of the Police Station the prisoners they captured after anti-Government riots had been suppressed.

Australian native tracker. They normally followed a trail on horseback

Police official in China   *RTHPL*

Egyptian gendarme   *RTHPL*

Havana policeman, 1899   *NYPL*

Turkish police outside the Central Police Station, Stamboul, 1895   *NYPL*

A John Leech cartoon that makes an ironical comment on the idea of employing women police   *Punch*

'Bull's Eye on Bobby'
Mr Bull *(takes Policeman's lantern)*. 'Thank you. I'll just have a look round myself. Strikes me the premises ain't as clean as they might be!'

The River Police at work, rescuing a would-be suicide, and charging a man at the station. They operated independently until 1839, when they were merged with the Metropolitan Police. Rowing and sailing boats were used until 1885, when steam launches were introduced.

The Black Maria, 1887   *RTHPL*

Really, policemen (most of them) are wonderful

Well before the turn of the century the police in Britain had been transformed from 'Peel's bloody gang' into the protectors of respectable society. There had been a disconcerting affair in the eighteen-seventies when Superintendent Frederick Williamson, head of the Detective Department, discovered that two of his four Chief-Inspectors, William Palmer and Nat Druscovich, and one Inspector, John Meiklejohn, had been taking bribes from a gang of racing swindlers. Another Chief-Inspector was tried, and was lucky to be acquitted. John Bull's feelings were expressed in the *Punch* cartoon on the opposite page. The Detective Department was thoroughly combed out and reorganized, with two new Chief-Inspectors and twenty new Inspectors, and in 1878 was renamed the Criminal Investigation Department. When this had been done, and a Director had been appointed from outside police ranks, it was felt that corruption had been rooted out. The London bobby (he was no longer called a Peeler) was everybody's friend.

In America the situation was different. European visitors were impressed by the thorough organization of police work in the big cities, 'so perfect, so symmetrical, so accurately planned', but appalled at the often slovenly and sometimes obviously vicious character of the police themselves. In the last decade of the century nemesis came to Inspector Byrnes. He was involved in the scandal brought to light by a Presbyterian Minister, who attacked the New York police for their complicity in the carrying-on of brothels and gambling houses. Everybody knew that rackets went on in New York, that policemen, lawyers and judges worked hand in hand with the political bosses of Tammany Hall, but Byrnes was America's most famous detective, and it was a shock that he should be accused. The case against Byrnes was not pushed home, although he never explained how he had amassed a fortune of nearly $500,000. New Yorkers took what comfort they could from watching the police at their yearly parade, thinking they looked a fine body of men.

New York annual police parade, 1899 *NYPL*

The march of science: photography

The early detectives were rough and ready men, sharp-witted, intelligent and often able to smell a crook a mile away, but generally of little education and contemptuous of scientific aids in finding a criminal. Conan Doyle's Inspector Lestrade seems to us a caricature, but in reality he was typical of the hard-headed policeman of his age, energetic and persevering in pursuing pickpockets and house-breakers but ill-equipped to deal with more complex crimes.

The uses of photography, however, were plain even to a detective on the Lestrade level. If you had a picture of your man then he could be identified when he turned up again. Criminals also realized this elementary fact, and many of them objected strongly to the photographic process. So a good many photographs were collected in police departments all over the world, but then the problem arose: what was to be done with the constantly growing and un-manageable pile of them? It was in relation to photography that many police departments faced for the first time the need for classification. How was this to be done?

At first photographs were classified by crimes, so that a man who had been robbed on the highway was shown pictures of highwaymen, but as photographs accumulated this became a lengthy business. A breakdown was made of crimes by methods used, and this proved much more satisfactory. It would be difficult to exaggerate the stupidity of most criminals. They may work their particular line with a fair degree of skill, but they are incurably repetitious, so that a racecourse pickpocket will never operate anywhere else. Sir Henry Smith, a Commissioner of the City of London Police, noted this fact ironically:

Criminals, if they will pardon me for saying so, show a strange want of originality. With strange stupidity the omnibus thief frequents the same line of omnibuses, returns to the same streets, and steals the same articles. In the higher walks of the profession these peculiarities are still more striking. The bank robber and the forger are fascinated by their own style of business. They never have an idea in their heads beyond bank robbery and forgery.

Photographing a criminal, New York. Inspector Byrnes is shown standing on the left of the picture *RTHPL*

24

These criminal habits extend even to a personal mode of operation, so that some housebreakers always pay a preliminary call posing as a salesman, others invariably use a jemmy on the kitchen window, and so on.

By the end of the century many police departments had moved well beyond a simple crime methods index. In Berlin, Vienna, and other German and Austrian cities, much more sophisticated cross-reference systems were being established. In one of them criminals were arranged according to height as well as crime, so that the category of housebreakers might be sub-divided into those who carried guns, used flashlights, always forced back doors, etc., with further sub-division by height. A witness able to say that a burglar was between five foot three and five foot six would be shown first the file corresponding to these heights together with any other characteristics noted. Often it was the right file. The virtues of organization were apparent. It was also becoming plain to the administrators of police systems that the higher the degree of co-operation between one police department and another, the more chance there was of catching an elusive criminal.

One of the first British police photographs (and a very bad one), taken in Glasgow, in 1865   *RTHPL*

A murderer, Pat Sheehan, sits for his portrait at the Pinkerton agency   *NYPL*

A prisoner being photographed in Siberia   *NYPL*

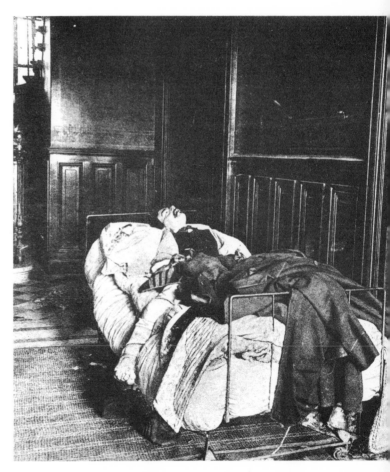

Photographing a corpse. Taken in the 1880s by Alphonse Bertillon

25

Bloodhounds, bicycles and handcuffs

The idea of using dogs for intimidating criminals was favoured much more in Germany, France and Belgium than in Britain. 'Their presence has a strong moral effect, and bad characters avoid towns where police dogs are kept', said the German Police Gazette, and the Belgian town of Ghent at one time had sixty-nine dogs on duty. As the Ghent chief of police wrote to the mayor, if a burglar jumped over a wall or swam across a river a dog could catch him easily, whereas a policeman 'would be hampered by his heavy uniform, and perhaps he could not swim'. These dogs were not used for tracking, but for service work with the police. They were specially trained to be savage and suspicious. In France various cross-breeds were used, in Germany Doberman Pinschers were much favoured, and in England such service dogs were generally Airedales.

The use of dogs as trackers was common in Canada and the United States, where a black-and-white Southern foxhound was much favoured, and attempts were made to develop bloodhounds for tracking in England and elsewhere. They had their triumphs – the Turkish Sultan Abdul Hamid was greatly impressed by the way in which bloodhounds and collies discovered soldiers who had been hidden in various parts of his palace grounds – but their uses proved extremely limited. It was essential that they should be on the scene while the scent was fresh, that police officers should not touch anything left by the criminal, and that other confusing cross-scents should be avoided. Dog patrols exist to-day in many cities – San Francisco inaugurated one in 1962 and have had great success with it – but scientific developments have largely superseded the use of tracker dogs.

Some police were mounted on bicycles from an early stage in the machine's existence. In 1879 Coventry put its police officers on locally-manufactured tricycles. The *Daily News* facetiously remarked that 'a defaulting debtor pursued by a constable mounted on a tricycle, and armed with a summons,

sounds more like a horrible dream than a probable reality'. By the end of the century, however, many forces had their bicycle squads. The horse was still much used, and superintendents in English county forces preferred to drive about in dog carts.

The number of handcuffs and leg-irons was legion. In the United States every state, and indeed every county, had particular preferences, and orders were placed through publications like *The Detective*. In Britain there was a regulation handcuff with a snap lock, but it was by no means universal. A pair of cuffs called the 'Snips' was often used, which operated on a central pivot that could be twisted by the constable to subdue his prisoner. In America, besides the cuffs and irons shown here, there was a combination cuff and leg-iron joined by a chain, and in France a 'letter lock' existed which could only be opened by operating the right code numbers. In Russia locks were both complicated and brutal. Murderers wore heavy leg-irons, which were not locked but rivetted to their ankles.

Tracking with bloodhounds in Epping Forest   *RTHPL*

Some of New York's bicycle policemen in the 1890s *NYPL*

ᴛʜᴇ Detective PUBLISHING CO., Inc.
1029 S. Wabash Avenue, CHICAGO, ILL.

TELEPHONE 1465 HARRISON   D. M. LA BOISSIERE, President.   CHAS. T. BRYAN, Vice-President.   ESTABLISHED 18

Reproduction of Gold Medal Awarded The Detective Publishing Company at the Louisiana Purchase Exposition at St. Louis, Mo., in 1904. Also received Gold Medal Award at the Jamestown Ter-Centenial Exposition, Norfolk, Va., in 1907. Both being for best and largest exhibit of Police and Sheriffs Equipment, and Bertillion and Finger Print Systems of identification, etc.

Manufacturers, Wholesale and Retail Dealers of all kinds of Equipment for Police, Sheriffs, Detectives, Penitentiaries, Reformatories, Jails, Asylums, City Marshals, Deputy Sheriffs, Constables and Peace Officers

PUBLISHERS OF ᴛʜᴇ Detective

OFFICIAL JOURNAL OF POLICE, SHERIFFS, AND ALL CLASSES OF PEACE OFFICERS, ETC.

In ordering goods, give name of each article and number, and also state if goods are to be charged to city, county, state, firm or individual

Remittances should be made by Chicago or New York Draft, Postal or Express Money Order, Registered Letter, City, County or State Checks, Orders or Warrants, payable to The Detective Publishing Co., Chicago, Ill., U.S.A.

=== **ALL GOODS GUARANTEED** ===

PEERLESS HANDCUFF.

Weight, 12 ounces.
Nickel plated or blue steel.. $10.00

No. 200
Tower Double Lock Hand Cuffs

Plated, $9.00   Polished, $8.00

No. 201
Tower Light Detective Hand Cuffs

Plated, $9.00   Polished, $8.00

No. 202
Tower Double Lock Hand Cuffs For 3 Hands

Plated, $11.00   Polished, $10.50

No. 203
Maltby Double Lock Detective Handcuffs

Plated only $7.00

No. 204
Chain Hand Cuffs, Detachable Comealong

Plated only $4.75

LEATHER HANDCUFF AND LEG IRON POCKETS.
Convenient to carry every day or on journey—prevents rusting. Strong and neat leather pockets for any style of handcuffs or leg irons. Write for prices.

No. 206
Mattatuck Double Lock Hand Cuffs

Plated only $6.00

No. 210
Bean's Giant Hand Cuffs

No. 211
Bean's Improved Hand Cuffs

Plated, $6.00   Polished, $5.00

No. 212
Tower Double Lock Bar Cuffs

Plated, $8.30   Polished, $6.80

Tower's Bean Handcuffs

Plated, $6.00   Polished, $5.00

No. 213
Five-Foot Chain and Ring

with Peerless cuff $7.50
with any other style of handcuff $6.50

No. 214
Oregon Boot or Leininger Shackle

11 lbs. Plated only $15.50
15 lbs. Plated only 16.40
Extra Key for Oregon Boot .. 1 00

No. 217
Mattatuck Legirons

Plated only $10.00

No. 220
Tower Double Lock Legirons

Plated, $11.30   Polished, $10.00

No. 222
Bean's Improved Legirons

Plated, $8.00   Polished, $7.00
Extra Keys for all Legirons..... .25

Spike Clog Shackle

Complete with Lock... .... $7.00
Extra Key Spike—Clog Shackle .75

Ball, Chain and Legirons
Any Style of Legiron

	Single		Pairs
12 lbs.	$10.30		$14.30
15 lbs.	10.75		14.75
18 lbs.	11.20		15.20
22 lbs.	11.80		15.80
25 lbs.	12.25		16.05
28 lbs.	12.70		16.70
32 lbs.	13.30		17.30
40 lbs.	14.50		18.50
50 lbs.	16.00		20.00

In ordering state distinctly whether wanted with single Legiron like cut shown above or with pair of Legirons.

TWISTER HOLDER

Designed to hang from suspender button. Released by quick pull. Out of sight.................. 25c

CHAIN TWISTERS.

The Improved Twister $1.00

Grooved Twisters $1.00

Plain Twister $1.00

Ball Twister $1.00

Leather cases for Peerless Handcuffs 2.50
Extra keys for Handcuffs and Legirons .... .25

NIPPERS OR COMEALONGS.

Phillips Nipper $1.50

PARTIALLY OPEN

Thomas Nipper $2.75

CELL PAILS

For Prisons, Police Stations, Hospitals, etc.

Porcelain Lined   Indurated Fibre
No. 224, $5.00 each   Prices on application

Bean's Sole Leather Clubs

8-inch with swivel............. $3.65
10-inch with swivel............. 4.00
12-inch with swivel............. 4.60
14-inch with swivel............. 5.25
16-inch with swivel............. 6.40

An advertisement supplement to the American official magazine *The Detective*, in the 1890s   *McDade Collection*

Prisons: separate or silent?

The great prison argument of the period was whether prisoners should be kept in confinement under the 'Separate System' or the 'Silent System'. Both had their beginnings in the United States. The separate system was put into effect in Philadelphia. Every prisoner was locked into his cell and had no communication with any other prisoner during the whole term of his sentence. The idea was that such separations would make the prisoners better men, and the Inspectors of the Eastern Penitentiary reported in modest self-congratulation in 1830: 'This mode of punishment, bearing as it does with great severity upon the hardened and impenitent felon, is eminently calculated to break down his obdurate spirit.' The advocates of the 'Silent System' thought such Philadelphian views inhumane. *Their* solution, exemplified in the practice of Auburn prison in New York State, was to keep the prisoner alone in his cell at night, but to permit him to work by day in association with others under the rigidly-enforced condition of total silence.

Charles Dickens, when he visited America in 1842, condemned the Philadelphia system, but was much impressed by Auburn. Delegates from England, France, Germany and Belgium came, saw, and were conquered – by the Separate System. In England Lord John Russell ordered the building of a model prison where the Separate System could be tried. This was Pentonville, completed in 1842. The prisoners were isolated, and even masked to avoid recognition. After five years a Commission reported on the results, and found them excellent. Complete separation, they said, was the only sound basis for 'a reformatory discipline'.

Such arguments, and the inhumanities to which they led, would seem incredible if they were not overwhelmingly documented. In America the Silent System triumphed, although the Separate System was tried for a time in a few states. The association of prisoners was used at first to increase the severity of punishment, but by the end of the century some prisons had accepted the idea that the men inside their walls might make something useful, like clothes and footwear. In Britain the adoption of the Separate System in most prisons led directly to sentences of penal servitude. Where the Silent System was in use it frequently provided an excuse for perpetrating appalling cruelties. The exposure of conditions in Birmingham prison made through Charles Reade's *It Is Never Too Late To Mend* led to a Royal Commission and the imprisonment of the prison Governor. In most of Europe the Separate System held sway. In Belgium prisoners wore hoods so that they should not see each other when exercising.

By the end of the century reformers had been at work effectively in improving food and working conditions, but the essential character of prisons remained unchanged. Most new prisons were built on the Auburn system, with blocks of individual cells several storeys high.

Henrico County Jail, Richmond, in the 1860s *NYPL*

Lincoln County Jail, Maine. Built in 1809, the first building in Maine specially constructed for the confinement of criminals. The granite blocks of which it was made were forty-one inches thick, and stone slabs were used for the ceilings *NYPL*

Oakum-room at the Middlesex House of Correction, under the silent system

A separate cell in Pentonville prison, about 1850, with hammock slung for sleeping and loom for day work   *RTHPL*

Convicts exercising in Pentonville prison yard. They are masked to avoid recognition of each other   *RTHPL*

American convicts at work *NYPL*

Methods of the Indian police

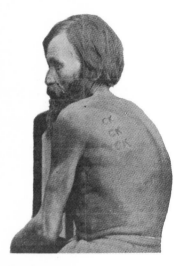

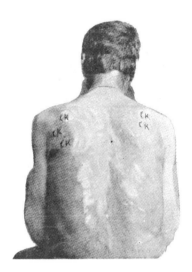

Russian convict branded after escape attempt *NYPL*

Executioner in Russian prison *NYPL*

Marks of a beating with the knout *NYPL*

Convicts engaged on railway construction in Siberia, 1898 *NYPL*

Exercising yard in English prison, turn of the century *Mary Evans Picture Library*

The lives of prisoners

The Separate and Silent Systems practised inhumanity in the name of reform. More primitive prison systems employed more obviously barbaric methods. Torture was common practice in the Far East, and to extract admissions from suspects Indian and Oriental police used a variety of methods, including the use of hot oil in the ears and nose, slivers of bamboo pushed under the nails, the use of the bastinado to break knee and ankle joints, and confinement in a cell containing quicklime. In Russia the knout was administered to the point of death, in many Eastern countries prisoners were chained together for days at a time . . . The list of tortures and cruelties is endless. A prisoner without wealth or social distinction had become a number in many countries outside Europe. If he died it was merely a matter of crossing that number off a register. A visit from the police soon put a stop to any questions asked by the dead man's family.

Yet the picture is not one of universal misery. In Russia political prisoners were treated with surprising leniency, and even in the countries most notorious for the horrors of their prisons, among them Turkey and Persia, friendly warders could be found. There were even prison Governors who thought it might be a good thing for men to learn a trade in prison so that they had a chance of entering society as something other than criminals when they came out. As yet, however, such Governors were only a small minority.

Prisoners and jailers in Persia *NYPL*

DOES CRIMINAL MAN EXIST?

Cesare Lombroso

The idea that there is a criminal type, and that it can be discovered by exact statistical analysis of various physical aspects of criminals, is particularly associated with the great Italian criminal anthropologist Cesare Lombroso. He had his predecessors, like Lauvergne, prison surgeon at Toulon, who examined many criminals to see what physical characteristics they had in common and made plaster casts of their skulls, or the psychologist Morel whose theories about the degeneracy of the habitual criminal were later popularised by Max Nordau. But Lombroso went far beyond them in thoroughness, studying the features and habits of thousands of criminals in his posts as Medical Superintendent of an asylum at Pesaro and later as professor of forensic medicine and of psychiatry at Turin. The conclusions he reached were put down in several books, of which *L'Uomo Delinquente* (1876) is the most famous.

While making a post-mortem examination of a brigand, Lombroso was struck by several characteristics which, when he found them repeated in other cases, convinced him that the born criminal had 'the ferocious instincts of primitive humanity', and that these were made evident by such anatomical features as very large jaws, high cheekbones, solitary lines in the palms, and what he called handle-shaped ears. He and his followers used ingenious instruments for making the necessary measurements to show whether a man was a born criminal or not.

Many of Lombroso's theories seem now self-evidently absurd, but it would be unjust not to say that he was a social scientist of scrupulous intelligence, who was concerned with every aspect of criminal life and habits, and who left behind him a mass of material upon which later scientific criminology was based. His theories also underwent considerable modification before his death in 1909. In his later years he was ready to admit that environment and social habits were important, although he never swerved from the belief that a criminal type, or several criminal types, existed and could be physically identified.

His theories were adapted by his most talented assistant Enrico Ferri, who laid more stress on the social background of crime while still emphasizing the importance of studying the criminal. The French criminologist Lacassagne thought of criminal activity as a sort of latent germ made active by society, 'the medium which causes it to ferment', and the German Adolph Prins asserted that 'criminality proceeds from the very nature of humanity itself'. The theory of the 'born criminal', however, was highly congenial to respectable society. Although Lombroso was a reformer his theories were often invoked as an excuse for not worrying too much about the background of criminals, or attempting their reformation. After all, if they were born to a criminal destiny, how could they be reformed?

Cesare Lombroso

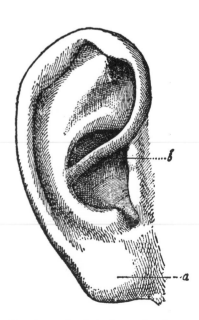

One type of criminal ear. Lombroso found that the lobe might be completely absent, or as in this case 'of huge dimensions and square in shape'.

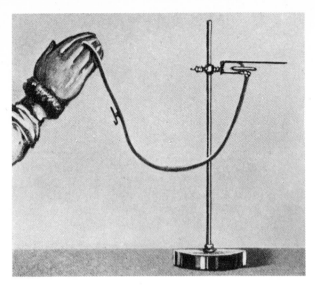

The volumetric glove, which might be called a crude form of lie detector. The glove was put on the wrist, hermetically sealed and filled with air. The suspect was then asked a series of questions, into which a meaningful one would occasionally be dropped. It was thought that in response to the meaningful question a sudden variation in the flow of blood in the hand would be shown.

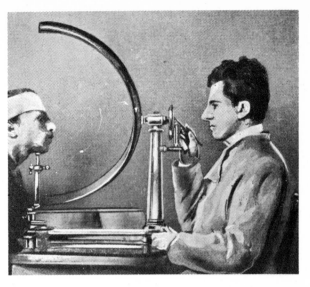

Landolt's campimeter. Lombroso believed that many criminals had a restricted field of vision, and the campimeter was used for testing this. A small ball was swung backwards and forwards, and the suspect's gaze followed it.

Weber's esthesiometer, which was used to test tactile sensitivity

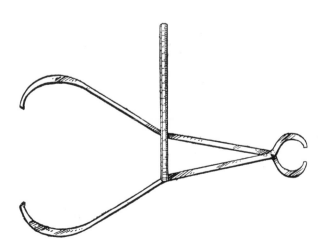

The pelvimeter, used for various measurements. In effect it was very similar to the calipers used by Bertillon

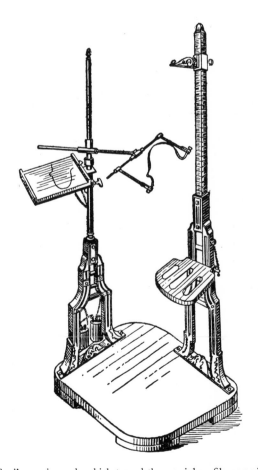

Anfossi's craniograph, which traced the cranial profile on a piece of specially prepared cardboard

Anthropometry and Alphonse Bertillon

Lombroso had propounded a theory which was of scientific interest but had little immediate practical use. The great scientific advance in criminology during the last quarter of the nineteenth century was made by a morose and sickly filing clerk in the Paris Prefecture named Alphonse Bertillon.

The advance was made first of all through the intelligent application of statistical laws. As Bertillon sorted his filing cards which vaguely characterized prisoners as tall, average or small in height, it occurred to him that an exact system of measurements would provide an infallible means of identification. Infallible? Well, if you measured not just a man's height, but also his head, ears, arms, fingers, feet, it would be found that no two men were identical in all these features. The idea was laughed at, and when in 1879 Bertillon advanced his theory in a report to the Prefect of Police it was rejected.

Three years later he was famous. His method had been given a brief trial, and during the course of it he had identified a man who called himself Dupont as an ex-convict named Martin. The identification had been made solely through the file records of Martin's measurements. This modest triumph was succeeded by others, and within a year Bertillon had identified nearly a hundred criminals by the method which he called anthropometry. The French press called it *bertillonage*. The system of measurement was adopted in most French prisons. Bertillon was made the Director of the French Police Identification

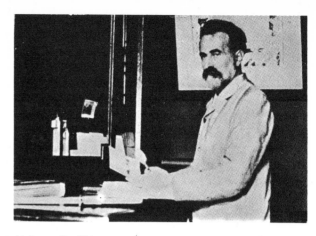

Alphonse Bertillon

Service and given several assistants. His fame spread to the rest of Europe.

Anthropometry took on greater exactness with the passing of time. Bertillon extended the number of the measurements he made to eleven. He also took advantage of the fact that over 60,000 photographs were in the police files to use a new method of criminal photography. He began by photographing prisoners himself and cutting up the pictures so that he could compare dozens of ears, noses and eyes side by side. He then gave instructions to police photographers, who were inclined to consider themselves as artists rather than craftsmen, that all pictures of

Bertillon measurements. Measuring the left foot   *RTHPL*

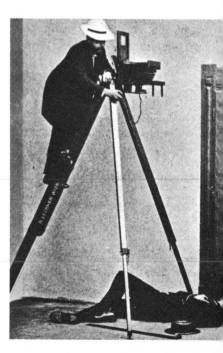

The ladder and camera devised by Bertillon for photographing the scene of a crime

prisoners must be taken both full face and profile, from the same distance, under the same lights, and with their heads in the same position. The picture appeared on every prisoner's card with his measurements. The first great triumph of the *portrait parlé*, as it was called, came in 1892 with the arrest of the Anarchist terrorist Koenigstein who used the name of Ravachol, by which he is now remembered. There was a *portrait parlé* for Koenigstein, and it confirmed beyond doubt that he was identical with Ravachol, after Ravachol had been arrested.

In the last decade of the century *bertillonage* was adopted almost everywhere. All the important countries of Europe used the system, occasionally elaborating it – in Italy Professor Ottolenghi combined Bertillon with Lombroso, using instruments to measure memory. Germany and Austria were wholehearted adherents, and so were Russia and Spain. 'Anthropometric cabinets' were set up in many prisons. At a conference held in the United States in 1896 it was found that 150 police forces and prisons were using some form of anthropometry, including Sing Sing prison. Only the British were comparatively lukewarm. Three police experts visited Paris, and

were impressed without being entirely convinced. They went back and recommended the use of five of Bertillon's eleven measurements. There had been much discussion in Britain about the possible uniqueness of fingerprints, and the British experts recommended that these should be taken and added to every convict's card.

Anthropometry had enormously increased the ease of identifying criminals after their arrest, yet it was showing also certain human limitations. Bertillon imposed his own fanatical standards of exactness on his subordinates, but supposing the man taking measurements was less careful? This possibility had been foreseen by the Police Prefect who originally rejected the idea, Gustave Macé, and it was one of the qualifications made by the visiting Englishmen. Melville MacNaghten, who later became chief of the C.I.D., used the measuring calipers so clumsily when invited by Bertillon to test the system personally that he nearly put out the subject's eye. It is not surprising that MacNaghten afterwards wrote of the difficulty of accurate measurement. 'Governors and warders in Britain did their best, and so did the police, but the results were pitifully small.'

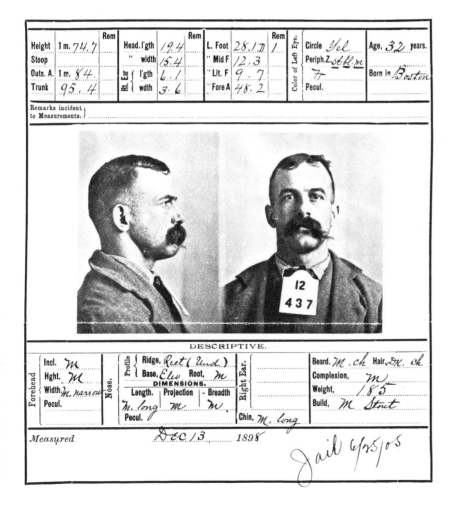

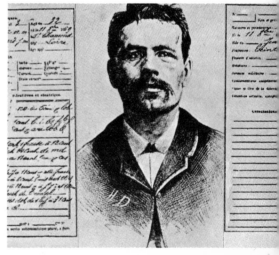

The Bertillon card on Koenigstein, which identified him as Ravachol

A wanted notice issued in Boston in 1898, showing the Bertillon measurements of the wanted man *McDade Collection*

The burglar and his tools

Most crime is humble, most criminals modest in their aims and intentions. Burglary, at least in England and in most of the United States, is an operation committed at night – that is, between 9 at night and 6 o'clock in the morning – in a dwelling house. Housebreaking is a different matter, because it need not occur at night and can concern any building. Both crimes involve 'breaking and entering'. The nineteenth century burglar used as wide a range of tools as his modern counterpart, and was equally devoted to a single method of entrance which he invariably repeated. All the operations shown here are American, but European practice followed them closely, although the chloroforming method shown seems both uncertain and unlikely.

The ladder shown is of steel wire bent at the ends, with two iron hooks for attachment to the window sill. A slight jerk from below released the hooks, so that the ladder fell. It was then flexible enough to be folded and dropped into a coat pocket
CP

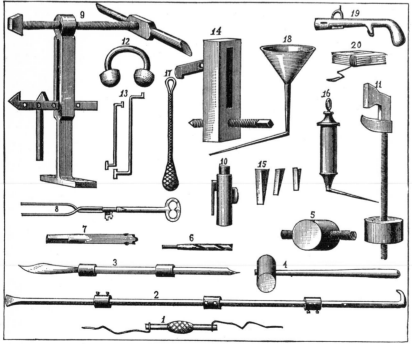

A set of burglar's tools   *NYPL*

1. Gag
2. Sectional jimmy
3. Sectional jimmy
4. Copper sledge
5. Lead sledge
6. Diamond drill
7. Diamond drill
8. Key nippers
9. Improved safe-opener
10. Glim
11. Used to obtain leverage
12. Knuckles
13. Skeleton keys
14. Wedge
15. Wedge
16. Powder blower
17. Slung shot
18. Powder funnel
19. Dummy pistol
20. Fuse

Where the shutter was wooden, as shown here, a long thin pliable knife was pressed into the crevice of the catch. It bent upwards on reaching the bevel and was then moved about to find the catch, which could easily be lifted or pushed aside. Window sashes were similarly 'sprung'   *CP*

This pair of nippers was a device particularly used in houses and hotels where residents turned the key and left it in the lock for safety. The nippers were put into the keyhole and twisted until the key unlocked the door. Courteous burglars relocked the door in the same way on leaving   *CP*

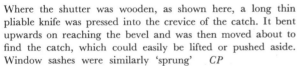

'Having overcome the difficulties of effecting an entrance, the first duty of the burglar is to discover if there are persons sleeping in the room', says a contemporary magazine. 'Should there be such, and should the bed be so placed that the burglar could not operate without awakening the sleepers, the anaesthetics are introduced. A small piece of sponge soaked with chloroform or ether is suspended by a string from a cane or other stick. This the cautious operator swings about from his perch by the window. A little experience will enable him to judge when the victim is sufficiently under the influence of the valuable assistant to permit him to search for "swag" or plunder.'   *CP*

A practised burglar could get everything out of a room almost noiselessly. The skill has not been lost to-day   *CP*

The Black Museum and Charles Peace

Several big cities have their museums in which relics of past crimes are preserved. Inspector Byrnes of the New York police had a room which he called the Mystery Chamber, where the walls were covered with photographs of arrested criminals, a rope hung from the ceiling, and death masks and bloody weapons were preserved in cabinets. Some of these items were withdrawn as too gruesome for public viewing, and the present New York Police Museum is a well-run but necessarily much tamer affair, although it contains interesting items from the Snyder-Gray case (see page 132).

Much the same applies to Scotland Yard's famous Black Museum. Permission to see it has to be specially obtained, and photography of any article is now strictly forbidden. The pictures reproduced here belong to a time before this ban came into force. In fact, however, the criminal relics contained in the Museum are not likely to upset any but the most susceptible. Among the most interesting are those relating to one of England's outstanding criminals, Charles Peace. It is too much to claim, as does one writer, that Peace was 'the greatest and most naturally gifted criminal England has produced', but certainly he is one of those figures, like Lizzie Borden in the United States, who has passed out of fact into popular mythology.

Peace was born in 1832, the son of an animal trainer. He suffered an accident in his childhood which left him permanently crippled. The remarkable thing about him is that his career up to the age of forty was that of a commonplace, not very successful burglar. The exploits that made him famous all took place during the last five years of his life. He carried out a series of daring burglaries in the Manchester area, which were notable for the use of an extraordinary skill in disguise. A police notice described him as 'almost a monkey of a man, with power of pulling about and altering his features so as to make his face unrecognizable even by his relations and intimates'. To hide the fact that he had lost one finger he wore a false arm made of gutta percha with a steel plate and hook on the end of it.

In 1876 Peace was interrupted by two policemen when about to burgle a house outside Manchester. He warned them, and then shot one of them, who subsequently died. Two brothers were arrested for the murder, and one was sentenced to death. Peace

A general view of the Black Museum. The ropes were actually used in executions   *Mirrorpic*

attended the trial, which he later said he had greatly enjoyed. At his home outside Sheffield, where he carried on a respectable trade as a picture framer, he had become friendly with a civil engineer named Dyson and his wife. Peace, although ugly, was an inveterate womanizer, and his pursuit of Mrs Dyson was so persistent that the husband and wife moved to another suburb of Sheffield to get away from him. Peace followed them. 'I am here to annoy you, and I'll annoy you wherever you go', he told Mrs Dyson. A few days later he quarreled with Dyson and shot him dead.

He now went on the run, disguised by dyed hair and spectacles. He delighted in danger, travelling once from Bath to Oxford with a police sergeant who had charge of a prisoner, and on another occasion actually lodging with a policeman. At another time still he astonished his wife by appearing in black coat and trousers, top hat, velvet waistcoat and kid gloves, accompanied by a small fox terrier. When the North of England finally became too hot for him, he made his way to London.

There ensued the two most successful years of his life. He rented a solid suburban villa in Peckham, established under one roof both his wife and his mistress, and there lived a life of extreme respectability as Mr Thompson, a gentleman of independent means with a taste for dabbling in scientific inventions such as an improved brush for washing railway carriages. By night Charles Peace practised his profession, usually driving to do a job in his pony and trap. A violin case contained his tools. Eventually he was caught while carrying out a burglary in Blackheath. He shot at and wounded a policeman before his capture.

The police had no idea of their prisoner's importance, but Peace was undone by his own ingenuity. He wrote a semi-illiterate letter to a fellow-inventor, and through it his identity as the respectable Mr Thompson became known. His mistress then told the police of his real identity. He was sentenced to life imprisonment for wounding the police constable at Blackheath, and taken to Sheffield to stand trial for killing Dyson. Moaning and groaning (he had injured himself when jumping from a train in an attempt to escape) and protesting his innocence, he was sentenced to death. He made a short speech from the scaffold to the reporters admitted to his execution, expressing his certainty of going to Heaven. A more practical observation was the one he made to the clergyman who attended him, and who was much impressed by his Christian feeling: 'My great mistake, sir, has been this – in all my career I have used ball cartridge. I ought to have used blank.'

Charles Peace *RTHPL*

Knives from the Black Museum. The one immediately in front was used in the murder of the actor William Terris in 1897 *Mirrorpic*

Relics of Charles Peace in the Black Museum, including his ladder, spectacles and gutta percha false arm *Mirrorpic*

Ladies at work

Women criminals – that is, professional criminals, for the woman who commits a crime of passion is in a different category – are generally the accomplices of men. 'As a rule women have a weaker moral sense', a male writer complacently remarked. 'They come more under the influence of feeling, and when once they stray from the right path they wander far, and recovery is extremely difficult'. Few women operate on their own, and few have ever become anything more than minor members of a gang headed by a man.

There are exceptions, of course. One of them was Mother Mandelbaum, the woman 'fence' of New York's Clinton Street, whose dealings were said to have extended through the whole of the United States, to Canada and Mexico. Under cover of her shop Mother Mandelbaum ran a 'bureau for the prevention of detection', bribing police officers, finding hideouts for criminals on the run, and backing them with cash when they needed it. She paid Howe and Hummel, the great shyster lawyers, a retaining fee of $5000 a year to look after her interests, and it was on their advice that she jumped her bail in 1884, after the proceeds of a silk robbery had been found on her premises. She spent the rest of her life in Canada.

She also ran a school for pickpockets in the Fagin manner, and it is Mother Mandelbaum's girls who are shown at work here, except for the lady garrotters. This popular form of attack in the London streets left the victim half or wholly strangled by means of a rope or scarf drawn round the neck from the back. A verse in *Punch* testified to its efficacy:

The old 'Stand and deliver's all rot.
Three to one; hit behind; with a wipe round the jowl, boys,
That's the ticket, and *Vive la Garrotte*.

Women were often used as garrotters because they could easily approach men on the pretence of being prostitutes.

Female garrotters at work in London

Siren shapes of the sidewalk – swindlers in petticoats and how they work

PICKING THE POCKETS OF A DRUNK.

THE HAT RACKET.

THE THOUGHT YOU WERE MY UNCLE DODGE

DIVIDING THE "SWAG"

SKINNING A STIFF.

THE LOST HER WAY RUSE.

41

Lamentation and Execution
OF JAMES LONGHURST

At Horsemonger Lane Gaol, on Tuesday, April 16th, for the wilful murder of Jane Sax,
a little Girl seven years old, at Shere, in Surrey.

Terrible Scene in the Prison with the Culprit.

James Longhurst, was executed this morning April 16, on the top of Horsemoner-lane gaol. Since his condemnation he has expressed contrition for his crime, and hoped that God would forgive him. Notwithstanding the prisoner appearing to be in a state of mind becoming his awful position, when he was taken down from the condemned cell to the yard to be pinioned a frightful scene ensued: The moment the culprit saw Calcraft, the executioner approach him with the straps to pinion his arms, he started back with an aspect of terror depicted on his countenance, and began to struggle violently with the turnkeys. The chaplain spoke to him and endeavoured to calm him, and this for a moment appeared to have the effect, but upon the executioner requesting that the culprit might be taken outside, as he could not see to fasten the straps properly, another fearful struggle ensued, and it required five warders to hold him, and it was necessary to throw him down and hold him on the ground while he was being pinioned, and one or two of the turnkeys were very much hurt by the kicks they received. The prisoner's conduct seemed to be actuated by an uncontrollable horror of the executioner and the apparatus of death. After he had been secured he walked quietly by the side of the chaplain until he arrived at the steps leading to the scaffold, and immediately he caught sight of the gibbet his horror appeared to return. He again struggled violently as well as he was able, and was forcibly dragged up to the steps and held under the beam by several turnkeys while the rope was adjusted round his neck, and as speedily as possible the bolt was drawn, and after a few struggles the wretch youth ceased to exist.

Good people all I pray draw near,
And my sad history you soon shall hear
And when the same I do relate,
I trust you will a warning take.

At Horsemonger-lane on the scaffold high,
For a cruel murder I was doomed to die

James Longhurst, it is my name,
I've brought myself to grief and shame,
Through the dreadful deed that I had done,
At Churchill-field, near Guildford town.

It was in last June, the twenty-eighth,
I did this deed as I now state;
An innocent child I there did slay,
And with a knife took her life away.

Poor Jane Sax, on that fatal day,—
A child scarce seven years of age;
In Churchill-field, I her did meet,
And shamefully did her illtreat.

Then coward-like I drew my knife,
To rob this helpless child of life;
I stabbed her in the throat—her blood did pour—
Then left her welt'ring in her gore.

Then I was taken for this cruel deed,
And sent for trial, as you may read;
At Kingston assizes, tried and cast,
Oh, would I could recall the past.

She cried for help did poor little Jane,
David Edsor to her assistance came;
Whilst I, a guilty wretch did stand,
And licked her blood from off my hand

The Judge said, James Longhurst you are guilty found,
You will go from here to London town
And there you'll die a detah of shame,
And meet your fate at Horsemonger-lane

While I lay in my prison cell,
My state of mind, no tongue can tell;
I could not rest by day or night,
Poor Jane was always in my sight.

My tender parents came to visit me,
My heart was breaking their grief to see
Tears from their eyes did in torrents fall
While for mercy to my God did call.

I hope that none will them upbraid,
While I am in my silent grave;
Farewell to all,—the bell does toll,
Have mercy, God, on my sinful soul.

A single page broadsheet mid-19th century

Commemorating the crime

Public passion for reading about famous crimes in detail was satisfied by the production of pamphlets and broadsheets. Fat pamphlets appeared dealing with every bloodthirsty crime, and broadsheets were issued either after sentence had been pronounced or on the eve of execution. Large crowds gathered for public executions. Many of them, like Charles Dickens, lamented the horror of the spectacle at the same time as they watched it. The scenes at the execution of Franz Muller (page 44) at Newgate were so disgusting that they led to an outcry in England against public executions. A crowd of 50,000 people, large numbers of them drunk, gathered to shout obscenities and to jeer at Muller when he appeared. According to *The Times*, robbery and garrotting were carried on openly, with little attempt by the police to check them. The last public execution in England was held in 1872.

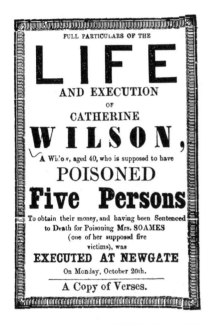

Title page of a typical pamphlet, mid-19th century *(top)*

A hanging in America, 1874

An American broadsheet. Because the murder occurred in Pennsylvania, which had a large German-speaking population, one side of the sheet is in English, the other in German *McDade Collection*

Train murder and robbery

A railway carriage with no corridor is in some ways a very suitable place for murder. There can be no witnesses, and the body is easily disposed of on the line. When Franz Muller, a young German living in London, tipped out the body of the man he had attacked with a life preserver and robbed, he must have thought that he was safe, particularly as four days later he had left England. The crime was committed on 11 July 1864, near Hackney in London and on the 15th Muller, who had been dissatisfied with the conditions of life in England, left for New York in the sailing ship *Victoria*.

He was caught through well co-ordinated police work. The man Muller left for dead – in fact he did not die until the night after the attack – was Thomas Briggs, chief clerk in a firm of City bankers. The murderer had taken Briggs's gold watch and chain and had left his own hat, which was lower in the crown than the high hat then commonly worn. Within a week a jeweller named Death had reported exchanging the chain for another bought by a man who came into his shop, and a cabman had remembered that his daughter had been given an empty cardboard box with the name 'Death' on it.

'Muller's Lament', a broadsheet referring to details of the case

The scene of the Merstham Tunnel murder in 1881. The murder took place inside the tunnel. The killer, Lefroy, maintained that he had been attacked himself, and was insensible at the time of the murder. He was arrested, taken to a house in Croydon, and then by some extraordinarily slack police work allowed to enter it alone. He naturally walked in through the front door and out of the back. Lefroy was later arrested, found guilty, and hanged

MULLER'S LAMENT.

Tune.—" The Roving Gardener."

My name is Francis Muller, an unhappy little man.
   So listen to my trials and my troubles;
It's true what the poet says, this life is but a span,
   And the world is made up of air bubbles.
So being short of tin, I thought some cash to raise,
   Likewise to cut a figure in this nation,
But my sad capers now has got me in a mess,
   And brought me too my present situation.

Oh, dear! have I got a chance
   To escape from my present situation?
I am afraid Dickey Calcraft will teach me for to dance,
   Which causes me great agitation.

They say I did a deed, all in the railway train,
   And another person's property did borrow;
But whether true or not, I am sure you can't me blame,
   If I speak not of that tale of sorrow.
Then I thought I'd take a trip to America,
   And being a bit of a soldier,
I thought I would join the Federal army—
   But the sequel it has to be told, sir.

I sailed in the Victoria,—just to take a trip,—
   Just thinking all was right and tight, sir;
But when they found in England I had given them the slip,
   They soon was down upon my flight, sir;
For the English detectives knew too much for me,
   They are too cute in this nation;
They soon made the sea far too strong for me,
   So I long'd to change my situation.

I tried to make myself agreeable while I was on board,
   And the passengers they thought I was a rum one

They said a murderer was on board, when the wind it roar'd,
   Or else that old Nick he was coming;
I tried to get a bite, but found I was not right,
   Just to amuse the passengers,
In a twinkling of an eye to put out of sight,
   Five pounds of German sausages.

I said I was a tailor, I was upon my word,
   When they said where is your bodkin and needle?
Says I, they are all right, along with my sleeve board,
   So I managed them for a-while to wheedle.
Just to make a shift I had to sell my shirt,
   It is truth now what I do tell ye,
For it is a fact, I cared not for my back,
   So as I feasted well my belly.

I thought I was all right, but I found out my mistake,
   So it took me by surprise, it must be granted;
When Inspector Tanner came on board, and said, your arm I'll take,
   For I tell you, Mr. Muller, you are wanted,
To the Police Court they took me in New York,
   Where amongst the Yankees I was mingling,
Then aboard the Etna they did me escort,
   And brought me back to old England.

I own I was a flat to keep the watch and hat,
   It has give my bowels such a shaking,
Just when the rolls are drawn, on some fine morn,
   I shall be strung up like a flitch of bacon;
So all young men take advice by me,
   No matter what country or colour,
For honesty is the best of policy,
   Take warning by poor Francis Muller.

London :—Printed for the Vendors.

The box had been given her by a friend, a young German named Franz Muller. The cabman also identified what quickly became known as the 'Muller Hat'.

Muller had gone to the United States on a sailing ship. Inspector Tanner of Scotland Yard, accompanied by a sergeant, and also by the jeweller and cabman, set off in a steamer. Their journey was just as dramatic as the later one involving Crippen, for there was no wireless telegraphy to give an assurance that Muller was in fact on board the *Victoria*. The steamer beat the sailing ship by twenty days, and public excitement was intense. When the *Victoria* arrived and was waiting in harbour a party of excursionists passing near it shouted: 'How are you, Muller the murderer?', a remark which remained unheard. Muller was extradited, tried, found guilty and hanged. The most deadly piece of evidence against him was the hat, and the Muller hat became immensely popular after his execution. It resembled very much the low-crowned hat favoured by Winston Churchill.

There was no railway murder in England for nearly twenty years after the Muller case, but a daring robbery had taken place in 1857. This was the theft of bullion from the gold van on a South Eastern Railway train carrying it from London to the Continent. The gold was sent in iron-bound boxes, and each box was deposited in a safe with two different locks and two keys. These keys were held by the traffic superintendent in London, the head of Folkestone railway office, and the skipper of the Channel boat.

The robbery was adroitly designed and executed. The two principals, Agar and Pierce, were both professional crooks. They bribed a train guard named Burgess, and a clerk in the traffic department in London named Tester. An impression of one key was obtained by Tester when a safe was sent to Chubb's for repair, and Pierce got the other by boldly walking into the Folkestone railway office when it was empty. Tester then told Agar and Pierce when bullion was being sent, and an equal quantity of lead shot was substituted for the bullion in the gold van. Bullion was unloaded at various points, and the boxes had reached Boulogne before the theft was discovered.

The affair had gone off wonderfully well, but the thieves were defeated by lack of that good faith which is so essential in business. Agar was arrested on a separate charge of uttering forged cheques, and sentenced to transportation for life. He asked Pierce to settle the rest of his share of the money on a woman named Kay, but Pierce made only a few small payments to her and kept the rest of the money. Agar heard about this, turned informer, and the other three men were arrested. The robbery was one of the most carefully planned and executed of its time.

Burgess, the train guard, in the bullion robbery

Tester, the bribed clerk

Agar, one of the principals

Ned Kelly and Captain Thunderbolt

The Kellys were the last and most famous of the gangs of bushrangers who flourished in Australia. The policy of transporting convicts to an under-populated country ignored the likelihood that some of them would continue criminal operations as soon as they escaped or were set free. They were often treated with the utmost savagery on the principle that punishment was an inducement to virtue. The colony was, as a writer of the time put it, a prison without walls or warders, without any system of reform or any thought of rational punishment. Most of the early bushrangers were convicts, like Dignum who killed seven of his companions when their provisions ran short so that there should be less mouths to feed, or the Jewish Davis who escaped from a chain gang working near Sydney and organized a gang which, although heavily armed, tried to avoid shedding blood.

The Kellys were not convicts, although their father had been transported to Tasmania from Belfast. The two principal members of the gang were Ned and his younger brother Dan, and their field of operation was the north-eastern part of New South Wales, which came to be known as the Kelly country. Many of the locals were opposed to all forms of authority, and quite a number were related in some way to the Kellys. Their sympathy for the outlaws was enhanced by a romantic strain in Ned Kelly, exemplified in the treatment of a constable who came to arrest him for cattle stealing and was permitted to leave after a scuffle in which he slightly injured his wrist. When the constable reported that he had been shot at, and the charge was altered from cattle stealing to one of shooting with intent to murder, Ned was furiously angry. The Kellys went on the run, and the next group of policemen who caught up with them were ambushed. One was shot when he tried to lay hands on his revolver, and another named McIntyre asked Kelly if they were going to shoot him.

'No, why should I want to shoot you?' Kelly asked.

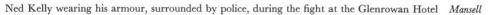

Ned Kelly wearing his armour, surrounded by police, during the fight at the Glenrowan Hotel   *Mansell*

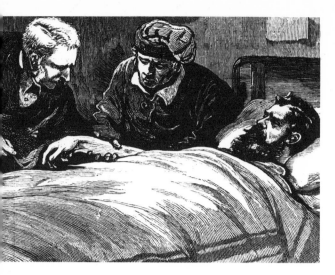

Ned Kelly in Melbourne Hospital after his capture   *Mansell*

A group photographed during the fight

'What brings you here at all? It is a shame to see fine big strapping fellows like you in a lazy loafing job like a policeman's.'

Soon after this two more troopers came up, and a gun battle ensued in which both were killed, although McIntyre escaped unharmed. A reward of £1000 a head was offered for the Kellys dead or alive, but it found no takers. The police were helpless in what was practically hostile country while the gang raided stores almost at will, taking hostages who were released unharmed after each raid. They netted almost £2000 by a raid on one bank, and held up another in the most daring manner, having first of all surrounded the police station, tied up one of its occupants and forced the other to act as decoy for the raid. It was a mark of the Kellys that they used violence only when compelled to do so, and on this occasion Ned Kelly harangued a crowd and told them that he was a martyr to police persecution.

The reward was increased to £2000 a man, and a number of Kelly sympathizers were arrested to encourage the others, without effect. They were finally caught when an attack planned on a train was foiled and they were shut up in a hotel at Glenrowan. As usual they were accompanied by hostages, and as usual also they wore protective armour covering head, chest, back and sides. They resisted a siege by more than thirty police for seven hours, but eventually Ned was captured and his three companions killed. There was a strong agitation for his reprieve, but it failed. 'Mind you die like a Kelly, Ned', his mother said on parting from him.

Captain Thunderbolt was the name used by an escaped convict named Frederick Ward, who is seen here with his (of course stolen) horse Talleyrand.

He was one of the most famous of the bushrangers who operated independently of any recognized gang. Thunderbolt's only regular companion was an intelligent half-caste woman who often dressed in men's clothes. He specialized in mail robberies, and like the Kellys tried to avoid personal injury to those he robbed. He once told a companion that the passengers on a mail coach should be left alone, because they must not hurt the ladies' feelings. Thunderbolt's activities lasted for seven years. In 1870 he was shot dead by a policeman in a gun fight.

Captain Thunderbolt, with his horse Talleyrand

The end of Jesse James

Two years after the capture of Ned Kelly in Australia, the greatest of the outlaws of the American Wild West was killed, and like Ned Kelly passed into legend. Jesse James was not caught in a gun battle, but shot in the back by a member of his own gang in his own respectable house at St Joseph, Missouri, where he passed under the name of Thomas Howard. Naturally enough a song told of the shooting:

Jesse James's lovely wife
Became a widder all her life,
    Though her children they were brave.
Oh, the dirty little coward
That shot poor Mister Howard
    And laid Jesse James in the grave.

The 'dirty little coward' was Bob Ford, one of two brothers who had been recruited by Jesse and Frank

REWARD!

- DEAD OR ALIVE -

$5,000.⁰⁰ ₓ ₓ will be paid for the capture of the men who robbed the bank at

NORTHFIELD, MINN.

They are believed to be Jesse James and his Band, or the Youngers.

All officers are warned to use precaution in making arrest. These are the most desperate men in America.

Take no chances! Shoot to kill!!

J. H. McDonald,

The reward notice that spelt doom for Jesse James *McDade Collection*

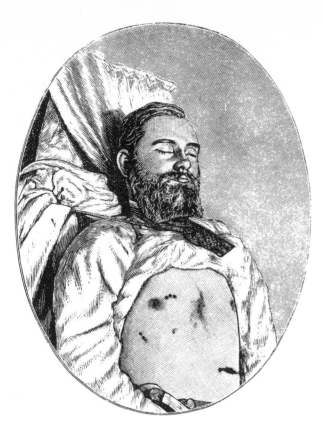

Jesse James after death. The scars on his chest are supposed to have been received during the Civil War *McDade Collection*

Bob Ford, who killed Jesse James *McDade Collection*

James into the gang to replace the Younger brothers, who had been arrested. Jesse James was doomed from the day when the Pinkertons persuaded the railroad companies to offer the enormous reward of $5000 for Jesse or Frank James. The Pinkerton National Detective Agency, the first and greatest of such agencies, was already nationally famous. They had discovered a plot against Abraham Lincoln before his assassination (see page 70), and had done espionage work on the Union side during the Civil War, but their principal source of revenue at this time was the protection of railway trains and mail coaches against the many gangs of armed bandits who plundered the expanding American West. A Pinkerton man had become a member of the sinister Molly Maguires, the secret society who terrorized much of Pennsylvania, and had played a major part in breaking them up. Another Pinkerton man, James W. Whicher, had been on the track of the James brothers in 1880. He had been recognized, killed, and left dangling from a tree with a note saying: 'Compliments of the James Boys to the Pinkertons.'

From the day that the reward was posted, Bob Ford determined to earn it. He waited his time and it came when they were due to leave to raid a bank. Jesse noticed that a picture of his favourite horse Skyrocket was hanging askew on the wall. He took off his holster, got up to straighten the picture, and Bob Ford shot him in the back of the head.

Jesse James's career has some similarity to that of Ned Kelly. Local Missourians, who did not love the railroad or the mail companies, exulted over his exploits and gave misleading information to sheriffs and Pinkerton men. But the Kelly legend was much nearer to truth than the legend of Jesse James. A follower of Quantrill's freebooters during the Civil War when he was a boy, Jesse grew up into a ruthless killer. Unlike the Kellys the James Gang left a trail of casual murders behind them – a boy of sixteen killed in one bank robbery, a cashier murdered in another, three civilians shot in a third. When they took to train robbery in the eighteen-seventies their first exploit involved killing the driver. Nor did the James brothers show the loyalty that marked the Kellys. After an unsuccessful bank raid in 1876, when the James brothers and the Youngers were all wounded, Frank and Jesse eventually made off, leaving the Youngers to fend for themselves.

A year after Jesse's death Frank James surrendered, handing over his pistols and saying that he wanted to end his days in peace. After a farcical trial he was acquitted and, generously allowed by the Governor of Missouri to settle down in his home state, lived quietly on his father-in-law's farm. He died, a respected and respectable citizen, in 1915.

49

Death by poison

Doctors have obvious opportunities for committing murder by poison, and Doctor William Palmer of Rugeley in Staffordshire took full advantage of them. Palmer was a genial man, the owner of several race-horses, who enjoyed the good life but lacked the income to support it. His career had been studded with unfortunate deaths before the sudden demise of his friend Alfred Cook. Among them were those of his mother-in-law from whom he inherited property, a racing friend to whom he owed £800, and his wife, who had recently been insured for £13,000. All these had gone unremarked but suspicion was aroused when a fellow racehorse owner named Cook was taken ill, and then died in agony after a visit from Dr Palmer, even though an aged doctor was found to say that death was due to apoplexy.

Some of the organs in Cook's body were submitted to Dr Alfred Taylor, the leading toxicologist of his day, and the author of the first standard work on medical jurisprudence. He found antimony in them, although he did not discover the strychnine from which Cook showed every sign of having died. When Palmer was arrested and tried, a sad tale of debt and forgery was revealed. It is hard to see how he could ever have been acquitted, but Palmer himself believed that the masterly conduct of the prosecution by the Attorney-General, Sir Alexander Cockburn, was responsible. He expressed himself in racing terms after he had been found guilty on 27 May 1856: 'It was the riding that did it.'

The Parisian operations of Dr de la Pommerais took place a few years after those of Palmer, and like Palmer's they were carried out purely for gain. He murdered first his mother-in-law, and then his former mistress, by administering digitalis. The

Dr de la Pommerais   *Mansell*

murder of his ex-mistress, Madame de Pauw, is of particular interest because the victim was induced to concur in it. De la Pommerais told her that she was to insure her life and then feign illness so that the insurance company would willingly settle an allowance on her during her lifetime to avoid payment of the capital sum on her death. The scheme was faithfully carried out by Madame de Pauw, and de la Pommerais took the precaution of making sure that she wrote to him giving the details of an illness which had been caused by an imaginary fall on the stairs. He then killed her by a large dose of digitalis, but suspicion was aroused by the unseemly speed with which he claimed the insurance she had made over to him. He was guillotined.

A certain doubt hangs over the cases of the three Victorian ladies pictured here. Madeleine Smith, the daughter of a good solid Scottish architect, was accused of giving a large dose of arsenic to her hope-

Dr Palmer of Rugeley   *RTHPL*

Palmer in the dock   *RTHPL*

lessly unsuitable lover Pierre Emile l'Angelier – not
because he was false to her but because she had tired
of the relationship and he was threatening to show
the letters she had written him to her father. This,
in the Glasgow of 1855, would have been quite
disastrous. The evidence against her was strong but
there were gaps in it, and the peculiarly Scottish
verdict of 'Not Proven' may be interpreted as the
jury's way of saying: 'Probably she did it, but any-
how he deserved it.'

Arsenic, in the form of flypaper, was also said to
have been administered by the 26-year old Florence
Maybrick, daughter of an Alabama banker, to her
50-year old English husband, when he died in 1889.
The case is a fascinating one, for certainly Florence
bought an extraordinary amount of flypaper just
before her husband's death, and certainly she was
seen soaking the papers in water, but then arsenic
was at that time much in use as a cosmetic and perhaps
she really did intend it for that purpose. And then
again Maybrick was in the habit of taking both
arsenic and strychnine in small doses, as a tonic and
an aphrodisiac. After his death a great deal of arsenic
was found in the house in bottles, glasses, rags, and
even in a dressing gown. At Florence Maybrick's
trial the medical experts were so totally at odds
about the cause of death that an acquittal was
confidently expected. The blunders of fact made by
Mr Justice Stephen in his summing up may have
contributed to the verdict of 'Guilty'. Her sentence
was commuted to one of life imprisonment, and in
1904 she was released. Like Madeleine Smith she
settled in the United States.

The ravishingly pretty Adelaide Bartlett was tried
at the Old Bailey in 1886 on the charge of poisoning
her husband with chloroform. There were many
suspicious circumstances, not least her friendship with
a young Wesleyan minister named George Dyson
who had bought chloroform for her a few days
earlier, but again the essential problem was a medical
one. How had the chloroform been administered?
Nobody would have drunk it voluntarily because of
the burning sensation it induced. Could she have
given it to him while he was unconscious? Even the
prosecution experts admitted that this would have
been a difficult operation, and that some would have
remained in the windpipe. And Edward Clarke,
counsel for the defence, pointed out that there was
no sign of chloroform in the windpipe.

Adelaide Bartlett was triumphantly acquitted. Did
she also go to the United States? Her later career is
unknown. Was she a poisoner who got away with
it? The caustic comment of Sir James Paget, consulting surgeon at St Bartholomew's Hospital, shows
what medical men thought of the verdict: 'Now
that it is all over she should tell us, in the interests
of science, how she did it.'

Madeleine Smith. Verdict: 'Not Proven'   *RTHPL*

Florence Maybrick. Arsenic in the fly papers?   *Mirrorpic*

Adelaide Bartlett. 'Now she should tell us
how she did it'   *RTHPL*

51

American firsts

The first American crime to attract national attention was also committed by a doctor, but a good-natured one, quite unlike the callous Palmer and de la Pommerais. Dr John White Webster, Professor of Chemistry and Mineralogy at Harvard in 1849, was chubby, amiable, a good husband and father. His weaknesses were a choleric disposition and inability to live on his meagre salary of $1200 a year. When in financial straits (and he was not often out of them) he borrowed from Dr Parkman, who had abandoned medicine in favour of the more profitable pursuit of acquiring and renting property. Webster gave Parkman a mortgage on his house and goods, including his valuable mineral collection. Parkman was naturally annoyed when he learned by chance that Webster had also borrowed money on the mineral collection elsewhere, and had given a bill of sale on it. From that time on Parkman pressed Webster for his money at all sorts of inconvenient times, even attending his lectures and making disparaging remarks about them. One day Webster could bear it no more. He picked up a handy stick, struck Parkman on the head and killed him.

They were in Webster's laboratory at the time. What better place could there be for disposing of a

Dr Parkman

Title page of book issued after the trial

The murder

body? The Professor of Chemistry set about his task with care, making only one fatal, elementary mistake. He cut up the body, put the head and some organs into the furnace, and placed other parts in a dissection vault. He carefully washed away all blood, and from time to time disposed of other parts of the body in the furnace. His manner was as jaunty as usual, and the only person who suspected him was the college janitor. Webster's propitiatory gift of a Thanksgiving Day turkey reinforced instead of stilling these suspicions, and after some investigation which included peeping through keyholes and under doors, the janitor dug under an exterior wall into the dissecting vault, and saw a pelvis and two pieces of leg. He went off immediately to tell the College authorities.

At the subsequent investigation Webster scoffed at the idea that the remains belonged to Parkman. 'This is no more Dr Parkman's body than it is my body', he said, and it is true that in the state of knowledge at that time the pieces could not have been positively identified. But, alas for human error. In the ashes of the furnace there were found, and quite positively identified by the dentist who had made them, Dr Parkman's new false teeth.

Kidnapping children for money is considered, with some reason, an American crime in particular. The first in a long series of similar horrific stories, among which the Lindbergh case stands out because of the parents' fame, took place in July 1874. It set a pattern for many others, in the way the child was taken, the ransom notes, the victim's eventual fate. Walter Ross, aged six, and his four year old brother Charley, accepted an invitation from two men passing by in a trap to go from their home in Germantown into Philadelphia to buy fireworks. Walter was given 25 cents to go into a shop, and when he returned Charley was gone.

Then came the ransom note, the first in American history, saying that 'charlie buster ros' would be returned unharmed if his father did not go to the police. Other notes followed, demanding $20,000 which Ross did not possess, giving reassurances about Charley, directing Ross exactly how to deliver the money. Some of the instructions resemble those given by Leopold and Loeb half a century later, in their use of a railroad car and their over-elaboration. Ross had already gone to the police. Later he consulted the New York police chief George W. Walling, who identified the ransom notes as the work of a crook named William Mosher. Nothing further happened until December when two burglars were shot in Brooklyn. One of them was Mosher, and he confessed before his death that he was one of the kidnappers.

What happened to Charley Ross? No trace of him was ever found.

$20,000 REWARD

Has been offered for the recovery of CHARLIE BREWSTER ROSS, and for the arrest and conviction of his abductors. He was stolen from his parents in Germantown, Pa., on July 1st, 1874, by two unknown men.

DESCRIPTION OF THE CHILD.

The accompanying portrait resembles the child, but is not a correct likeness. He is about four years old; his body and limbs are straight and well formed; he has a round, full face; small chin, with noticeable dimple; very regular and pretty dimpled hands; small, well-formed neck; full, broad forehead; bright dark-brown eyes, with considerable fullness over them; clear white skin; healthy complexion; light flaxen hair, of silky texture, easily curled in ringlets when it extends to the neck; hair darker at the roots,—slight cowlick on left side where parted; very light eyebrows. He talks plainly, but is retiring, and has a habit of putting his arm up to his eyes when approached by strangers. His skin may now be stained, and hair dyed,—or he may be dressed as a girl, with hair parted in the centre.

DESCRIPTION OF THE KIDNAPPERS.

No. 1 is about thirty-five years old; five feet nine inches high; medium build, weighing about one hundred and fifty pounds; rather full, round face, florid across the nose and cheek-bones, giving him the appearance of a hard drinker; he had sandy moustache, but was otherwise clean shaved; wore eye-glasses, and had an open-faced gold watch and gold vest-chain; also, green sleeve-buttons.

No. 2 is older, probably about forty years of age, and a little shorter and stouter than his companion; he wore chin whiskers about three inches long, of a reddish-sandy color; and had a pug-nose, or a nose in some way deformed. He wore gold bowed spectacles, and had two gold rings on one of his middle fingers, one plain and one set with red stone.

Both men wore brown straw hats, one high and one low-crowned; one wore a linen duster; and, it is thought, one had a duster of gray alpaca, or mohair.

Any person who shall discover or know of any child, which there is reason to believe may be the one abducted, will at once communicate with their Chief of Police or Sheriff, who has been furnished with means for the identification of the stolen child.

Otherwise, communications by letter or telegraph, if necessary, will be directed to either of the following officers of

PINKERTON'S NATIONAL DETECTIVE AGENCY,

Viz:
BENJ. FRANKLIN, Sup't, 45 S. Third St., Philadelphia, Pa.
R. A. PINKERTON, Sup't, 66 Exchange Place, New York.
F. WARNER, Sup't, 191 and 193 Fifth Avenue, Chicago, Ill.
GEO. H. BANGS, Gen'l Sup't.

ALLAN PINKERTON.

PHILADELPHIA, September 1st, 1874.

(POST THIS UP IN A CONSPICUOUS PLACE.)

Wm. F. Murphy's Sons, Stationers, Printers, 509 Chestnut St., Philada.

The reward advertisement for Charley Ross *McDade Collection*

Multiple murder

Cases of multiple murder are not so rare as is generally supposed. After a murder has been successfully committed for gain, the certainty that one will not be caught seems to grow with each crime. Or, putting it another way, most people regard human life and the human personality as sacred, and automatically refuse to contemplate certain actions. For those who lack this regulator of conduct, murder and cruelty have no limits. The three murderers recorded here stand for thirty others.

The most remarkable of them was Herman Webster Mudgett, who called himself Harry Howard Holmes. Holmes was hanged in Philadelphia in May 1896 for the murder of Benjamin Pitezel. The murder was part of an insurance fraud by which Holmes insured Pitezel's life, chloroformed him, and then combined with a shyster lawyer to identify the body. The insurance company was deceived, but Holmes had unwisely confided the general plan of the crime to a convict with whom he was in prison, and this undid him. In the background of this crime were many others. First, the murder of three children of the Pitezels, who had come with him to identify their father. Detective Frank P. Geyer found, after months of patient research, that Holmes had gassed two of them and probably beaten the third to death. Then bigamy – he had at least three 'wives' – forgery and

patent medicine swindling. And last, wholesale murder, committed in what came to be known as the 'Murder Castle', which he had had built for him in Chicago in 1893. This extraordinary house at 63rd and Wallace Streets, Chicago, contained several air-tight chambers with secret entrances and false ceilings or walls, a room lined with asbestos to stifle screams, and a death-shaft through which bodies dropped from the secret rooms into a cellar containing vats of quicklime and a crematory. Here Holmes killed by his own account twenty-seven people, mostly young women. Detectives who explored the cellar found so many skulls and teeth that they put the number of his victims at two hundred.

Holmes was a polite and charming man with a guileless expression, hypnotically attractive to women. So also was Alfred Deeming, alias Williams, who murdered his wife and four children at Rainhill, near Liverpool, went to Australia and disposed of a second wife, and was set to marry a third when he was arrested near Perth in 1892. Deeming, again like Holmes, was an accomplished swindler. He had travelled in many countries, worked elaborate confidence tricks in Johannesburg, posed as an Australian millionaire in Antwerp and as an English peer in Montevideo. His murder method always involved the use of cement. He had used it to cover the flagstones

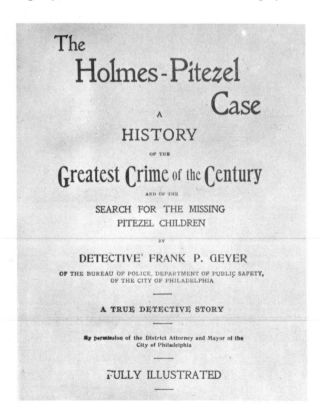

Title page of the book written about H. H. Holmes by the detective who searched for and finally discovered the missing Pitezel children CP

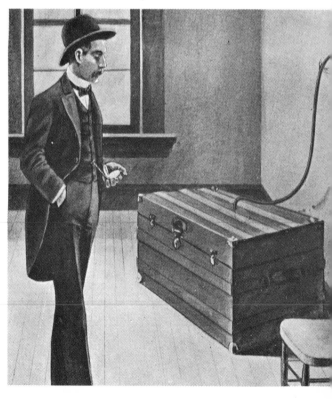

Holmes consulting his watch while gassing two of the Pitezel children

Katie Rounsville giving evidence at Deeming's trial. Cement was ready for her

that concealed his first wife and their children, his second wife was embedded in it, and he had it all prepared for Katie Rounsville, whom he was about to marry under the name of Baron Swanston when arrested. He was thought to have committed several more murders which were not brought home to him.

One interesting aspect of Deeming's trial is the plea made by the Inspector-General of Lunatic Asylums that he was an 'instinctive criminal' and not responsible for his actions. Such arguments did not appeal to an Australian jury at that time, and Deeming was hanged at Swanston Jail, Melbourne, on 23 May 1892.

Jean-Baptiste Troppmann was a less interesting and complicated character than Holmes and Deeming. In 1869 he was still in his teens, 'with an open countenance and soft sensuous eyes that sometimes flashed fire', when he decided to murder the whole family of a well-to-do man named Jean Kinck to obtain their money. Kinck, who must have been extraordinarily credulous, was told by Troppmann that he had found a gold mine in the Vosges Mountains. He was easily persuaded to give the youth a power of attorney to act in his name before they went to look at the gold mine. Troppmann poisoned him on the journey by the use of prussic acid. He then went to Paris, used Kinck's name to send for his wife and their six children, and murdered them all. He was caught when enquiring at Le Havre about the possibility of taking passage to the United States.

Alfred Deeming, confidence trickster and multiple murderer

Jean-Baptiste Troppmann. He murdered a family of eight

Jack the Ripper

I'm not a butcher, I'm not a Yid,
  Nor yet a foreign Skipper,
But I'm your own light-hearted friend,
  Yours truly, Jack the Ripper.

This little verse was one of the many anonymous communications sent to Scotland Yard in 1888 about the murders in Whitechapel. They caused terror throughout London – it is difficult to see why, since they were all confined to one part of the East End – and were a subject of national interest for months. Queen Victoria took a characteristically positive interest in them. 'All these courts must be lit and our detectives improved', she wrote to the Prime Minister, Lord Salisbury. 'They are not what they should be.' Salisbury called a Cabinet meeting specially to discuss the Ripper, but the effects of its deliberations were slight. He was never caught, and there is no certainty of his identity. Here are the facts.

Between August and early November 1888, six prostitutes were murdered in the dangerous, badly-lit area which embraces Whitechapel and Stepney. All had their throats slit by a long-bladed knife, and the last five were savagely mutilated. The mutilations varied – in one case the intestines had been pulled out and draped over the right shoulder, the face disfigured, the lobe of the right ear cut through obliquely and the lower eyelids nicked – but they were always done with some skill. Given time, as he was in the sixth murder which was carried out indoors, the Ripper carried out even more savage mutilations. It was after this sixth murder that the Queen wrote to her Prime Minister, and that something approaching lynch law prevailed in the East End. Slowly the passion died away and slowly, as weeks changed into months and there were no more murders, it was realized that Jack the Ripper's career was over.

Who was he? The police officers who worked on the case, and some who did not, have put down their views in print. He was, wrote the head of the C.I.D., (Sir Robert Anderson), a low-class Polish Jew. Sir Robert was tempted to name him in his memoirs, but

The discovery of the first victim, by PC John Niel

The last Ripper murder, that of Mary Kelly

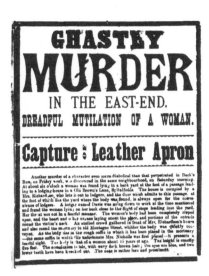

A broadsheet announcing the second murder and also saying wrongly that 'Leather Apron' had been captured

A *Punch* cartoon blaming the murders on official neglect of the slums. The police also came in for a great deal of blame.

refrained from doing so. Sir Melville MacNaghten, who succeeded Sir Robert, thought that the Ripper committed suicide about 10 November, a convenient explanation. His candidate has been traced as a barrister, who drowned himself in early December. His connection with the case was extremely slight, and it seems that he lacked the necessary surgical skill. Another candidate was Alfred Deeming (see page 55), who was certainly not the Ripper, and another still was the poisoner George Chapman, who was believed to be the Ripper by Chief Inspector Abberline, who worked on the case. Chapman had the necessary surgical qualifications, but the improbability of a poisoner being also a sex maniac intent on mutilation need hardly be pointed out. Theories that the Ripper was a seaman, a midwife and a policeman have also been advanced.

The most engaging theory is that advanced by Donald McCormick in *The Identity of Jack the Ripper* (1959). McCormick's Ripper is Alexander Pedachenko, a shadowy Tsarist secret agent sent to London to discredit the Anarchists. According to this theory Pedachenko, who had been a barber's assistant, joined pleasure to duty by committing these particular crimes. The *Ochrana Gazette*, circulated by the Tsarist secret police, is said to have named him as 'wanted for the murder of five women in the East Quarter of London'. But the Pedachenko theory remains no more than that. One authority for it is Rasputin, another a very dubiously accurate doctor.

The Ripper has been the central figure in dozens of books, plays, films and operas, of which the latest is his cinematic encounter with Sherlock Holmes. His identity remains enigmatic.

Forty whacks

In its essentials the case is simple. The facts are easily put down. Why should it have been a puzzle for more than seventy years?

On 4 August 1892, Andrew J. Borden of Fall River, Massachusetts, and his wife were both hacked to death by blows from what may have been an axe. Who killed them? This is one of the few murder cases in real life with the classic closed circle pattern of the detective story. Outsiders can be ruled out for various reasons. The only possible suspects were John Vinnicum Morse, an uncle paying a visit – but he had an alibi showing that he was nowhere near at the time; Emma Borden, Lizzie's elder sister – but she was away staying with friends, and only the most desperate ingenuity can place her on the scene; the Irish maid Bridget Sullivan; and Lizzie Borden herself, who was arrested, tried and acquitted. She spent the rest of her life in the little Fall River community, and died there in 1927.

The case against Lizzie was that she disliked her stepmother intensely, that she had set the stage by talking about premonitions of trouble, that she had tried to buy prussic acid, that her story after the murders had been strange and confused, and that she burned a dress three days after the crime. Moreover, she said that she had been in the hayloft of the barn adjoining the house at the time of the murder, and who would have spent such a very hot day in a hayloft? The case was very thin, and against it was the fact that although the crime was singularly bloody there was no blood on Lizzie. Had she, as Courvoisier did before her and as William Wallace was said to have done later, stripped naked for the murders, dressed hurriedly afterwards and later burned the dress?

It was certainly right, on the evidence, that Lizzie Borden should have been acquitted, but public opinion did not think so.

Lizzie Borden took an axe
And gave her mother forty whacks,
When she saw what she had done
She gave her father forty one.

A rear view of the Borden home. In the right foreground is the barn where Lizzie Borden said she went on the morning of the murder *CP*

Lizzie Borden. A photograph at the time of the trial *CP*

So far the popular verdict, which was endorsed by Edmund Pearson, the scholarly American chronicler of real life crime. But in 1961 Edward Radin published a fresh study which showed conclusively that Pearson's account of the case, long accepted as authoritative, had been slanted against Lizzie even to the point of tampering with the printed evidence. Radin had a candidate of his own, one rarely considered: Bridget Sullivan. He pointed out that she had just as much opportunity to commit the crime as Lizzie and that the rumours of Bridget having been paid off afterwards for keeping silence were utterly untrue. But although his theory is ingenious, it is hardly convincing. The likelihood remains, as it has always been, that Lizzie Borden killed her father and stepmother in a fit of passion. If a more solid motive is needed, should not the $175,000 she inherited with her sister be given consideration?

But of course such simple observations will not convince those who are assured of Lizzie's innocence. The debate continues.

A scene at the trial, Lizzie leaning forward

A drawing made during the trial. Lizzie has her hand on her chin. Her sister Emma has a hand over her eyes *CP*

The Benders

The home of the Benders on the prairies in south eastern Kansas. The region was lonely, and the Bender house served as a store by day, an inn by night. It became a recognized stopping place for travellers, but what happened to those who stayed there? Nobody worried much about them – it was a stop on the way to Indian territory – until Dr York vanished after a night at the Benders, and was sought for by his brother, a Colonel at Fort Scott. The Benders vanished suddenly and a search revealed eleven graves in the orchard. They had all been killed by a sledgehammer, except a little girl who had apparently been buried alive. Most of the bodies were identified, and Dr York's was among them. The Benders were never certainly heard of again   *NYPL*

John Bender, the father. The family consisted of Old Man Bender, of German origin and aged about 60, his raw-boned wife who was a few years younger, their son who was in his late twenties, and their daughter Kate   *NYPL*

Kate Bender was a spiritualist, and gave lectures in various nearby Kansas towns as well as calling on the dead to speak – a task for which she was well equipped. 'Professor Miss Kate Bender can heal disease, cure blindness, fits and deafness', said her advertisement in local papers. And no doubt, with the aid of her family, she could   *NYPL*

The Stauntons

Here are two horrifying families of the eighteen-seventies, one American, one English. The Benders killed many people, the Stauntons destroyed only one, yet they are fitting companions to face each other on the page.

Harriet Staunton. Born 1841. Pleasant, neat and careful in dress, affectionate but just a little weak in the head. Could not spell, and found letter writing difficult. In a small way an heiress, with an inheritance and a reversion of nearly £4000. Left her Essex home in 1874 to visit cousins in London *RTHPL*

Louis Staunton was twenty-three, an impecunious auctioneer's clerk when he met Harriet. 'Of the type which housemaids call handsome', somebody said. Proposed to Harriet, was accepted. Marriage strongly opposed by Harriet's mother on the ground of her feeble-mindedness, but it took place in June 1875. Child born in the following spring *RTHPL*

Patrick Staunton. Louis's elder brother. He and his wife Elizabeth took Harriet to live with them in August 1876, in their desolate cottage at Cudham near Sevenoaks in Kent. The baby was already there *RTHPL*

Alice Rhodes was Louis's mistress. Lived with him, at first in London with Harriet in the same house, then near Cudham where she passed as Louis's wife *RTHPL*

Louis Staunton

Patrick Staunton

Alice Rhodes

Harriet Staunton

The scene at the inquest. The baby died of neglect early in April 1877. Louis, using the name of Harris, ordered the funeral. Harriet died a few days later. She had been literally starved to death, weighing only 5 stone instead of a normal weight of nearly double that. Her body was filthy and covered with vermin, the hair matted. She had been given only dry bread and tea for months, kept shut up in her room and shouted at if she left it. When her boots fell off her feet from age and use she walked in bare feet. The Stauntons were tried and sentenced to death, but the possibility that Harriet might have died from tubercular meningitis caused the sentence to be commuted to life imprisonment. Alice Rhodes, who had no direct part in Harriet's death, was acquitted *RTHPL*

Michel Eyraud *CP*   Gabrielle Bompard *CP*   Gouffé *CP*

Detection by science, pertinacity and luck

Detection at this time – detection as distinct from
Bertillon's methods of identification – was a matter of
science, pertinacity and luck. These are well shown
in three French cases of the period.

Forensic science took a leap forward in 1889 when
Professor Lacassagne of the University of Lyons was
able to identify a corpse found in a sack in the river
Rhône as that of a bailiff named Gouffé, who had
vanished from his Paris home. Gouffé had been
murdered for his money by a man named Eyraud and
a prostitute named Gabrielle Bompard. They had
then wrapped the body in a sack, put the sack inside
a trunk, taken the trunk by train to a point near
Lyons, and dumped it in the river, where the trunk
broke and the body dropped out. The detective work
involved was remarkable. Goron, the Chef de la
Sûreté, traced the trunk from Paris to Lyons through
an only partly-legible label. Lacassagne's pathological discoveries, undertaken after an autopsy had
been conducted three months before by one of his
pupils who had decided definitely that the body was
not that of Gouffé, were more remarkable still. By
measurement and comparison of the bones he es-

The trunk in the Gouffé case after reconstruction.

tablished that the dead man had walked with a limp, had suffered from inflammation of one ankle and also from water on the knee. It was found that this was precisely Gouffé's condition. His height was assessed through the bones, his age through the teeth. Both corresponded to those of Gouffé. Finally the last stumbling block was overcome. The corpse had black hair, Gouffé's had been brown, but Lacassagne had already observed that hair could change colour inside a coffin. He obtained Gouffé's hairbrush, compared the hairs on it with those on the head of the dead man, and was able to say positively that the corpse was that of Gouffé.

The case of Henri Pranzini involved dogged detective work. When the body of Madame de Mantille was found in her apartment in the Rue Montaigne in Paris, together with those of her maid-servant and the servant's child, clues were not lacking. There were bloody fingermarks (but this was in 1887, before the days of fingerprinting), and the murderer had left his detachable shirt cuffs and a belt with the name 'Gaston Geissler' inside it. Geissler was searched for, and a description of him was obtained. At the same time a description of the jewellery stolen from the apartment was issued, and a man was found trying to sell some of it. But this man gave his name as Pranzini, and claimed that he was a Swedish doctor.

Were Pranzini and Geissler one and the same? There was no means of knowing, and if Geissler was not found the case against Pranzini would certainly fail. Goron, at this time only Assistant Chef de la Sûreté, spent several weeks travelling from Brussels to Cologne to Berlin to Breslau before he traced a valise found in 'Geissler's' hotel to a man named Guttentag, whose innocence was proved by the fact that he had been in prison when the murders were committed. The way was now clear to bring a case against Pranzini, and eventually a genuine Geissler was discovered, against whom Pranzini had a bitter enough grudge to leave the belt and cuffs as a false trail.

Luck however, as Goron once observed, is often the detective's finest collaborator. Prado, who called himself at times the Count de Linska, also murdered a woman for her jewels. Almost a year later he was arrested, but only for common theft. While he was in custody he was seen by two women friends who were also under arrest, and one of them handed to the police a scrap of paper which she had kept after a violent quarrel with Prado. It contained the address of the jeweller in Madrid to whom Prado had sold the jewels obtained through the murder. If he had not been arrested at just that time ... Prado could consider himself unlucky.

Prado

Pranzini

63

Murder in church

The fascination of the murders that took place in San Francisco's Emanuel Baptist Church lies not only in the macabre setting, but in the total disregard shown by the murderer, William Henry Theodore Durrant, of the trail of witnesses who saw him do everything but actually commit the crimes. It is almost as though he had wished them to be publicly known.

Durrant was undoubtedly schizophrenic. He was a devout young man, assistant superintendent at the Sunday School, so polite, kind and well liked that many people refused to believe in his guilt in the face of overwhelming evidence. Some of his fellow medical students regarded him as rather dismally pious. There were rumours of quite different behaviour on his part, but they were not generally believed. He was, after all, a genuinely good young man.

On 3 April 1895, Durrant met a tall, dreamy, pretty girl of twenty-one named Blanche Lamont after she came out of High School. They knew each other well, and had often been out together. He made no attempt to conceal his actions, and the two were seen together on the cable car, crossing Twenty Second Street, and actually entering the church. A woman who lived opposite saw Blanche, a tall girl in a floppy hat, go in the side gate, followed by young Theo Durrant. That was at half past four. At five o'clock the church organist arrived and found his friend Theo looking pale and tired after, as he said, breathing escaping gas from a jet he had been fixing upstairs. During that half hour Durrant had strangled Blanche, presumably after she refused to have intercourse with him, dragged her body upstairs into the Sunday School room and then further up and up, right into the belfry tower. There he took off her clothes and left her, putting two wooden blocks under her head to hold it in place and crossing her hands over her.

Blanche Lamont's disappearance caused her family great anxiety, but Theo Durrant was above or beyond suspicion. He told another woman friend named Minnie Williams, who also attended the Emanuel Baptist Church, something about Blanche's disappearance which upset her. Nevertheless nine days later, on 12 April, Minnie Williams left the house where she worked as a maid (her place in the social scale was much lower than that of Blanche Lamont) to meet Durrant. Again there was an unbroken chain of witnesses who saw them together, and there was even a man named Zengler who saw them enter the church. Zengler was suspicious about what went on in the church, and he waited until Durrant reappeared alone. Then, apparently satisfied that nothing untoward had happened, Zengler went home.

Within the church Durrant had had intercourse with Minnie and had then gagged and murdered her, using a knife to slash her wrists, forehead and body. Blood spurted over the walls. He may have had intercourse with her again, and he then stuffed the body behind an open door in the Library. It was found there the next day by women coming to decorate the church for Easter.

At his trial Durrant was perfectly calm and cheerful as he asserted his innocence. He spoke of having prophetic dreams in his cell and of following his sister to Germany and pursuing his medical studies at Heidelberg. (His sister later became famous as a dancer under the name of Maude Allan.) In very few murder cases has there been so little room for doubt, yet his speech from the scaffold convinced two of the men detailed to supervise the hanging that Theo Durrant was innocent.

Theodore Durrant *McDade Collection*

The Emmanuel Baptist Church in San
Francisco   *McDade Collection*

Blanche Lamont, the first of the murdered
girls   *McDade Collection*

65

Robbing the Bank of England

One of the most audacious swindles of the century was that practised by George Bidwell and his brother Austin, with their accomplices George Macdonnell and Edwin Noyes. It was nothing less than an attempt to rob the Bank of England. Austin opened an account there, and paid in a perfectly genuine bill of Rothschild's for £4500. Having established confidence 'he then said that he was going to manufacture Pullman cars in a large way in Birmingham, and obtained the Bank's agreement to the discounting of bills. These bills, all of them excellently forged by Macdonnell, were presented for more than £100,000 and duly cashed. The forgers were undone only by gross carelessness. On two of the forged acceptances Macdonnell had forgotten to insert the date. They were

supposed to have been drawn by Rothschild's, and when the Bank of England returned them to have the dates added, the game was up.

It was usual for swindlers at this time to have some skill in forgery, or at least to be in touch with a forger. Walter Sheridan, who was said by some to have been the moving spirit behind the Bidwells' enterprise – he was certainly justly contemptuous of the carelessness which caused it to fail – was both an accomplished forger and a swindler. Beginning in a small way, as the pupil of a hotel thief, Sheridan became a specialist in defrauding banks. He was, as can be seen from the illustration, impressively respectable in appearance, and frauds of various kinds made him a man of property. The Pinkertons were put on to his track,

The trial of the Bidwells, Macdonnell and Noyes at the Old Bailey in 1873 *RTHPL*

The arrest of Walter Sheridan by a Pinkerton man

and for some time Allan Pinkerton and his son stayed in a Michigan hotel owned by Sheridan in order to get a picture of him. Caught, tried and acquitted, he launched an immensely successful series of forged bonds and securities. Sheridan's usual approach was to ask for a loan on bonds which he offered for security, and his success was based on the excellence of his forgeries. Having made a million dollars and ruined several Wall Street brokers he went to Europe, where he expressed himself ready to settle for life.

His end was sad and, for such a man, unworthy. Unable to resist the lure of his own country he returned to the United States, started a bank of his own (of all foolish things!) and lost his money in deplorably wild, and honest, speculation. He was arrested by a Pinkerton man when about to launch a fresh series of forged securities, and his subsequent life was spent in and out of prison.

Edward Ketchum, an American forger, practised a variety of hands. These two forged letters from non-existent members of his family were carried by him to support his assumed character as a Western merchant. The gold cheque was also forged by him and he gave value for money, as it were, by having the word GOLD actually printed in gold letters running across the cheque

The con man of all time?

Was the Tichborne Claimant the con man of all time, laying claim to be the vanished Sir Roger Tichborne when he was in reality Arthur Orton, the son of a Wapping butcher? Certainly the imposture was immensely successful. Roger Tichborne had disappeared from South America in 1853; the Claimant came to England from Australia in 1865. He was accepted without question by his mother, Lady Tichborne, by the family solicitor, and by some others who had known Roger, rejected by far more including, naturally enough, those whose inheritance he was claiming as his own. In the legal battle lasting for years which ended in his total defeat and sentence to 14 years' imprisonment, the Claimant made an enormous number of glaring mistakes – he had forgotten his mother's maiden name, knew nothing about the family estates, could recall no details of the school where Roger Tichborne had been educated, thought that Caesar was written in Greek, and believed that Virgil was a general or a statesman. Roger Tichborne spoke French well, the Claimant was almost totally ignorant of it.

Yet there was something to be said on the other side. When the Claimant fined down in prison from his monstrous weight of 24 stone to something like 10 stone, his letters changed altogether in style and

An unusual picture of the Tichborne Claimant *RTHPL*

The hut at Wagga Wagga in Australia, where the Claimant lived *RTHPL*

Mrs Gordon-Baillie

Hugh L. Courtenay *RTHPL*

character, becoming quite remarkably literate. In one he quoted from the Psalms in Latin, and these letters were utterly out of character for the ignorant butcher's son Arthur Orton. He retained many passionate adherents. Was it not possible to discover some physical marks which would have clinched the matter? Strangely, it was not. Bertillon said that a simple comparison of the Claimant's lobeless ear with that of Roger Tichborne disproved his case, but it was said in reply that mental disturbances, including sunstroke, could be responsible for such a change. Tattoo marks were invoked, various measurements were called into question, there was even discussion of a malformation of the genitals which the Claimant had and which Roger Tichborne may have had. With our knowledge of the personality changes which can occur through changes in weight, we can grant that the whole question is more complicated than Victorian writers were willing to admit. As Douglas Woodruff said at the end of his masterly and surely definitive account of the case, published in 1957: 'The great doubt still hangs suspended.'

In 1885 there appeared in London a tall fair-haired lady, always very elegantly and even floridly dressed, named Mrs Gordon-Baillie. She was the friend of a baronet in his eighties who had made himself personally responsible for her, but when he went into bankruptcy after spending £20,000 on her, Mrs Gordon-Baillie survived. A year or so after his bankruptcy she was passionately championing the cause of the crofters in the Scottish island of Skye. She went to Australia to obtain a grant of land where they might settle, and the Victorian Government gave her 70,000 acres. Before the crofters could leave for Australia, however, Mrs Gordon-Baillie had been arrested. She had floated so long on the sea of prosperity by the old practice of ordering goods, paying for them with a cheque above their value, and taking the change in cash. The cheques, of course, were worthless, but when they were dishonoured she paid importunate tradesmen with the cash obtained from other worthless cheques. The London-Australian blaze of glory was the peak of a career which had been marked by many similar swindles.

Hugh L. Courtenay, alias Lord Beresford, alias Sir Harry Vane of Her Majesty's Light Infantry was born in England, 1852, the son of a lodge-keeper named Clinton. A lord about town in New York while still in his twenties, and then Sir Hugh Courtenay of the Royal Navy in Baltimore, where the young ladies cut off the buttons of his uniform for souvenirs, Clinton was a typical con man, bouncing back from prison sentences for fraud and forgery into one of a variety of uniforms. Most of his operations were carried out in the United States.

The death of Lincoln

The shooting of President Abraham Lincoln, unlike most political murders, had a purpose. John Wilkes Booth was a fanatical sympathizer with the South in the Civil War, and although he had spent the war years in the North, where he was in demand as a tragic actor, he had made no secret of his view that the country would benefit if the South won the war. He believed also that if Lincoln was killed the Southern cause might still triumph, even though General Lee had surrendered.

It is probable that to-day we should regard Booth's acting as mere rant, but he cannot have been as bad an actor as he was a conspirator. In Washington taverns he talked incessantly about what he would do, saying that he would kidnap Lincoln and take him in chains to Richmond. He ruled among his little band of associates by passion and gimcrack eloquence rather than intelligence, and it is not surprising that nobody took his boasting seriously.

At the same time, it is true that the President was scandalously unguarded. He had asked for a body-guard, but when he attended the performance of a play called *Our American Cousin* at Ford's Theatre on 14 April 1865, the one man provided was away drinking when Booth went to the President's private box, walked in unquestioned, pointed his Derringer behind the President's ear, and shot. He then jumped to the stage in what he must have visualized as a triumphant dramatic leap. He caught his foot on a spur, landed awkwardly and fractured his shin, but in the general confusion managed to escape. Lincoln was taken to Peterson House nearby, where he died within a few minutes.

The conspirators had planned triple assassinations, but George Atzerodt got drunk and did not attempt to kill Vice-President Andrew Johnson, and although young Lewis Paine stabbed Secretary of State William H. Seward, he did not kill him. Booth's end had its own pathos. He was on the run for twelve days with another of his group named David Herold, but his dream that he would be welcomed as a hero in the South proved to be wholly wrong. A doctor put his leg in splints, but nobody in Maryland or Virginia would take him in. When, exhausted and desperate, they were surrounded by soldiers in the barn of Garrett's Farm in Bowling Green, Virginia, Herold surrendered. 'I'll shoot it out with the whole damned detachment', Booth cried. After the barn had been set on fire, however, he was shot by Sergeant Boston Corbett, who said that his order to shoot had come from the Almighty. Atzerodt, Paine, Herold and Mrs Suratt, the wife of another of the conspirators, were later tried and hanged

John Wilkes Booth *RTHPL*

Boston Corbett, the Sergeant who shot Booth *RTHPL*

The assassination. Booth fires with his one shot Derringer   *RTHPL*

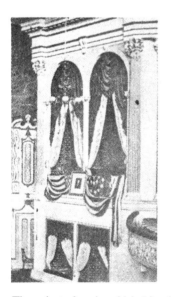

The private box in which Lincoln was sitting at the theatre
NYPL

Peterson House, where the President died   *NYPL*

The execution of four of the conspirators   *McDade Collection*

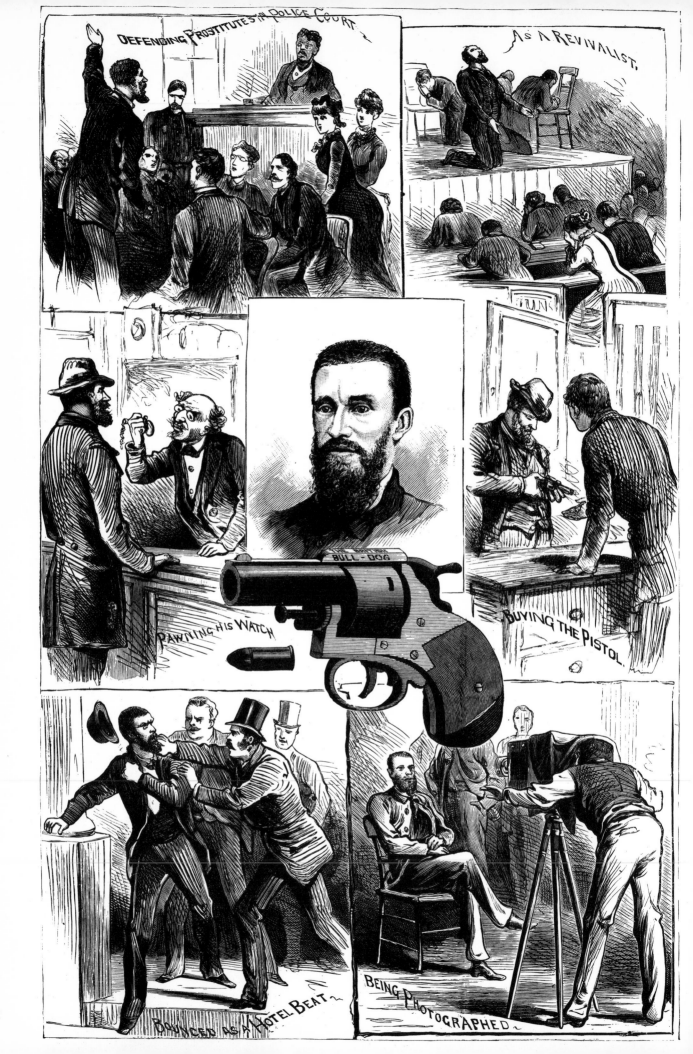

DEFENDING PROSTITUTES IN POLICE COURT.

AS A REVIVALIST.

PAWNING HIS WATCH.

BULL-DOG

BUYING THE PISTOL.

BOUNCED AS A HOTEL BEAT.

BEING PHOTOGRAPHED.

The murder of President Garfield

If Booth showed almost megalomaniac vanity, Charles Guiteau was without doubt insane. He had been a lawyer – he specialized in defending prostitutes even after contracting syphilis from one of them – and had travelled through New England as a generally unsuccessful lecturer and preacher. He has also served a short prison term for fraud. He considered himself still an evangelist when in 1880 he received divine instruction that he should work for the election of James A. Garfield at the Presidential election. Garfield probably never read the speech he wrote, 'Garfield Against Hancock', and certainly never delivered it, but after Garfield's election Guiteau decided that his efforts deserved the Austrian ambassadorship as his reward.

Like other men, Guiteau found his hopes disappointed when he went to Washington to claim his due. He wrote letters to the President, he saw Secretary of State Blaine, he modified his demands first to the Paris consulship and then even to a mere pension for an old soldier who had served in the Civil War. It was to no effect. Guiteau bought a revolver and followed Garfield as he left the White House to go to the Baltimore & Potomac Railway station. In the station waiting room he pulled out his .44 calibre Bulldog revolver and shot Garfield twice in the back. Taken to prison, he began at once to write his memoirs.

One of the bullets had lodged near Garfield's pancreas and could not be removed. Shot on 2 July 1881, he lingered on in pain through the summer, and died in mid-September. The letter found on Guiteau when he was arrested had of course been written in anticipation of this event. 'I presume the President was a Christian, and that he will be happier in Paradise than here', he wrote, adding that he felt no personal ill-will. 'His death was a political necessity. I am a lawyer, theologian, politician. I am stalwart of the stalwarts; I was with General Grant and the rest of our men in New York during the canvass. I am going to jail.'

The assassination of Garfield was a meaningless end to Guiteau's meaningless life. On the scaffold he recited a poem he had written, before being hanged.

A press view of the assassination *NYPL*

There were seven attempts to assassinate Queen Victoria during the sixty-odd years of her reign, of which this was the first. In June 1840 an eighteen-year old potboy named Edward Oxford fired two pistol shots at the Queen and Prince Consort in Constitution Hill, from no more than five yard's distance. They were not hit. Quite unmoved, they drove on to their destination, the Duchess of Kent's house in Belgrave Square. The Queen's Prime Minister wrote: 'Viscount Palmerston humbly trusts that the failure of this atrocious attempt may be considered as an indication that your Majesty is reserved for a long and prosperous reign.' *RTHPL*

The assassination of Sadi Carnot, President of France, in June 1894, was said at the time to be the culmination of a series of Anarchist attacks on public figures. Two years earlier Ravachol (see page 35) had planted bombs in the houses of the Judge and Public Prosecutor who had officiated at the trial of some Parisian Anarchists. In 1893 Auguste Vaillant had tried to blow up the French Chamber of Deputies with a bomb which exploded prematurely, precipitating only a shower of nails. Yet although the Italian Santo Geronimo Caserio, who killed Carnot, belonged to Anarchist groups, there is no doubt that he acted as an individual. He chose Carnot because the President had refused to grant Vaillant a reprieve. His weapon was a fancy dagger with an ornamental handle and a six inch blade.

Carnot went to Lyons to open a big French Colonial Exhibition. He had attended a banquet and was on his way to the theatre when Caserio broke through the cordon surrounding him, jumped up on to the President's landau and struck so powerfully that the dagger went up to the hilt in Carnot's body.

The security arrangements were so wretchedly inadequate that Caserio nearly got away. When he was caught he was almost lynched. An operation was performed on Carnot while fireworks in honour of his visit lit up the sky. It was in vain. He died within a few hours. Two months later his killer's head fell on the guillotine *NYPL*

Queen Victoria
Carnot
McKinley

The Temple of Music at Buffalo, where McKinley was shot on 6 September 1901 *NYPL*

The last picture of McKinley, taken as he mounted the steps of the Temple *NYPL*

The assassination shown in a contemporary painting. Czolgosz approached with the gun concealed by a handkerchief *NYPL*

Leon Czolgosz, shown here in his cell after arrest, was the unstable, neurotic child of a Polish immigrant family. He had approached more than one Anarchist group, but they were suspicious of his vague talk of revolution, and it seems that he acted entirely on his own. Czolgosz had nothing against McKinley, but he had grown to hate America, which kept his parents poor. He bought a short-barrelled .32 calibre Ives-Johnson revolver, attended the great Exposition being held at Buffalo, where McKinley was to make a speech, advanced on the President and shot twice through his handkerchief. McKinley, shot through the stomach, died within a few hours. It had been a meaningless crime, like that of Guiteau, a mere expression of personal inadequacy. When the police asked Czolgosz who he was, he replied: 'Fred Nieman'. *Fred Nobody*: Nobody killed the President *NYPL*

20th century first half

INTO THE FINGERPRINT AGE

The ineradicable print

The greatest single scientific discovery made in forensic science was undoubtedly the realization that every fingerprint shows markings that are unique. Fingerprinting as a form of signature had been common in Japan and China for many years, and in the early nineteenth century the engraver Thomas Bewick placed his thumb-mark, with his name attached to it, as a colophon to some of his work. In Bengal it was customary for illiterates to make their mark by wetting the tip of one finger with ink and then pressing it to paper. All these, however, were marks made for security rather than identification, and so was the Chinese banking practice of placing thumbmarks on notes, the mark being placed partly on the note and partly on the counterfoil so that they matched.

The idea that fingerprints might be unique occurred to a Scottish physician named Henry Faulds, when he was working in Tokyo. In the eighteen-seventies Faulds collected a good many fingerprints, and by chance became involved in a case of theft in which prints of sooty fingers had been left on a wall. A man had been arrested, but Faulds found that his prints were obviously different from those left on the wall. Later this man was released and another man arrested. Faulds compared the prints of this fresh suspect with those on the wall, and found that they corresponded. A second similar case convinced Faulds that he had made a revolutionary discovery, and in 1880 he wrote to the English journal *Nature* about it.

The letter was read by William Herschel, a civil servant working for the East India Company in Bengal. He promptly wrote to *Nature*, claiming that he had used fingerprints for identification twenty years before Faulds. The claim had some justification. In 1858 Herschel had asked an Indian named Konai to sign an agreement made for some road metalling with the palm of his hand, using the oil-ink kept for the official seal. Herschel's object was to impress Konai with the solemnity of the contract, but he became scientifically interested in the subject. In 1860, while working as a district magistrate, he took up fingerprinting in earnest, and some years later solved the problem of paying allowances to Indian soldiers who all looked very much alike to him, and who often sent friends and relations to collect their pension twice over. He first of all made a register of their fingerprints, and then made them 'sign' for the payments by pressing their inked fingers to the receipt. He found no difficulty in checking these prints. He also made tests which convinced him that fingerprints were ineradicable and did not change with the years, and in 1874 wrote to the Inspector-General of Bengal prisons suggesting that finger-printing would provide 'the means of verifying the identity of every man in jail'. The Inspector-General was not impressed, and Herschel dropped the idea.

Faulds's letter reawakened his interest, and an unedifying controversy ensued about credit for the discovery. Herschel became famous, the peppery Faulds was more or less ignored. Yet it was Faulds rather than Herschel who first realized the uses of the ineradicable mark in criminal investigation.

A Chinese bank note, showing the thumb print at the right hand side

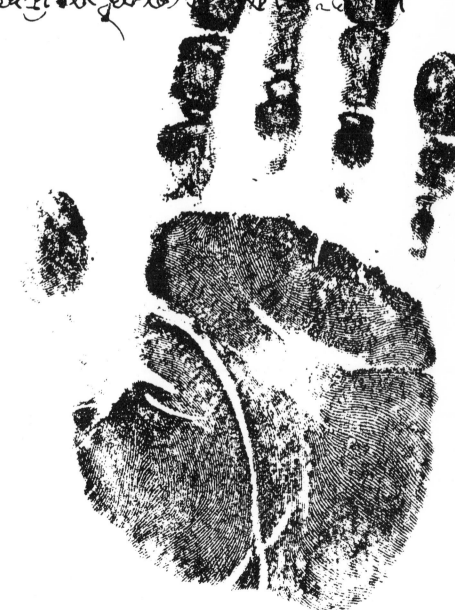

The contract for 2000 maunds of road-metalling, made in 1858 between Herschel and Konai, in Konai's handwriting

Konai's 'signature' by means of his palm print

William John Herschel

Devising a system

When a scientific discovery has been made the next question is always: how do you use it in practice? The development of fingerprints owed most to Sir Francis Galton, the credit for adapting them into a system for criminal investigation belongs to Sir Edward Henry and Juan Vucetich.

Galton, a cousin of Charles Darwin, was one of those scientific all-rounders who flourished in the Victorian age. He was a physician who never practised, a disciple of Lombroso who was also much impressed by Bertillon, a traveller who in the adventurous Victorian tradition tried to discover the source of the Nile. His prime interest was anthropology, and his secondary one the almost untouched field of statistical research. His contribution to the development of fingerprinting was in the field of classification. After endless investigation of deltas, arches, loops and whorls, Galton distinguished four basic types of fingerprint that he thought might serve as a basis for a system of registration. His *Fingerprints* (1892) greatly impressed the police members of the Troup committee who later visited Bertillon (see page 35).

Galton himself never devised a workable registration system, but Sir Edward Henry, who did so, owed his first instruction in fingerprinting to Galton. Henry, who was Inspector-General of Police in Bengal, had been using *bertillonage* with moderate success. On a home leave in England he visited Galton, took away a portmanteau full of photographs, and after his return to India devised the cataloguing system which became established throughout the world. Henry discerned five basic patterns, assigned code numbers to them, and then broke

Sir Francis Galton. Discovering deltas, arches, loops and whorls

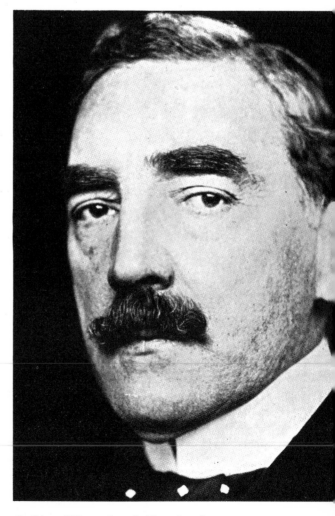

Sir Edward Henry. A workable registration system

down these main patterns into a great many sub-divisions. He invented a new terminology for the relationships of Galton's loops and whorls, and set up a fingerprint registration system in Bengal. Within months anthropometry had been replaced by dacty-loscopy, as it was called, throughout British India. In 1900 Henry's report to a London committee impressed them so much that fingerprinting was made the official criminal identification system in Britain. Henry was appointed head of the C.I.D., and in 1903 became Police Commissioner.

The great Argentinian police criminologist Juan Vucetich was an enthusiastic advocate of finger-printing almost from the day in 1891 when he read an article by Galton and realized the immense possibilities of a fingerprint system. Quite independently of Henry he devised his own coding for basic patterns, and worked out sub-divisions which were not identical with Henry's but were equally effective. Within a year a murder in Buenos Aires had been solved through a bloody thumb mark left on a door. In 1896 Argentina became the first country to base its system of identification upon fingerprinting. In 1901 Vucetich attended a Scientific Congress in Montevideo and expressed himself in scathing terms about anthropometry.

His success had been immense, and his fertile mind conceived the idea of international identification bureaux which would exchange information. But Vucetich's passion for logical completeness ruined his career. It seemed to him obvious that every human being should have his fingerprints taken, and in 1916 after years of controversy the Argentine Govern-ment passed a law authorizing the fingerprinting of the whole population and of all resident foreigners. The storm of protest was so great that the scheme was hurriedly abandoned (it has never yet been put into effect in any country), many records were destroyed, and Vucetich was forced to resign his official post. He died in retirement in 1925.

Juan Vucetich. He wanted to fingerprint the whole population of Argentina

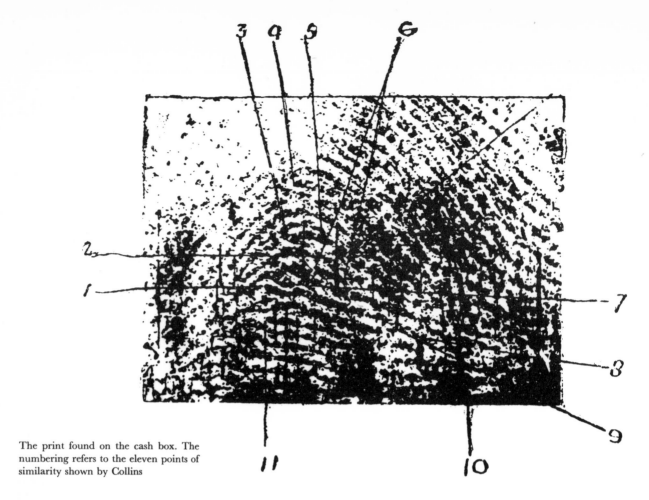

The print found on the cash box. The numbering refers to the eleven points of similarity shown by Collins

The thumbprint of Alfred Stratton

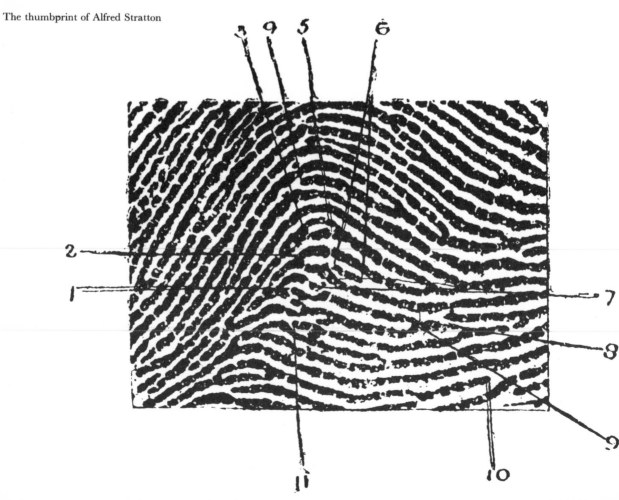

The Stratton case

It was one thing to devise an excellent registration system for fingerprints, another to get prints accepted as evidence in an English court. On Derby Day, 1902, fifty-odd men were arrested on Epsom racecourse. They were fingerprinted, the impressions checked with the fingerprint file, and more than half were found to have criminal records. In this way fingerprinting provided a useful check on criminals using false names, but the real test was whether a jury would accept fingerprints as evidence. In September 1902, prints on freshly-painted woodwork played a part in the conviction of a man arrested at Denmark Hill in London on a charge of burglary, but there was other evidence which might have led to a conviction. The first true test came with the murder of an elderly couple named Farrow who lived above a little oil and paint shop in London's dingy suburb of Deptford. This was obviously murder for money, and a small cash box with a japanned surface was found under a bed.

The surface of the box was ideal for taking prints, and a clear thumb-mark was found on the tray inside the box. A detective sergeant had moved the tray, but his prints proved to be totally unlike the thumb mark. Local enquiries identified the likely murderers as two young toughs named Stratton. They were arrested, charged with murder, and their prints were taken. 'I shall never forget the dramatic entry made into my room by the expert an hour or two later', Melville MacNaghten says in his memoirs. ' "Good God, sir" ', he exclaimed, with pardonable

Henry Faulds in old age

excitement, "I have found that the mark on the cash-box tray is in exact correspondence with the print of the right thumb of the elder prisoner." ' Perhaps the expert did not express himself in precisely those pedantic words, but in any case the discovery led to a historic trial. There was very little solid evidence against the Strattons. Could a conviction be obtained on the print?

The prosecutor was Sir Richard Muir, who had also prosecuted in the burglary case, and had thoroughly familiarized himself with the new science. His exposition of the thumb print found was lucid and simple, and he employed Detective Sergeant (later Inspector) Collins to point out on a blackboard the eleven points of similarity between the thumb print of Alfred Stratton and the print found on the tray. The defence had their own experts, one of whom was Henry Faulds. The feeling that he had been deprived of his rightful share of glory in discovering the importance of fingerprints was now strong in Faulds's mind, and he said that he found discrepancies between the prints, discrepancies which were in fact a matter of more or less pressure being applied. Collins demonstrated this when he took the prints of the jurymen several times in succession, and showed that similar discrepancies occurred in them. The jury were convinced. The verdict was guilty.

Within a few years fingerprinting had replaced anthropometry throughout Europe. In some cases the enlightened police chiefs who had acclaimed Bertillon's system showed that they remained enlightened by abandoning it. America lagged behind a little, but in 1906 a New York detective named Farrant arrested an Englishman on suspicion of theft, sent his prints to Scotland Yard, and received in return a fingerprint card identifying the man as a well known hotel thief. By 1910 almost every country in the world had adopted fingerprinting, although some of them also sent out anthropometric measurements on their 'Wanted' notices. The permanence, as well as the uniqueness, of fingerprints had also been proved. Experiments were made by cauterizing and burning the fingertips to try to get rid of the tell-tale papillary lines. They all failed. The lines quickly grew again.

Alone among criminological scientists Bertillon refused to believe that 'tiny spots on human fingertips' could compete with his system. When he died in 1914 anthropometry still reigned in France. A few weeks after his death his own country abandoned it in favour of fingerprinting.

New homes, new machines

During the first years of the century police departments all over the world were occupied in modernizing themselves. This implied not only obtaining money to buy new equipment, but also having police officers who could use it. There were policemen in high places in almost all forces who said that the methods used in their youth were good enough for the present day. They were slowly weeded out and replaced by men who had their emotional roots in the twentieth century. These new men were aware of wireless telegraphy, and were prepared to see the horse replaced by the motorcar.

The first building occupied by the U.S. Department of Justice in Washington, from the 1880s to 1899. The Department had four floors of the building, which housed between 150 and 200 employees. They were allotted a single telephone *FBI*

The old Hall of Justice, San Francisco *SFPD*

The Department's second home, from 1899 to 1917 *FBI*

San Francisco mounted police on parade *SFPD*

A modern view of New Scotland Yard   *Metropolitan Police*

A Peking Black Maria   *NYPL*

A motor police patrol car, a great innovation in South America, in Rio de Janeiro, 1907   *NYPL*

Some of the last of the horse-drawn police wagons, outside Fresnes Prison, Paris   *RTHPL*

Modernization can be painful

The process of modernization was often painful. The idea that women might be employed for police work was both repugnant and ridiculous to many people, and until 1907 physical examination of women suspects was conducted in England by a male police sergeant. The first woman to go 'on the beat' wearing uniform was Teilmann Idsen, and doubts were expressed about her safety. 'If the experiment proves successful a regular corps of police Amazons will be formed and distributed throughout the country', a commentator wrote, and Amazonian strength was thought essential, as the picture of a police matron suggests. The 1914–18 War, which solved so many similar problems for women, brought general acceptance of the role as uniformed police which they now play all over the world.

For the most part the police readily accepted that they were the paid servants of any state – Communist, Fascist, or empire-building Japanese. Their rebellious moments are worth recording. One in England was the police strike of 1918, when the men demanded both pay increases and recognition of the National Union of Police and Prison Officers. Several thousands of police marched from Smith Square in London to Tower Hill behind a single bagpiper, who had brought his pipes down from Scotland. They got their pay rise, with a pension for their widows, but official recognition of the Union was refused. The strike led to the resignation of Sir Edward Henry, who was held responsible for allowing the pay negotiations to hang fire. Another strike in 1919 for Union recognition was poorly supported, and many of those who joined it were dismissed.

Teilmann Idsen, who in 1911 became the first uniformed woman police constable in the world. She was stationed at Aalborg, in Denmark *NYPL*

Right: Police matron attached to New York City Police *NYPL*

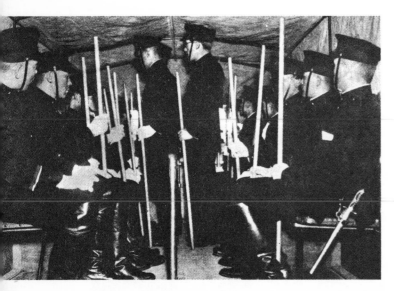

Japanese 'thought police' look out for thought criminals with dangerous ideas. They are equipped to deal with dangerous thoughts by physical means. *NYPL*

When the Japanese invaded Manchuria they made great efforts to train a loyal local police force. Here a young Chinese student in the Police School at Hsinking is interrogating a suspect (*right*). The Japanese instructor (*left*) gives advice and criticism *NYPL*

A rare picture of a Russian policeman and woman in the early nineteen-thirties *NYPL*

A smart group of Polish women police in the 1930s *Mansell*

London, August 1918. The police go on strike *RTHPL*

Early 20th century. A squad of Indian police at riot drill

Mexican rurales under the Diaz regime. Before his fall in 1911 they formed one of the most savagely repressive police forces in the world *NYPL*

Old and new

The different developments of police forces is one of the prime facts of their history. This is true not only of poor and backward countries like some of the South American Republics, nor is it simply a matter of the police being the servants of a repressive regime, as in Mexico and Spain. The New Zealand police, for instance, are in many ways among the most forward-looking in the world. A Police Training School was opened in 1898, and a fingerprints registration system was adopted in 1904. A C.I.B. (Criminal Investigation [Detective] Branch) has existed since 1886, and comparison with other forces shows how well aware New Zealand police officials were of some modern techniques. But no patrol car system existed in the country until 1938, and two-way radios were not introduced until ten years later. No criticism of the New Zealand police is implied. Often a comparatively small force is hampered by lack of money, and in such a country as New Zealand native police may have a part to play even in modern society. In the use of new scientific devices, and particularly in the development of radio communication, the New York police have a wonderful record. Comparisons are unwise, but many big American and European cities did not use radio systems until the end of the twenties.

A Bedouin in the Iraq Desert Patrol. The silver star bears the words 'Iraq Police' *NYPL*

A Maori policeman of 1910, with his billy *NYPL*

Motorized police in Philadelphia, on their way to deal with a tram strike *RTHPL*

The Manhattan Telegraph Bureau, New York, 1898   *NYPD*

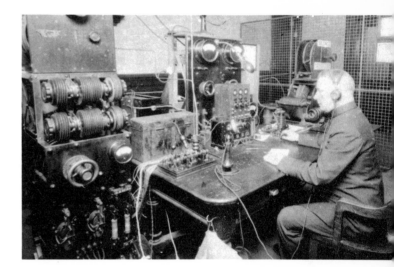

'KUVS' Radio Station, Manhattan, 1916   *NYPD*

New York's first two way police radio car, 1917   *NYPD*

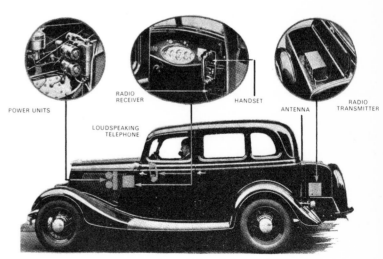

Police car with two way radio equipment, 1930s   *NYPL*

Science and disguise

The Gouffé case (page 62) had shown how useful dental characteristics could be in establishing identity, and by the beginning of the century many police forces realized that careful examination of a dead person's mouth might provide important clues. In the case shown below all marks of identification had been removed from a dead woman's body, and she had been so badly burned by the sun as to be unrecognizable. The Chief of Police at Colorado Springs provided twenty lines of information about her dental structure, adding that the dental chart was the only remaining evidence of identification, and asking other police chiefs to 'call the attention of dentists in your city' to the chart.

Contrary to general belief disguise did not go out with Sherlock Holmes, although it has always been favoured by some forces and deprecated by others. French detectives between the wars were particularly fond of disguising themselves, particularly when trying to penetrate militant Left-wing organizations and criminal gangs, and the Turkish police, as can be seen from the illustration, had a regular make-up department. The 'young women' in the illustration (a recent picture) are all men. These New York detectives act as decoys in areas where muggers operate, ready to cosh an unescorted woman on sight, and take her handbag. Such assignments are thought to be too dangerous for women police. The decoys are armed, and have had considerable success in checking violence against respectable women.

At the Police Training School in Hendon the instructor shows recruits how defaced numbers on licence plates, and other number alterations, show up under infra red photography *Mirrorpic*

An interesting detail from a 1904 Wanted notice, showing the attention already paid to dental characteristics *McDade Collection*

DESCRIPTION OF NUDE BODY OF MURDERED WOMAN
Found on Cutler Mountain, December 17th, 1904.

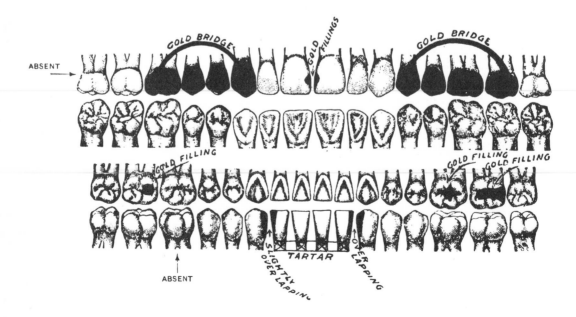

Le Bozec the bookseller's tout *NYPL*

Inspector Le Bozec of Marseilles disguised as a dock labourer *NYPL*

Le Bozec undisguised *NYPL*

Le Bozec as accomplice of a murderer, who carried gloves in his left hand *NYPL*

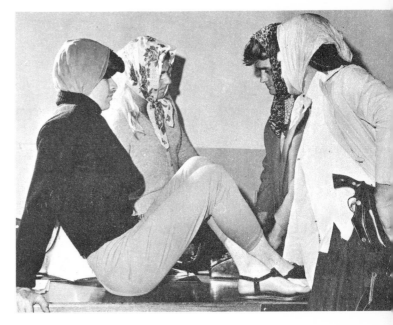

The make up room at a Turkish police institute *NYPL*

Why does the attractive young woman need a revolver? *NYPD*

A prison experiment set up by the Cuban Government on the Isla da Pinos, sixty miles off the Cuban mainland, during the 1920s. This was one of several circular cell houses with doorless cells permitting free communication. The houses were watched over from a heavily armed central guardhouse. All work was carried on by prisoners, who ran their own farm. Escapes were punishable by death, and were rarely attempted *ILN*

One of the circular cell houses. Each of them held 900 prisoners. At the back is a good conduct building with larger cells *ILN*

The baseball ground of the Isla da Pinos prisons *ILN*

Some prisons are modernized

'Moral regeneration should be the primary aim of prison discipline and hope should always be a more powerful agent than fear.' This pious resolution was passed at a London Congress in 1872, but little was done to put it into practice during the next half century. Most of the genuine reforms in prison life and treatment took place in European countries with enlightened administrators, like the Scandinavian countries or Germany under the Weimar Republic. The Cuban Isla da Pinos experiment, shown above, became eventually chiefly a home for political prisoners of the hated General Machado, and later of Batista. In Britain the living conditions of prisoners undoubtedly improved, but prisons still remained houses of correction, where reform was no more than an idea which even the best-intentioned Governors found impossible of achievement. In the United States things were far worse. Silent and Solitary systems had long ago been abandoned, and in 1919 John Lewis Gollin, an official observer, found several Negro men, one Negro girl and one white girl sharing a room in a South Carolina prison. This was exceptional, but the overcrowding and the generally insanitary conditions were not. Buckets were standard equipment in many American prisons in the thirties, prisoners were packed together often regardless of their records, and bribery and enforced homosexuality were the rule, not the exception. James Spenser, the Englishman who worked for Al Capone, described in *Limey* the activities in San Quentin of a Mexican who acted as labour boss, took money from the 'prison aristocracy', and terrorised the prison guards – who nevertheless got their cut from his activities.

Not all prisons were like this, and certainly not all prison officers accepted tamely what went on inside prison walls, but the atmosphere was not likely to turn prisoners into good citizens.

A prison at Stuttgart, Germany. The prisoners, boxed off from each other, are listening to a concert *Mary Evans Picture Library*

Aerial view of a modern prison near Copenhagen, 1932. Between the spokes of the wheels were the exercising yards *Wide World*

And others are not

Dartmoor can serve as an example of the many prisons in which reform could operate only in the most limited way because the gloom of the surroundings and the wretchedness of the prison conditions affected everybody – Governor, warders and prisoners. It was built at the beginning of the nineteenth century to house French prisoners taken in the Napoleonic wars. These prisoners were treated with a savagery that made many of them less than human beings. A group who called themselves the Romans sold all their clothes and exchanged their rations, to gamble and obtain tobacco. They hunted for scraps of food, caught and ate rats, and engaged even more than most prisoners in homosexuality. A little later American prisoners were put into Dartmoor, when the United States declared themselves at war with Britain in 1812. Charles Andrews, a young American who spent three years there, wrote:

Any man sent to Dartmoor might have exclaimed:
'Hail, horrors! Hail, thou profoundest hell!
  Receive thy new possessor.'
For everyone ordered to this prison counted himself lost.

For a good many years Dartmoor was unoccupied, until it became a convict prison in 1850. Mutinies and escapes were common, and a rigidly disciplinarian regime was instituted in 1865. It was designed to break the spirit of the prisoners by forcing them to do useless work like stone-breaking, and to make sure that they would not escape by guarding them closely. Everything was done to make the prisoner obedient, including the instruction that he must turn his face to the wall when a visitor passed, a procedure ordered 'to avoid assaults or familiarity'. In spite of the close guard, escapes were often attempted under the cover of the famous Dartmoor fog, but few prisoners got away. In 1932 there was a mutiny, and although it was tame by the standards of other countries, with little violence and no deaths,

SENTENCE NO. OF YEARS	NO. OF PRISONERS.					
	A	B	D	E	HOS.	TOTAL.
5	103	114	64	12	5	298
5-10	83	63	46	8	2	202
10-15	11	3	25	6	2	47
15 & OVER	2		7	1		10
LIFE.	7	6	8	1	1	23
TOTALS.	206	186	150	28	10	580

The Summary Board in the Deputy Governor's office, showing length of sentences and number of prisoners *Mirrorpic*

the prisoners obtained complete internal control for a short time. Some improvement in conditions ensued, but the prospects of Dartmoor prisoners were correctly assessed by Sir William Joynson-Hicks, who was far from a liberal Home Secretary. When he was asked what hope there was for the men on the Moor he answered: 'Honestly, very little. It is really a cesspool of humanity.' A campaign to close Dartmoor has continued from the mutiny until the present day. It has had no success, chiefly because Britain is short of prisons. Men are still shut away in the cesspool of Dartmoor, and as nearly as possible forgotten.

Prisoners at work quarrying stone
Mirrorpic

A general view of Dartmoor prison *LEA*

The entrance gate. Above it is the inscription 'Parcere Subjectis': Spare the Vanquished. A prison officer rendered it as: 'If you once come in you don't get out again' *LEA*

White prisoner being beaten. Place, an American prison. Period, end of 1920s *UPI*

Whipping post at which Negro is being beaten. Place, Wilmington, Delaware, U.S.A. Period, 1920s *UPI*

Posed picture of the cat o' nine tails about to be used. Taken for a French paper, with the approval of the Home Secretary at the time, Winston Churchill. Place, Wormwood Scrubbs prison, England. Date, 1910 *Mirrorpic*

Punishment often remains barbaric

The pictures on this page need little gloss. Flogging is still a legal punishment in some Southern States in America. In England it was forbidden by the Criminal Justice Act of 1948 except for prison mutiny and gross violence to prison officers, but respectable housewives are continually demanding the return of the cat as a punishment for particularly brutal crimes. But of course vicious punishment is not confined to beating. Steam heat, cold water, solitary confinement in agonizingly cramped conditions, are still in use, and it is said that an unofficial injunction to young policemen in some forces is: 'If you beat them, make sure it doesn't show.' It should be added that these pictures can be shown only because the United States and Britain are such open societies. Punishments involving torture, like those used by the French police forces against Algerian nationalists, have been amply proved, but there are no photographs to illustrate them.

Right: Sweatbox in which a convict was found dead. Hands are tied, the chain prevents all but slight head movement. Place, Jacksonville, Florida, U.S.A. Period, 1920s *UPI*

In this corridor four convicts were baked to death when the steam pipes were turned on full blast as a punishment. Place, County Jail, Philadelphia, U.S.A. Period, 1920s *UPI*

MURDER, SCANDAL AND CORRUPTION

Cheerful Charlie Becker

The scandal of New York's police administration, in which the police openly took bribes from gambling houses and brothels, and faked charges against those who refused them a rake off, broke wide open in July 1912, when Herman Rosenthal, who ran a gambling house, was shot dead outside the Café Metropole on West 43rd Street.

The murder was the result of a feud between Rosenthal and Charlie Becker, the strong man of the New York police force. Becker was the trusted personal assistant of the phenomenally stupid Police Commissioner Rhinelander Waldo, who placed him in charge of a special crime squad which Becker used for his protection racket. When Rosenthal refused to contribute to the defence of Becker's press agent, who was up for trial on a murder charge, his gambling place was raided and smashed up by the police. On learning that Rosenthal had talked to a reforming District Attorney named Charles S. Whitman, Becker got in touch with gangster Jack Zelig, then imprisoned in the Tombs, and offered him freedom and $2000 for the murder of Rosenthal. Zelig was released and enlisted four young thugs. It would be all right to kill Rosenthal in public, Becker told them, if it were done in front of a policeman.

Rosenthal was shot down in the street in front of a policeman, but it was not all right. Whitman was on the scene quickly, and was given the number of the getaway car before the police could shut the mouth of the witness who had seen it. From that point the casually-planned murder collapsed. The four gunmen

Lieutenant Charles Becker. The totally crooked cop *UPI*

were arrested, together with some of Becker's collectors, and they talked. The involvement of Becker was so thorough that neither his high reputation nor the Judge's evident determination to get a 'Guilty' verdict could save him. He was tried a second time, because of the Judge's prejudice at the first trial, found guilty again, and sent to the electric chair. The corruption of a society in which some politicians and policemen were on the make survived him.

News headlines on the Becker case *NYPL*

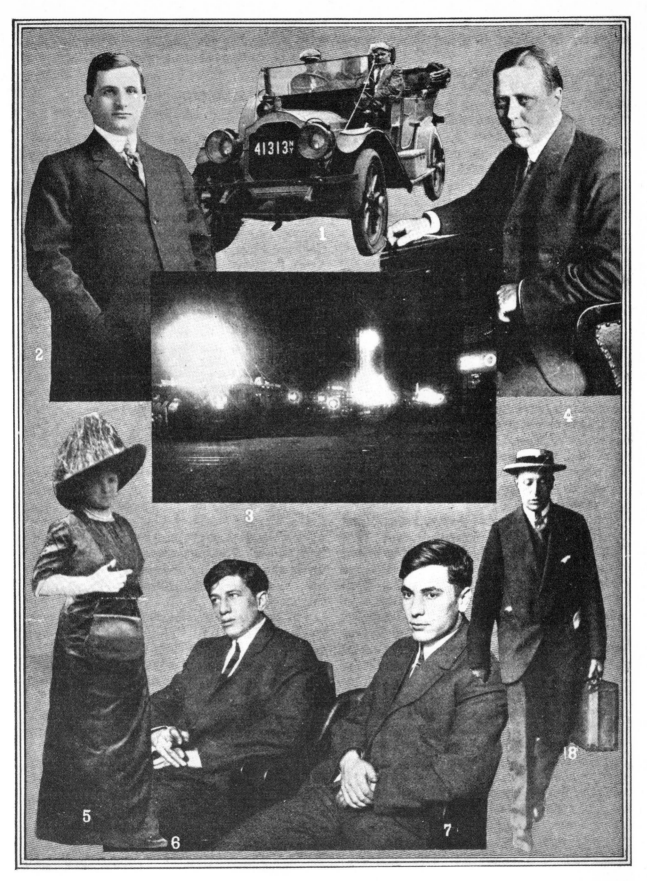

2. shows the victim, gambler Herman Rosenthal, and 4. is Rhinelander Waldo, the New York police commissioner. Between them is the grey car which carried the gunmen. 5. is Mrs. Harry Vallon, wife of one of Becker's chief *aides*, and 8. is Sam Schepps, said to have paid out the money for the murder through gangster Jack Zelig. Gyp the Blood and Lefty Louis, two of the killers, are 6 and 7. The centre picture, shows brightly lighted West 43rd Street where the murder took place   *NYPL*

The scandals that rocked France

Early in 1914 Gaston Calmette, director of *Le Figaro* and probably the most influential journalist in France, began a press campaign to force the retirement of the Finance Minister, Henri Caillaux, whom he believed to have treasonable contacts with Germany. For more than two months Calmette printed two attacks a day on Caillaux, in print or in cartoon form, often in both. At last he decided to print politically compromising letters written by Caillaux in the distant past. It was too much for Mme Caillaux, the Finance Minister's second wife. She bought a Browning revolver from a gunsmith after first trying out a Smith & Wesson, went to the office of *Le Figaro* and shot Calmette dead. With characteristic confidence she said to those who tried to detain her: 'Let me go, I am a lady, I am Madame Caillaux. I have my car waiting to take me to the police station.'

Her confidence was not misplaced. Thousands of people followed Calmette's coffin, the Government was rocked, Caillaux had to resign – but Mme Caillaux emerged scatheless. Her trial turned into a furious political dispute about whether Caillaux was, as Calmette had suggested, in German pay. And the jury decided that his wife had been telling the truth when she said that the revolver she had bought just before visiting Calmette's office had gone off by mistake because of her slight acquaintance with it and that, as she put it, the bullets had followed each other automatically. They found her not guilty of murdering Gaston Calmette. Strong in the consciousness of innocence, and never for a moment losing her magisterial calm, Mme Caillaux walked

Mme Caillaux at Madame Tussaud's. In wax she appears as calmly magisterial as in life *RTHPL*

out of the Assize Court of the Seine – free.

Twenty years before Caillaux was accused by Calmette, Captain Alfred Dreyfus of the French General Staff was also accused of treasonable communication with a foreign power. He was sentenced to life imprisonment, sent to Devil's Island, freed in 1899, and finally rehabilitated seven years later. He had been convicted only because of the strong anti-Semitic feeling in the French Army, and the lies told by Major Henry of the Intelligence Bureau, who committed suicide when his disgrace was imminent. In fact the *bordereau* about French military secrets

The funeral of the victim, Gaston Calmette. Generals and politicians led the mourners *RTHPL*

The trial, with M. Caillaux giving evidence. It turned into a political battle, in which at times the murder was almost forgotten *Mary Evans Picture Library*

that Dreyfus was found guilty of writing was the work of another officer named Esterhazy.

The case divided the whole of France into pro- and anti-Dreyfusites, and was the greatest *cause célèbre* of the age. Its most direct criminal connection is with Bertillon, who was approached at an early stage and asked if Dreyfus had written the *bordereau*. He was not in any way a handwriting expert (and experts already consulted had expressed doubt), but he was told by the General Staff that Dreyfus was certainly guilty and that the handwriting evidence was of secondary importance. He decided that Dreyfus had written the *bordereau*, but that he had used several disguised hands in which to do it. This extraordinary theory did not convince the Court, but they were swayed by the magic of Bertillon's name. Bertillon himself was strongly anti-Jewish, and he never admitted his mistake. When Esterhazy's writing was shown to him beside that of the *bordereau*, and he was told that this could not possibly be the work of Dreyfus, who was on Devil's Island, he replied: 'Then the Jews have trained someone to imitate that hand, and they have succeeded in producing one identical with it.'

The *bordereau* in the Dreyfus case, with (*right*) the handwriting of Dreyfus

101

And two that rocked New York

The crime was straightforward. On 28 June 1906, Harry Kendall Thaw shot and killed Stanford White, the sandy-haired red-faced internationally famous architect, whose sex life was as florid as his design for Madison Square Garden. The shooting took place, appropriately enough, on the roof of the Garden, at the opening of a review called *Mam'zelle Champagne*. Behind it lay an extraordinary story which was slowly unfolded to fascinated newspaper readers at Thaw's two trials. It became clear that his wife Evelyn had not overstated the case when she said: 'Harry, I'll stick to you, but my, you're in an awful mess.' Evelyn did her best for her husband by telling on the witness stand how Stanford White had seduced her when she was a showgirl in the 'Floradora' company, and only fifteen years old. There had been a room with a red velvet swing in which White pushed her almost up to the ceiling, a studio where she had posed in a 'gorgeous Japanese kimono', and then a fateful night when she had been given too much champagne, had fainted, and found herself in a room where the walls and ceiling were covered with mirrors. She had, she learned, been seduced.

She went on to say that she had told Thaw this story before their marriage, and that he had been deeply upset by it. Was Thaw, then, simply a wronged husband, was Evelyn as innocent as she was enchan-

Left: Harry Thaw, rich boy, jealous husband, sadist, killer   *UPI*
Right: Stanford White, designer of Madison Square Garden   *UPI*

Evelyn Nesbit Thaw, in her 'gorgeous Japanese kimono'   *UPI*

102

tingly pretty? Alas, under severe cross-examination by the District Attorney, William Travers Jerome, it was made plain that neither of these people were quite as they had represented themselves. Evelyn had been one of White's mistresses for a considerable time, and had received a regular weekly sum of money from him, she had been cited as co-respondent in a divorce case, she had travelled to Europe with Thaw as his wife before she married him. And Thaw himself? This 34-year old son of a Pittsburgh millionaire was revealed as a sadist who on his trip to Europe with Evelyn had rented an isolated castle in the Austrian Tyrol (some of the details in the case are like bits of a Gothic romance) and there beat her with a cowhide whip so savagely that she had to stay in bed for three weeks. Other beatings had followed. Nevertheless, Thaw had been passionately indignant about her seduction, and always referred to White as 'the Beast' or 'the Bastard'.

Delphin M. Delmas, Thaw's principal counsel, made an appeal for Thaw as a wronged husband shooting his wife's seducer, but this proved too much for the jury, which disagreed. A second jury heard a brothel keeper give details of the beatings inflicted by Thaw on young girls in an apartment he hired from her. A history of mental disorder in the Thaw family was introduced into the case, and he was found insane. Had the Thaw millions been at work? They certainly operated to ensure his freedom in 1915. He died just before the Second World War. Evelyn, who had been the coolest person at the trial, was divorced from Thaw immediately after he was set free. She lived on into a respectable old age.

The murder of Joseph Elwell, an unsolved mystery, took place in 1920. Elwell was a Brooklyn salesman who had made a fortune from his skill in playing cards. *Elwell on Bridge* and *Elwell's Advanced Bridge* were said to earn him $10,000 a year, in addition to the money he made by playing bridge and by teaching the game. He became a racehorse owner, he bought a yacht, he collected pictures. His principal collection, however, was women. After parting from his wife he had dozens of mistresses.

When Elwell was found in an armchair in his pyjamas with a bullet hole in his forehead it seemed likely that he had been shot by a woman. But had he? Elwell was a vain man, and he was not wearing one of the forty toupees he kept to conceal his baldness, nor his fine white teeth. A woman's husband, then? But how had the man got in, when both front and rear doors were securely locked? And Elwell had been killed early in the morning, as was proved by the fact that he had collected the 7 o'clock mail – a bloodstained letter lay open in his lap. The early morning seemed somehow not quite the time for a wronged husband to pay a murderous visit. Was it a sneak thief? But nothing had been taken. There were many promising suspects, but all the clues led nowhere. The murderer of Joseph Elwell remains unknown.

Joseph Elwell. A racing stable, an art collection, books on bridge *UPI*

The chair in which Elwell was shot *UPI*

The hoax of the century

One day in 1906 the peaceful little town of Köpenick, a few miles east of Berlin, suffered a military invasion. Six fusiliers and four grenadiers disentrained, marched out of the railway station and towards the Town Hall. At their head was an elderly Captain, in the uniform of the Prussian Guards.

At the Town Hall the Captain halted his men, posted one at each of the three doors, and told them that nobody was to enter or leave without his permission. With the rest of the men he marched into the office of the burgomaster, Dr Langerhans, and told him that he was under arrest. Asked for a warrant, the Captain replied that his soldiers were his warrant. He was taking Dr Langerhans to Berlin as his prisoner.

The Captain's incisive military manner was impressive. Dr Langerhans made no further protest, and the Inspector of Police made no protest at all when the Captain told him to make sure that there were no disturbances in the square while he was carrying out his mission. The Inspector did as he was told. The Captain found the town Treasurer, placed him under

The Captain in his uniform
Mansell

A German cartoon about the hoax   *Mansell*

The Captain of Köpenick comes out of prison *Mansell*

arrest as well, and gave the unhappy Dr Langerhans permission to say goodbye to his wife. It was not goodbye, however. She insisted on accompanying him.

At this point the Captain's activities were interrupted by the arrival of the deputy chief of police from a neighbouring district. He saw the crowd in the square, pushed past the fusilier on guard, and asked what was going on. The Captain explained that some irregularities had been found in the financial affairs of the town, and that he would be grateful for help in keeping order out in the square. The police officer was happy to oblige a Captain in the Guards. He kept good order in the square.

Now came the most delicate part of the operation. The Treasurer had been told to balance his books and produce the money. He did so. The Captain took charge of the sum of just over 4000 marks, and gave a receipt. The Treasurer quaveringly said that this could be done only on the burgomaster's orders, but the Captain pointed out that the burgomaster was under arrest. 'I am now the highest authority in Köpenick. Is that understood?' he asked. It was understood.

He had already told a police sergeant to commandeer two closed carriages, and now gave his final instructions. The corporal of the fusiliers was to accompany Dr and Frau Langerhans and the Treasurer to military headquarters in Berlin. The police sergeant would go with them. The rest of the soldiers would guard the Town Hall for half an hour and return to barracks. After making these arrangements, the Captain left.

That evening, 'the prisoners from Köpenick', as they were called, arrived at military headquarters in the Unter den Linden. They saw one police and

military figure after another, and were interviewed eventually by the Berlin Chief of Police and the Adjutant-General, Count Moltke. The appalling truth became known. The Captain was an impostor.

The Captain of Köpenick was a shoemaker in his late fifties named Wilhelm Voigt. He had spent almost half his life in jail, a mark less of his criminal nature than of the fact that once in prison it is hard to keep out of it. He had seen the uniform in a shop, bought it, and had then boldly commandeered his fusiliers and guards when he saw them marching in the street. Respect for the uniform had been so great that nobody had noticed his shabby shoes nor the fact that he had put the cockade on his peaked cap the wrong way round, with the Prussian insignia above that of Imperial Germany.

The whole world – including all but the military caste in Germany – rocked with laughter at the simplicity of the deception and the demonstration that in Prussia, as one German paper put it, 'they will all lie on their bellies before a uniform'. The laughter increased when the Captain was caught, and his real status and occupation were learned. His trial was conducted in a light-hearted atmosphere, and he was released from prison after serving only twenty months of a four year sentence.

He emerged to find himself famous. Rejecting many offers of marriage he took instead to the stage, where he appeared dressed in a splendid uniform. He obtained a passport – which he said had been the original object of the imposture – and had some success in London music halls and in New York. He did not, however, receive the Nobel Peace Prize, of which a British magazine had suggested he would be a worthy recipient.

Here's What "Sells" Spanish Prisoner Victim

Barcelone 2/1/41

Dear Sir

Being imprisoned here by bankr—
me to obtain a sum of *360,000 dollars*
being necessary to come here to raise t—
paying to the Register of the Court the exp—
cover my portmanteau containing a s—
hidden two checks payable to bearer —

As reward I will give up to you —
dollars. I cannot receive your answ—
can send a cablegram to a person of —
deliver it me, addressed as follows —

Awaiting your answer to instru—
only sign now

First of all answer by cable,

DEPOSITARÍA JUDICIAL

TALÓN NUM. ▨▨ POR VALOR DE ▨▨▨ PTAS. ▨▨▨ CÉNTS.

Termina el plazo de posesión el día ▨ de ▨▨▨ de 19▨▨

TRIBUNAL DE 1.ª INSTANCIA DE ESTA CIUDAD

El tribunal compuesto de los Sres. Magistrados expresados al margen, ha dictado la siguiente

Sentencia:

Aplicando los artículos del Código Penal núms. 4̶1, 412 y 507.

SEÑORES

D. JUAN SERRANO.

DR. D. EUSEBIO SOL

▨▨▨ ▨ ▨▨▨.

Debemos condenar y condenamos á ROBERTO DE SILVA, ex ban
quero, de 48 años de edad, viudo, natural de Santa-
Cruz de Tenerife (Islas Canarias) a la pena de
3 años de prisión y a la multa de 13.000 Pesetas,
por el delito de quiebra fraudulenta estimada en
2 Millones de Pesetas y perpetrada en Tenerife el
5 de Abril de 1923.

Lo condenamos asimismo al pago de las costas y gastos de su proceso,
que ascienden a la suma de 1,987 Pesetas 40 Centimos, que
junto con las 13.000 Pesetas de multa hacen una su
ma total de CATORCE MIL NOVECIENTAS OCHENTA Y SIETE
PESETAS CUARENTA CENTIMOS—VALOR ORO—

(—14.987 Pesetas 40 Centimos, valor oro—)

Y si en el plazo de ciento veinte dias contados desde el pro-
nunciamiento de esta sentencia, no ha satisfecho dicha cantidad, todos los
objetos de su propiedad serán vendidos en licitación pública.

Por esta nuestra sentencia así lo pronunciamos y mandamos su ejecu-
ción habiendo sido publicada y sellada por orden del Excmo Sr Presidente de esta Audencia.

BARCELONA 30 de MAYO de 19 23.

Es copia,

El Presidente, *L. Castillou*

El Secretario, *J. Ruiz*

Detención de un Banquero

Hace poco tiempo la policía tuvo conoci-
miento de que un banquero de las Islas Canarias llamado Roberto de Silva, se había fugado
dejando un pasivo de cerca de dos millones de
pesetas.

Dadas las órdenes oportunas para la vigilan-
cia de la frontera, ayer en el tren exprés de la
mañana, don Roberto de Silva que viajaba
acompañado de su hija hermosa joven de 16
años de edad, fué reconocido y arrestado cuan-
do se disponía a internarse en Francia

El banquero y su hija fueron conducidos a la
comisaría y más tarde llevados a presencia del
Sr. Juez de Guardia, quien dispuso que inme-
diatamente fuera puesta en libertad la hermosa
joven y dictó auto de prisión contra el banquero fugado. La separación de estos fué en extre-
mo emocionante, desarrollándose entre ambos
una tristísima escena

El equipaje del banquero no lo constituían
más que dos maletas de mano que le fueron se-
cuestradas y registradas sin que se encontrase
ninguna cantidad, aunque es sabido que se llevó
de Canarias una importante suma

Como las Islas Canarias son posesiones espa-
ñolas y la ley ordena que los indígenas detenidos en la península sean juzgados por los Tribu-
nales de la capital más próxima de donde son
detenidos, el proceso contra el banquero Roberto de Silva se verá en Barcelona

V.° B.°
El Presidente,

Newspaper Translation

A Banker Arrested!

Some short time ago the police were notified that a banker named Roberto de Silva
from the Canary Islands had absconded.
leaving a deficit of nearly two million pesetas. Necessary instructions having been
given to the police at the frontier, Roberto
de Silva, accompanied by a beautiful girl
of 16, said to be his daughter, was recognized and arrested on trying to enter France.

The banker and his daughter were taken
to the Commissary of Police and later appeared before the judge, who disposed that
the beautiful young girl should be immediately set at liberty, and that the absconding
banker should be remanded. The moment of
separation between the two was one of extreme emotion and produced a very sad
scene.

The baggage of the banker, which was
only made up of two portmanteaux, was
seized and searched, though nothing was
found, though it is known that he took a
large sum with him on leaving the Canary
Islands.

As the Canary Islands are a Spanish possession and the law established that natives
shall be tried at the nearest county town to
where arrest is made, the trial of Roberto
de Silva will be held in Barcelona.

TRANSLATION OF SENTENCE

In accordance with Articles of Penal
Law, 411, 412 and 508 etc.

We, the Tribunal, after pronouncing
verdict, condemn and order Roberto
de Silva, ex-banker, 48 years old, widower, born in Santa Cruz de Tenerife,
Canary Islands, to be sentenced to the
penalty of three years imprisonment
and to pay a fine of thirteen thousand
pesetas as costs for his fraudulent
bankruptcy, valued at two million pesetas, committed on the 5th April, last.

We also condemn him to pay the
costs of this process amounting to 1,-
987 pesetas which, together with the
amount of the fine amounts to fourteen
thousand nine hundred and eighty-
seven pesetas forty centimes in gold.
(14,987 pesetas, 40 centimes).

And if in the interval of 120 days
counting from the date of this sentence, the aforesaid amount has not
been liquidated, all objects of this property will be sold by public auction.

Barcelona, 30th May, 1933.

Some of the documents in a version of the 'Spanish Prisoner' fraud   *McDade Collection*

Simple but effective weights and measures frauds. From left to right are a weight filled with cork, one with the bottom hollowed out and a wooden weight thinly coated with lead *RTHPL*

The tricks that go on forever

There are many frauds which have been practised successfully, with minor variations, for nearly a hundred years. One of them is the Spanish Prisoner story. The essentials of this are always the same. A man has been given a prison sentence – in the version shown here for embezzlement, at the beginning of the century generally for gun-running – but his money has been put in a safe place. The plan of this place, however, is in a portmanteau which has been seized by the authorities, or by his creditors. If £500 is paid (the sum varies) the portmanteau will be released (or the necessary documents obtained), and the money can be collected. The prisoner will reward his benefactor with £5000 (again the sum varies) to be taken from the money. The prisoner's lovely daughter – there is always a lovely daughter, and her photograph is enclosed – will meet the benefactor at. . .

It may sound unconvincing, but the art of the trick is to provide so many details that the gull is deceived. He sets off for the meeting place, Spain or France or Italy. Sometimes he meets the lovely daughter, sometimes an important business or military man. He may redeem the portmanteau, he may be sent on to some other meeting place. But somewhere along the way he parts with his own money, and there is never any reward at the end of the trail.

Among other time-tested swindles are the long firm frauds by which an absconding firm defrauds those who have given them credit, innumerable varieties of confidence trick in all of which the con man appears to be trusting *you* with *his* money, and of course the badger game, in which a respectable man is in a bedroom – generally a hotel bedroom – with an agreeable and agreeing woman, when the woman's husband bursts in. The 'husband' – the inverted commas are not always necessary – threatens exposure, and the victim pays up.

Generally the sum of money involved is small, but

in 1919 the badger game was played for very high stakes with the nephew of an Indian Maharajah. Sir Hari Singh, or as he was known throughout the affair, Mr A, was the heir-presumptive of the immensely wealthy Maharajah of Jammur and Kashmir. He was introduced by his A.D.C. Captain Arthur to a fascinating lady named Mrs Robinson, and was in a Paris hotel with her when her 'husband' entered. The inverted commas are fully justified here, for the entrant was in fact Montague Noel Newton, a solicitor for whom shady is far too friendly a term. Captain Arthur advised the Prince that scandal must be avoided at all costs, and the costs were high. Sir Hari signed two cheques, each for £150,000, leaving the payee's name blank. The cheques went in due course to William Cooper Hobbs, the chief managing clerk of a firm of solicitors which in fact he controlled. Hobbs opened an account in the name of Charles Robinson, and drew out the money. Disaster came when the real Robinson discovered that his wife had got only £21,000 out of a much larger sum, and indignantly tried to obtain the rest of the money. Hobbs went to prison for two years, and Sir Hari Singh returned to Kashmir, wiser, sadder, and poorer.

William Cooper Hobbs. The badger game played with the nephew of a Maharajah *LEA*

Great British swindlers

The end of the nineteenth century was the heyday of the great British financial tricksters, who used the laxity of the Companies Acts to promote visionary companies designed to exploit non-existent gold fields in Australia or Siberia, or copper mines in Spain, or motor cars that ran on water. These villains often had an agreeable panache, and their frauds on a simple public were carried out with immense audacity.

Consider the operations of Ernest Terah Hooley, who once said: 'Any fool can sell what people want. I can sell them things they neither want nor need.' Hooley had literally dozens of peers on the boards of his mostly fraudulent companies. He paid a standard rate of £10,000 for a duke and £5,000 for a peer. By use of judicious bribes he became High Sheriff of Cambridgeshire and Huntingdonshire and a member of that sanctum of Toryism the Carlton Club. Not all of Hooley's companies were fraudulent – he bought the Dunlop Tyre Company in the eighteen-nineties, re-selling it within a few months at a paper profit of £2 million, and he was the founder of Schweppes – but his handling of them was invariably dishonest. He was made bankrupt, not once but four times, and more than once saw the inside of a prison. He died in 1947, penniless.

In the eighteen-nineties and afterwards, Hooley occasionally passed on an awkward client to Horatio Bottomley, like a doctor asking for a second opinion.

Bottomley was the most remarkable of all British swindlers. He promoted dozens of bogus companies, and was finally sent to prison for a fraud connected with Victory Bonds. But Bottomley was more than simply a cheat. This squat frog-faced man who breakfasted off kippers and champagne was a spell-binding orator on recruiting platforms, the founder of the paper *John Bull*, and for many years Member of Parliament for South Hackney. His personal influence during the 1914-18 War was tremendous, and after it he formed the Independent Parliamentary Group, supported by six M.P.s, under the slogan 'Business, Brains and Bottomley'. The Bottomley dream ended when in 1922 he was sent to prison for 7 years. In prison he wrote doggerel 'Songs of the Cell':

Of fair estate and good repute,
He fell against the Law,
And, though his hands were free from guilt,
Was drawn within its maw.

When he came out the golden touch was gone, and he died in poverty, cared for by a devoted woman friend. He had extraordinary qualities, and just a touch of the honesty he lacked might have taken him into the Cabinet.

Like Bottomley and Hooley, Whittaker Wright lived luxuriously, with a Park Lane mansion, a yacht

Ernest Terah Hooley *Mirrorpic*

Jabez Balfour, 'the Napoleon of Finance' *RTHPL*

at Cowes, and an extraordinary country house containing a theatre and a glass-roofed room under a lake through which fish could be seen. Like Hooley again he used titled guinea pigs for the mining companies he promoted successfully in the eighteen-nineties. When one company became shaky he floated another, building an intricate network of companies which transferred shares to each other to conceal the crumbling structure. After the Official Receiver began to investigate the companies in 1902, Wright fled the country. He was arrested in America, extradited, tried, found guilty, and in January 1904 sentenced to 7 years' penal servitude. He asked for a final consultation with his solicitor, and in the consultation room committed suicide by taking cyanide.

Jabez Balfour was like Bottomley a Member of Parliament, and like Wright fled the country when his Liberator Permanent Benefit Building Society collapsed, but there the resemblance ends. Balfour was a model of the Victorian hypocrite, a teetotaler, and a pious advocate of good works, who was at the same time making a fortune by cooking the books of his companies. Extradited from the Argentine, he was sent to prison in 1895 for 14 years.

D. S. Windle finds a place in this gallery because of his name. He cashed a series of cheques on a non-existent account, and not until the fraud had been discovered was it realized that the signature 'D. S. Windle' on the cheques could be read as Damned Swindle. 'Windle', who refused to give his real name, went to prison for 18 months.

D. S. Windle in the dock at Bow Street, 1909 *Mirrorpic*

Horatio Bottomley addressing a recruiting meeting during the 1914–18 War *Mirrorpic*

Whittaker Wright (with box in front of him) in Court *RTHPL*

The classic cases of mistaken identity

In November, 1896, a teacher of languages named Ottilie Meissonnier was walking down Victoria Street in London when a man tipped his hat to her and addressed her as Lady Everton. The hat-tipping served as an introduction and, charmed by the politeness of his manner and impressed by his casual mention of the six gardeners he employed on his Lincolnshire estate, Ottilie invited him to tea. There she was gulled by the oldest and simplest kind of confidence trick. She learned with pleasure that her visitor was a cousin of Lord Salisbury, at that time Prime Minister of England, and with more pleasure still that her charms had so much overwhelmed him that he was going to take her on his yacht for a trip to the Riviera and would provide her with a suitable wardrobe for the journey. He made out a list of the clothes she needed, generously wrote a cheque for £40 to cover their cost, and took away two wrist watches and her rings, which he said he would replace with more valuable pieces.

Within a few hours Ottilie discovered that the cheque was worthless. She had been the victim of a man known to Scotland Yard as Lord Wilton and Lord Willoughby, whose technique did not vary and was remarkably successful. A few weeks later Ottilie Meissonnier was again walking down Victoria Street. Under the light of the street lamps she saw Lord Salisbury's 'cousin', and demanded the return of her watches and rings. The man boldly went up to a policeman and complained that a strange woman was pestering him. They went to Rochester Row police station. . .

The man's name was Adolf Beck. He had lived a rather erratic but not criminal life in South America, Norway and England, and he was entirely innocent of stealing the watches and rings. Nevertheless, Ottilie and other women who had been cheated identified him without hesitation in a line-up where the other men did not greatly resemble him. Two policemen who had been responsible for arresting a man named John Smith who had carried out similar frauds several years earlier, also identified Beck as the man they had caught. The man arrested and convicted previously had left scraps of writing. They were compared with Beck's by a handwriting expert. They were dissimilar, but the expert had a simple explanation – obviously they were disguised. The Judge, by unfortunate chance, was the man who had sentenced John Smith, and he had no doubt that John Smith stood before him again. Beck's protests were unavailing against the cloud of witnesses. He was sentenced to 7 years' penal servitude, and in prison was given John Smith's number. He had, so far as the authorities were concerned, been identified as John Smith even though records showed that John Smith had been circumcised and this man was not.

Beck spent five years in prison. Three years after his release he was again accused by a young woman of stealing money and jewellery from her. He was arrested again, briefly tried, and found guilty. He was awaiting sentence when the police learned that a man had just been arrested who had used precisely the 'Smith' approach. Detective Inspector Kane went to see him, and noticed immediately the strong resem-

Adolf Beck *RTHPL*

William Thomas, alias John Smith *RTHPL*

blance between the two men. The swindler, whose real name was William Thomas, had committed all the frauds attributed to Beck.

Beck was freed, and given £5000 compensation for his years in prison. It is hardly surprising that he spent the money recklessly, and was destitute when he died in 1909.

Beck would have been saved if a fingerprint system had been used in the 1890s, but what could have saved Oscar Slater? This German Jew, whose rather dubious activities included dealing in jewellery, was accused in 1909 of killing with a hammer an old woman named Marion Gilchrist. The crime was committed in her Glasgow apartments, and Slater became implicated because a large crescent-shaped diamond brooch had been stolen, and it was learned that he had pawned what was called 'a valuable diamond brooch'. It proved subsequently that the brooch had been pawned some time before the murder, but by that time the hunt for Slater was on.

He had sailed with his mistress in the *Lusitania* for the United States. When the ship arrived off Sandy Hook six detectives went out to arrest him. He was sent to the Tombs and then extradited to Scotland. His trial was overwhelmingly prejudiced by his foreign origin, his way of life, and by what was interpreted as his flight overseas. Witnesses who had seen somebody leaving Miss Gilchrist's house, and had been very vague about the man's appearance, now unanimously identified him as Slater. There was practically no evidence against him except that of these unreliable witnesses, but the Glasgow police, having fixed on Slater as the murderer, made no attempt to look elsewhere.

The conduct of the trial was disgraceful. The Lord Advocate, Alexander Ure, who prosecuted, made an extraordinary number of unjustified assumptions which Lord Guthrie, who tried the case, did almost nothing to controvert. Slater, Ure said, had lived on the proceeds of prostitution (an assertion never proved), and 'all moral sense in him has been destroyed'. Was he not therefore obviously capable of murder? He was found guilty by a majority verdict, and sentenced to death.

He was reprieved, and the rest of his story belongs to Sir Arthur Conan Doyle, who led the agitation which ended in 1927 with Slater being given his freedom. In the meantime several people who testified on his behalf had suffered for it, like Detective Lieutenant Trench, who was dismissed from the Glasgow police force after more than twenty years' service. Slater was offered the inadequate sum of £6000 compensation, which he accepted without question. In 1936 he married a woman much younger than himself, and lived on peacefully until his death in 1948.

Oscar Slater in 1908 *RTHPL*

The hammer with which Miss Gilchrist was said to have been killed *RTHPL*

Oscar Slater in Hyde Park in 1928, after his release *RTHPL*

Real pearls, doubtful diamonds, a spiked suit

In October, 1912, a Hatton Garden diamond merchant named Max Mayer bought a necklace consisting of sixty-one perfectly graded pearls, joined with a diamond clasp. He paid £123,000 for it, confident that he would make a handsome profit, and in June of the following year sent it to Paris in response to an enquiry. It remained unsold, and Mayer's Paris agent carefully repacked it, together with three loose pearls, in a morocco leather case, put the case in a special wooden box, and sent it by registered post. When the parcel arrived at Hatton Garden the leather case contained some French newspaper and eleven pieces of French sugar. The pearls had gone.

The puzzle of their disappearance could be simply stated. Either the pearls had never been posted in Paris (but the French agent was unimpeachably honest) or they had been stolen *en route* (but the police convinced themselves that this was not the case) or they had been taken in London. But how? Sir Richard

Muir said sarcastically that the upshot of police enquiries was to prove that the necklace had not been stolen at all. It might never have been found but for the activities of two young diamond merchants named Brandstatter and Quadratstein, who were eager to get the substantial reward offered. Brandstatter heard rumours of a big pearl deal being done in London, connected with the most famous British fence of the time, Cammie Grizard. Brandstatter and Quadratstein met Grizard and a friend of his named Silverman, and a day came when all four gathered in a Holborn teashop. A fifth man entered, Grizard asked him for a match, and the stranger threw down on the table a match box containing three beautiful rose-tinted pearls. They were the loose pearls that had been sent with the necklace.

The negotiations ended in the arrest of Grizard, Silverman and the other man, James Lockett, but then it was impossible to discover the necklace. It

James Lockett, one of the thieves involved in the pearl robbery *Mirrorpic*

The £150,000 pearl necklace, and the matchbox in which it was found *Mirrorpic*

was found a fortnight later by a man named Horn, who saw in the gutter at Highgate a small brown box. He opened it. Inside was the matchbox, and inside the matchbox was the necklace.

And how was the theft committed? Like many puzzles, its solution is disappointingly simple. Silverman had an office near to Max Mayer's, and had prepared a stamp which imitated Mayer's special seal marked 'MM'. With the co-operation of a postman he took in the package for a few minutes, opened it, substituted newspaper and French sugar for the pearls (a nice touch to place the theft in France), re-sealed it, and handed it back in time for postal delivery to Mayer.

The achievement of Lemoine the diamond maker was that in 1905 he managed to convince Sir Julius Wernher, President of De Beers Diamond Mines, that he could make artificial diamonds. Wernher was present at some experiments made by Lemoine, and he signed a contract saying that when further tests witnessed by experts had been carried out he would pay Lemoine 125 million francs for his formula, as a means of safeguarding the diamond industry.

Wernher, with a diamond expert from South Africa and several from other countries, attended Lemoine's Paris laboratory for a final demonstration. The Frenchman placed his special mixture (made by the secret formula, of course!) into a cylinder, put the cylinder into an electric furnace, took it out white hot and produced from within – a diamond! The experts were momentarily convinced by this old trick, but within days Lemoine had been charged with fraud by Wernher, who had realized that the diamond was contained in the mixture. Lemoine escaped before coming to trial and continued to make dia-

Lemoine the diamond maker   *RTHPL*

monds for the credulous, without ever finding again so notable a believer as Sir Julius Wernher.

Lacombe was a French criminal terrorist operating in the early years of the century, who is notable only for the leather suit he wore, which was studded from top to bottom with two inch steel spikes, fastened from inside and pointing outwards. Police who tried to arrest him had their hands badly lacerated. On another occasion, when the suit was of no help to him, he escaped by throwing a bomb at the pursuing police. When finally caught Lacombe composed a long memoir in prison, justifying his actions on the ground that they were based on an idealistic view of the universe. Sentenced to be guillotined for several murders, he committed suicide by jumping from a prison building to the stone flags below.

Lacombe's cuffs, shoulder straps and revolver

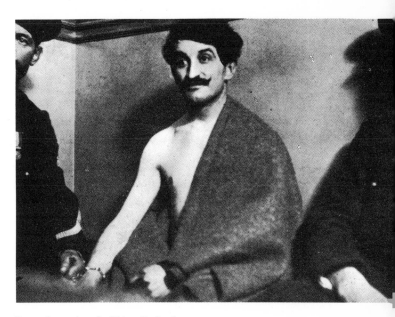

Lacombe, stripped of his spiked suit

A lawyer's mistake and a comely widow

Lawyers have such excellent opportunities of embezzling their clients' funds that they rarely resort to murder. William Marsh Rice, however, was not the client of lawyer Albert T. Patrick, and it was this very fact that led to Patrick's plan for getting hold of his fortune. The plan, ingeniously devised and executed, was ruined by an elementary mistake.

Rice was an old and extremely eccentric Texan millionaire, who came to live in New York after the death of his wife. He had founded in Texas the William M. Rice Institute for the Advancement of Literature, Science and Art, and in order that this not very flourishing project might endure he made a will leaving most of his money to further its welfare. He then settled in a Madison Avenue apartment with a youthful secretary named Charles T. Jones.

Rice had never met Patrick (and was never to meet him), but he knew the lawyer by name, and disliked him. Rice was engaged in a bitter dispute about the validity of his wife's will, and Patrick was acting for the other side. When, therefore, Patrick called one evening to try to see Rice and effect a compromise settlement, he was told by Jones that Mr Rice would not see him. Patrick was a bluff, engaging figure, and his remarks to Jones on the monstrous injustice of Rice's will, in which so much money went to the ridiculous Institute and so little to the faithful Jones, fell on fruitful ground.

After several evening visits to the apartment when Rice had gone to bed, Jones became Patrick's willing tool. He typed a new will, and Patrick traced Rice's signature on each page of it. The Institute vanished from this will, and by a thoughtful stroke Rice's relatives received more money in the new will than they had in the old. And the principal beneficiary? Jones, one might think, but Patrick shook his head at this. For Jones to receive a large part of the estate would look suspicious. The bulk of Rice's fortune was left to – Albert T. Patrick. There was a gentleman's agreement, as one might call it, that Patrick would pay Jones $10,000 a year.

Now came the question: why should Rice leave his money to a complete stranger? Patrick and Jones set out to prove that Patrick, so far from being a stranger, was Rice's intimate, valued friend. A great many letters were typewritten to prove this, apparently written by Rice to Patrick, cheques were forged to show that the signature on them and on the will was identical, a typewritten order was given for securities and cash in various safe deposits to be handed to Rice's valued friend Albert T. Patrick. On all of these documents Rice forged Patrick's name.

But there was a stumbling block. Rice, although a feeble old man in his eighties, seemed to be positively improving in health. When the old man suddenly decided to spend millions of dollars on reconstructing

William Marsh Rice *UPI*

Albert T. Patrick (right) under arrest, handcuffed to a detective, on his way to Sing-Sing *UPI*

a mill in Texas, the conspirators acted. Jones killed Rice one night by placing a chloroform-soaked towel over his face. A death certificate was given without question, cremation was ordered. All had gone well. But Patrick was undone by his own greed and Jones's carelessness. Eager to lay hands on ready cash, he made Jones fill out cheques for $250,000, to which he forged Rice's name. On one of these cheques Jones wrote Abert instead of Albert T. Patrick, and when the bank telephoned and asked Mr Rice to confirm personally that the cheque was in order, Jones lost his nerve. Both men were arrested.

They were charged with forgery, then with murder. Jones turned States' Evidence. Patrick was sentenced to death in March 1902, but the sentence was commuted to life imprisonment. In 1909 he cried to the Appeals Court: 'Give me liberty or give me death.' Liberty was granted him in 1912. Death came in 1940.

Belle Gunness was a comfortable hardworking woman who had bad luck with her husbands. The first died from heart failure in Chicago, a sorrow slightly alleviated by the fact that two insurance policies on his life had recently fallen due. She remarried, and settled happily with her husband and children on a farm in Indiana – but in 1904 a meat chopper fell from a shelf and killed him. Desperate for companionship, she inserted an advertisement saying that a 'Comely widow who owns a large farm' wished to 'make acquaintance of a gentleman equally well provided, with view of joining fortunes'. Well provided gentlemen came – from Wisconsin, Minnesota, South Dakota and elsewhere – but evidently they did not suit her, for she did not marry again. They may have been put off by her evident intimacy with a worker on the farm named Ray Lamphere.

In April 1908, shortly after she had quarrelled with Lamphere and dismissed him, the Gunness farm was burned to the ground. Belle Gunness and her three children died in the fire, and Lamphere was convicted of murder by arson. In the back yard of the farm parts of twelve dismembered bodies were found. They included Belle's adopted daughter, and also parts of the well provided gentlemen from Wisconsin and Minnesota and South Dakota.

Belle Gunness *UPI*

The Gunness farm at Laporte, Indiana. The letters mark the places where bodies were found *UPI*

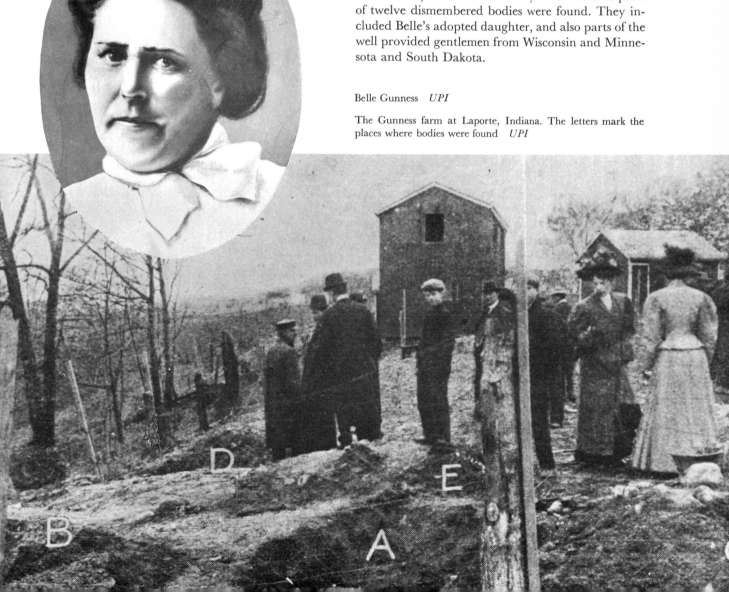

The Daily Mirror

THE MORNING JOURNAL WITH THE SECOND LARGEST NET SALE

No. 2,230. Registered at the G. P. O. as a Newspaper. MONDAY, DECEMBER 19, 1910 One Halfpenny.

HOW THREE LONDON POLICEMEN WERE MURDERED BY FOREIGN BURGLARS WHO WERE TRYING TO BREAK INTO A JEWELLER'S SHOP.

Sergeant Tucker, who died shortly after receiving his injuries. A bullet lodged in his throat.

Sergeant Bentley, who died in hospital on Saturday. A bullet penetrated his neck and shoulder.

Constable Choate, who succumbed to his wounds on Saturday. He was shot in several places.

The Siege of Sidney Street

In the early years of this century the Anarchist movement flourished in London's East End. Balts, Letts, Poles, Russians came to England to escape the Tsarist police. They found London congenial and comparatively free, and met in cafés and at the Anarchist club in Jubilee Street.

Most of these Anarchists were, as the journalist Philip Gibbs said after visiting the Club, as tame as rabbits, but a minority combined practical crime with theoretical Anarchism. In December 1910, a group of rather more than a dozen of them rented two small houses in a cul-de-sac called Exchange Buildings. From one of these houses they bored a way through into a jeweller's shop in the parallel street of Houndsditch. They made so much noise that the man living next door to the jeweller notified the police. A policeman called at No. 11 Exchange Buildings, was dissatisfied with his reception, and returned with six colleagues in uniform and two in plain clothes.

The Anarchists made little distinction between Tsarist and English police. No doubt they expected to be shot at or clubbed, and they began to shoot first. The policemen, of course, were not armed. One was killed outright, two others fatally injured, and four wounded. The leader of the Anarchists, George Gardstein, was shot accidentally by one of his own men. He died that night, and during the next few days several of the group were arrested.

Others, however, remained at large, and on 2 January 1911 the police were told that two of them were hiding in a second floor room at 100 Sidney Street, near the scene of the robbery. They surrounded the house, and the other occupants were evacuated. Only two men were left there, Fritz Svaars and a man known only as Josef. At about 7.30 in the morning the police flung gravel at the windows. The Anarchists at once opened fire, and a police sergeant was wounded. The police had been armed, and firing continued all the morning. At about 10.30 a company of Scots Guards arrived from the Tower of London, and four of them tried to force an entrance at the back. They retired, one of them wounded. An hour later Winston Churchill, then Home Secretary, came to take command.

No further attempt was made by police or soldiers to rush the building. The shooting continued until 1 o'clock, when the house burst into flames. The police refused to allow firemen to approach because of fear that they might be shot, and Svaars and Josef, defiant to the last, burned to death. Several firemen were injured a little later, when the roof collapsed.

That was the end of the siege, which was conducted with unnecessarily large forces. All of the men arrested were acquitted, because there was no proof that they had been associated with the murders. Several mysteries remained unsolved, the chief one being the identity of the mysterious figure known as 'Peter the Painter'. Was he in fact a Tsarist *agent provocateur*, sent to provoke the Anarchists to violence? The question has never been finally settled.

Scots Guards facing the house in Sidney Street, policemen crowded behind   *Mirrorpic*

Winston Churchill, then Home Secretary, views the battle from a gateway   *Mirrorpic*

Peter the Painter   *Mirrorpic*

BEFORE AND AFTER THE CRIME: SERAJEVO'S TRAGIC PART IN HISTORY.

PHOTOGRAPHS BY FRANZ PLANER AND RUDA BRUNER-DVORAK.

HOW THE ARCHDUKE AND DUCHESS BEGAN THEIR DAY AT SERAJEVO:
THE ROYAL CAR STARTING.

HOW THEY LEFT SERAJEVO: THE COFFINS BEING CONVEYED THROUGH THE TOWN
TO THE RAILWAY STATION.

JUST BEFORE THE CRIME: THE ARCHDUKE (1) THE DUCHESS (2), AND GENERAL
POTIOREK, GOVERNOR OF BOSNIA (3), IN THE CAR ON LEAVING THE TOWN HALL.

JUST AFTER THE ASSASSINATION: THE ARREST OF THE MURDERER, PRINZIP (X) WHO
SHOT THE ARCHDUKE AND DUCHESS AFTER THEY HAD LEFT THE TOWN HALL.

RACE-HATRED AROUSED BY THE CRIME: THE DESTRUCTION OF SERVIANS' HOUSES
AND HOTELS BY THE CROWD AT SERAJEVO.

ANTI-SERVIAN RIOTS AT SERAJEVO: A SERVIAN TAILOR'S PREMISES PLUNDERED
AND ITS CONTENTS THROWN INTO THE ROAD.

Our photographs illustrate some of the principal events in the Austrian royal tragedy at Serajevo, from the moment when the Archduke Francis Ferdinand and his wife set out in their motor-car to the time when their dead bodies were conveyed from the town in their elaborate coffins. After the assassination, it was reported that Cabrinovitch, the bomb-thrower, had received the bomb from Belgrade; and that Prinzip, the actual assassin, had spent some time in the Servian capital. The bitterest feelings were aroused, and it was rumoured that the crime was the outcome of a Pan-Serb agitation. The premises of Servians in Serajevo were attacked by infuriated mobs of the Moslem and Croatian inhabitants. Some 200 houses and shops belonging to Serbs were demolished, the Servian club, a Servian school, and two hotels. Martial Law was proclaimed.

Left: The full page of illustrations and captions from the *Illustrated London News*, exactly as it appeared in July 1914 *ILN*

A shot of Princip being dragged away after the assassination *RTHPL*

The end of a world

It was the end of the world, or at least of the European world, but nobody recognized this at the time. The murder on 28 June 1914 of an obscure Austrian Archduke, at a town in Bosnia which few people had heard of, did not appear among the really important news on the middle page of *The Times*, and although after a week or two the *Illustrated London News* published a full page of photographs, the assassination got rather less prominence than the Caillaux case (see page 100), and certainly took second place to the rumours of mutiny among British troops at the

Curragh in Ireland. In countries outside Europe, and also in the United States, the crime received still less notice.

The Archduke's assassination was organized by an officer group among the Serbian general staff who hated Austrian rule, and carried out by a group of students headed by Gavrilo Princip, who fired the fatal shot. A monument to Princip and the other conspirators now stands in Sarajevo, where there are no memorials to the Archduke. It was really the end not only of his life, but of his kind of world.

Another Yugoslav assassination that did not change the world. The murder of King Alexander of Yugoslavia and the French Foreign Minister, M. Barthou, by Petrus Kaleman *RTHPL*

'My mother was a buss horse'

'My mother was a Buss horse, my father a Cab driver, my sister a Roughrider over the Artic regions, my brothers were all galant sailors on a steam-roller.' So George Joseph Smith rebuked the father of his second victim, Alice Burnham, for an enquiry about his background. Smith was an extraordinary man, who hated women but was evidently immensely attractive to them. It is significant that he had little education and that he always approached women who were, as he once put it, a cut above him. He began with petty larceny, moved on to bigamy, and ended with a murder method which for a time baffled forensic science.

In 1910 Smith married under the name of Williams a bank manager's daughter named Bessie Mundy. When he found that her money was tied up in an unbreakable trust he decamped with her ready cash, leaving a letter in which he accused her of infecting him with venereal disease. It is almost unbelievable that, when they met by chance two years later, Bessie immediately went to live with him again. This time the trust was broken by the making of a will in his favour. As soon as this had been done he took her to stay in Herne Bay, and bought a tin bath of the kind that has to be filled with a bucket. He then went with the mesmerised Bessie to a doctor, explaining that she suffered from fits. A couple of days afterwards she drowned in her bath, a cake of soap clutched in her hand. Obviously, the doctor agreed, she had had a fit. The money was paid over, and Mr Williams returned the bath because he had no further use for it. He then vanished, and George Joseph Smith sent for his real wife (who believed him to be a respectable antique dealer) to join him so that they could take a holiday at Margate.

The same pattern was twice repeated, with Alice Burnham and a clergyman's daughter named Margaret Lofty. Neither had much money, and Smith made his profit by insuring their lives. He chose houses with bathrooms (his first question, at one lodging, was 'Have you a bath?'), and took his wife to a doctor in both cases. The report of Margaret Lofty's death was seen by Alice Burnham's father, who informed the police. They realized that Smith was a murderer, but there was no sign of violence on the bodies. How had he done it? Not until Detective Inspector Neil, on the advice of the pathologist Dr Bernard Spilsbury, had carried out experiments with a young woman swimmer in which he pulled her legs up out of the water and nearly drowned her, was Smith's precise method of operation understood.

Like Smith, Dr Arthur Waite killed for money, yet his actions like Smith's had obviously some deeper motivation. After a chequered youth – even his degree in dental surgery had been obtained by chicanery – Waite married an heiress, and set out to kill the rest of her family. His victims proved highly resistant. He administered arsenic, ground glass and various germs to his wife's aunt without noticeable effect. His mother-in-law proved an easier proposition. When she came to stay with the young couple in New York, Waite put tubes of pneumonia, diphtheria and influenza germs in her food. Not surprisingly, she became ill. He finished her off with a dozen 5 grain veronal tablets, and had her quickly cremated. His father-in-law, a drug millionaire named John E. Peck, then came to stay. Large doses of germs had not the slightest effect on him. He thrived on a nasal spray filled with tubercular bacilli. Even huge doses of arsenic did not kill him, and at last Waite was forced to the comparative crudity of using chloroform and then holding a pillow over Peck's face. His attempt at another quick cremation was checked by suspicions in the Peck family, and at his trial Waite made a full, calm admission of what he had done. At the autopsy after his electrocution, scars from an early meningitis illness were found on the right side of his brain.

Dr Arthur Warren Waite *UPI*

A posed picture in Waite's apartment. Left to right, Detective Schindler, mystery writer Arthur B. Reeve, Detective Taylor and Ray C. Schindler, head of a famous New York Detective Agency *UPI*

George Joseph Smith, with his first known victim, Bessie Mundy *LEA*

Phyllis Dimmock, victim in the Camden Town murder *Mirrorpic*

The postcard in the Camden Town case, which led to Wood's arrest *Mirrorpic*

The only photograph ever taken showing a Judge wearing the Black Cap to pronounce sentence of death. The Judge is Avory, the case that of a chauffeur named Thomas Allaway who killed a girl at Bournemouth in 1922 *Mary Evans Picture Library*

The defence counsel and the hanging judge

Of the several great defence counsel acting in criminal cases during the twentieth century in England, Sir Edward Marshall Hall is the most famous. His great rival in his own period, the first quarter of the century, was Sir Henry Curtis-Bennett. A little later Sir Patrick Hastings rose to fame, and so did Lord Birkett. (The titles are those they achieved.) The changed approach of criminal counsel in English courts is well shown by the characters of these famous barristers. Marshall Hall was handsome, excitable, and at his best when able to identify himself strongly with his client's cause. Curtis-Bennett was plump, jovial, and deadly in cross-examination. Both conducted many hopeless defences. Marshall Hall, for instance, was the counsel for 'Brides in the Bath' Smith, and Curtis-Bennett was a junior counsel for the defence in the Stratton fingerprint case, and defended Major Armstrong (see pages 83 and 125). Both men were histrionic performers in a way that would now be quite unacceptable to juries. In 1922, when defending Madame Fahmy, who had shot and killed her brutal Egyptian husband in the Savoy Hotel, Marshall Hall crouched and snarled so convincingly in the role of the villain from the East that the jury acquitted Madame Fahmy in spite of the fact that she had shot her husband at point blank range. Hastings was famous in both criminal and civil actions. One of his celebrated cases was that of Elvira Barney (see page 131). He was a sharp, concise cross-examiner, in many respects a far less flamboyant Marshall Hall. Birkett, lucid, logical, imperturbable, hardly ever raising his voice above the tone of conversation, was the model of the modern counsel who avoids any kind of dramatic show because he knows a modern jury would dislike it.

One of Marshall Hall's triumphs was the Camden Town murder in 1907, when a commercial artist named Robert Wood was accused of murdering a prostitute named Phyllis Dimmock in her lodgings. One of the most important pieces of evidence was the postcard which Wood had sent to the girl, signing it 'Alice', and arranging to meet her at a pub called The Rising Sun. There was a great deal of evidence against Wood, but Marshall Hall believed passionately in his innocence, and successfully cast doubt on the evidence of some of the Crown witnesses. Wood went into the witness box – before the Criminal Evidence Act of 1898 he could not have done so – and was the first man accused of murder to be found not guilty after giving evidence. The case was a tribute to Marshall Hall's power over a jury. It remains officially unsolved.

The most famous criminal judge of the time was Mr Justice Avory. He had been an icy, merciless counsel (he prosecuted in the case of Adolf Beck) and became an icy Judge, one who disregarded all except purely legal considerations. He was on the Bench from 1910 until his death in 1935 and in his later years would sit with eyes closed, apparently inattentive, until an incautious statement or an unjustified reply would lift his eyelids and prompt a hawk-like swoop on counsel or witness. He was known as a 'Hanging Judge', and the element of mercy was certainly not conspicuous in his character.

Sir Edward Marshall Hall *LEA*

Mr Justice Avory *LEA*

The gentle poisoner: Crippen and others

Crippen in the dock   *LEA*

'Belle Elmore', Crippen's murdered wife   *LEA*

Ethel le Neve in boy's clothing   *LEA*

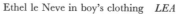

Poisoners are generally ineffectual characters, who feel compelled to lay claim by poison to the rights which life has denied them. It is often possible to feel sympathy for their predicament, although not for their attempted solution of it.

Take the case of Dr Hawley Harvey Crippen, who has achieved a notoriety that he hardly deserves. Crippen was an insignificant, rather amiable little man, completely overpowered by his wife, who after conspicuously failing to become an opera singer under the name of Belle Elmore, devoted herself to ruling her husband's life, even to the extent of ordering his clothes. Was it not natural that Dr Crippen should look warmly upon the neat little typist Miss Le Neve, so quiet and pleasant? And since Belle was by no means faithful, who can blame him? Blame enters only when Crippen is moved for once in his life to decisive action, poisoning his wife with five grains of hyoscin, cutting her up and disposing of some parts of the body under the floor of his coal cellar.

His attempts to persuade Belle's friends that she had gone to Los Angeles, died there and been cremated, were not assisted by the fact that Ethel le Neve appeared in his company at a dinner dance wearing one of Belle's brooches. More plausibly, he told the police that his wife had left him for another man, and suspicion had been temporarily lulled when Crippen lost his nerve. The flight he attempted by boat to Quebec under the name of John Philo Robinson, with Ethel le Neve accompanying him disguised in boy's clothing, was the single romantic incident in a humdrum life. The Crippen case became historic partly because wireless telegraphy was used for the first time to prevent a criminal's escape, in the form

Seddon (head on side) and his wife in the dock at the Old Bailey *LEA*

of a message sent by the captain of their boat, the S.S. *Montrose*, to London. Inspector Dew, the pertinacious officer in charge of the case, sailed after Crippen in a faster boat, and arrested him in the captain's cabin. His trial in October 1910 was almost a formality. Ethel le Neve was acquitted.

Major Armstrong, a dapper little solicitor who practised in the small town of Hay on the Brecon border, was essentially in the Crippen mould. He was married to a severe, strong-minded woman who thought nothing of telling him in public that it was his bath night, or that he should not have another drink, and when early in 1921 she died, the Major's many friends were inclined to regard it as a happy release. But the fact that he had poisoned his wife successfully went, as one might say, to Armstrong's head, and he made determined attempts to poison Oswald Martin, the rival solicitor in Hay, offering repeated invitations to tea which Martin refused after the violent pains he had suffered when eating a buttered scone at one tea party in Armstrong's house. Refusal became even more difficult when Armstrong invited Martin to come to his office for a refreshing cup of tea, for their offices faced each other in the High Street. Eventually Armstrong was arrested, Mrs Armstrong was exhumed, and more than 3 grains of arsenic were found in her body. He was hanged at Gloucester Prison on 31 May 1922.

Frederick Seddon was cast in a different pattern. He was a grasping, miserly insurance agent, who in 1911 took in as lodger an equally mean woman lodger named Miss Barrow. When she died after making over her money to him for an annuity, Seddon gave her a pauper's funeral. Her indignant relatives went to the police, and exhumation of the body revealed the presence of arsenic. Seddon was thought to have used arsenical fly papers and dissolved them in water, although the purchase of them was never brought home to him. Seddon was found guilty, his wife acquitted. He then made a remarkable twenty minute speech, which ended by his signifying to the Judge that they were both Freemasons. Mr Justice Bucknill was moved to tears, but he still pronounced sentence of death.

Major Armstrong arriving at Court after his arrest *LEA*

125

The motor bandits and the French Bluebeard

The division between anarchy and professional crime was a loose one in the early years of the century. Were the Motor Bandits Anarchists? They would have been disowned by Kropotkin and by Emma Goldman, but they had certainly been influenced by the activities of French Anarchists. It was only a step from the belief that propaganda by the deed was more important than verbal argument, to the view that armed robbery was not only profitable but also politically virtuous.

Jules Bonnot, with the small group he led, was responsible for a series of extremely daring crimes in the early months of 1912. They began with an attack on a bank messenger in a busy Paris street, and continued with other robberies carried out with a recklessness that implied utter disregard of personal risk. In March, after abandoning their gray De Dion-Bouton car, the Bonnot group stopped a man driving a racing car through the forest of Senart. They killed the driver and the two mechanics with him, drove to Chantilly and held up a bank there, killing three more people and getting away with 80,000 francs. After splitting up they evaded capture for another month. Bonnot escaped sensationally from a room in which he had been cornered, killing the deputy chief of the Sûreté and severely wounding another detective. At the end of April Bonnot and his companion

Dubois were trapped in a house that was part of a small Anarchist community. A full scale siege was conducted by nearly two hundred police. It ended by them dynamiting the house. As they approached the smoking ruin they found Dubois dead and Bonnot dying. Bonnot sought fame as well as what he regarded as glory. He left a will in which he said: 'I am a celebrated man. Ought I to regret what I have done? Yes, perhaps, but I am not more guilty than the sweaters who exploit poor devils.'

The most remarkable thing about Landru, 'the French Bluebeard', is that although he certainly murdered eleven women, and according to the French police killed many more, no real trace of them was ever found. How did he manage to dispose of them, living as he was for two years of the murder period with a French girl who impressed the Court as completely honest when she said that she never for a moment suspected anything wrong? How was it that the oven of his villa at Gambais yielded no more than a few unrecognizable bone splinters? The questions were never answered. The only bodies found in the garden of his villa were those of three dogs.

Landru was a Lonely Hearts killer, like Belle Gunness before him and Fernande and Beck later on,

The gray De Dion-Bouton car of the Bonnot gang. The man in the car is the chief of the Sûreté, M. Guichard. The bearded figure talking to him is Alphonse Bertillon.

Jules Bonnot at the wheel of an electric brougham. He had been engaged as driver by an Englishman named Ashton-Wolfe (in the brougham) who worked for the Sûreté

who graduated to murder from various types of fraud. He had been several times in prison when, in 1914, he began to advertise in matrimonial papers as an affectionate widower with a comfortable income who wanted to marry a widow. His contacts with the eleven known victims were carefully traced, and it was plain that under his several names of Fremyat, Dupont, Guillet and Cuchet he had taken them to his villa and that they had disappeared. There was much other evidence against him, building up to a case of overwhelming strength. The women did not marry him, and were not insured, so that Landru's profit from each individual death was comparatively small.

It is interesting that, when arrested in the name of Cuchet, Landru was identified by his Bertillon measurements and not by his fingerprints, although they must have been on the file. He behaved with verve and humour at his trial, offering his place in the dock to a woman who could not find a seat in Court, and saying calmly after he had been declared sane that this was a proof of his innocence, because the crimes of which he was accused could only have been committed by an insane man. He was found guilty in spite of a remarkable two day speech by his counsel, Maître Moro-Giafferi, who stressed the failure to link Landru with the missing women. He was guillotined on 23 February 1922.

Landru in Court   *RTHPL*

Landru and some of his victims   *RTHPL*

Sacco and Vanzetti: myth and reality

A rusty wagon pulled by a bay horse stopped in Wall Street one day in 1920, opposite J. P. Morgan and Company. Who drove it, and what happened to him, was something nobody ever knew. Just after midday there was a tremendous roar as a bomb in the wagon, covered with what were afterwards reckoned to be 500 lbs of sliced-up lead window weights, exploded.

Wall Street was crowded at the time and the number of killed ran into dozens, the injured into hundreds. The horse and wagon no longer existed. A clerk in the J. P. Morgan office was killed, hundreds of windows were blown out, the area of devastation extended thirty yards, the area of damage half a mile. It was the worst bomb outrage in American history, and in spite of careful and continuous police work over a period of years, nobody was arrested and nobody knows who set the bomb. It may have been the Irish Sinn Fein, it may have been the Anarchists, it may have been one of the many individuals who hated Wall Street and J. P. Morgan...

The Wall Street bomb had an effect on the fate of Sacco and Vanzetti. Did they stage a hold-up outside a shoe factory near Boston on 15 April, 1920, killing two men and stealing the factory payroll, or not? In the Red-baiting wave of 1920 and 1921 encouraged by the Attorney-General, Mitchell Palmer, on the basis that foreign revolutionaries were trying to overthrow the American Government, their guilt was taken for granted. The men were Italians, they were

Parts of bodies on the sidewalk after the Wall Street explosion *UPI*

A general view of Wall Street after the bomb exploded. Every window in the area was blown out *UPI*

Anarchists, they were carrying guns, and Sacco's pistol was a .32 of the type that shot one of the men who died. The conduct of their trial in an atmosphere of extreme political prejudice, with frequent references to wops and dagos and an almost incredible summing-up by Judge Webster Thayer, who made no bones about his hatred of foreigners ('Did you see what I did to those anarchist bastards?' he asked afterwards), caused liberal feeling to be stirred on the other side. A belief in the innocence of the two men was engendered, almost as automatic as the Red-baiters' belief in their guilt. The innocence of Vanzetti the fish peddler and Sacco the factory worker who never gave trouble were taken as proved by the small army of American intellectuals who organized protest and fund-raising meetings in their defence. The agitation about the injustice of the case in a dozen different countries assumed not only that the trial had been grotesquely prejudiced, but that the verdict must be wrong. And when, after six years of delays, appeals, and demands for a new trial, Sacco and Vanzetti went to the electric chair at Boston's Charlestown Prison, while riot squads armed with automatic rifles broke up street meetings, and sympathetic strikes took place in Central and South America, and riots in Paris and Cherbourg, the creative literature about the martyrs began to pour from the presses. Eugene Lyons's biography, Edna St Vincent Millay's poems, Lola Ridge's 'Two in the Death House', Maxwell Anderson's plays *Gods of the Lightning* and *Winterset*, a dozen novels – these only scratch the surface of the imaginative literature dealing imaginatively with the case.

Most of this literature makes an assumption of innocence which cannot be justified. The most recent book about the case, Francis Russell's *Tragedy at Dedham*, comes to the conclusion, largely on the ballistics evidence, that Sacco was certainly guilty. Yet it is no reflection on the ballistics evidence given by Calvin Goddard in 1927 to say that so much chicanery took place on the part of both prosecution and defence that it is impossible to be sure that the bullet he compared with those fired from Sacco's gun had not been planted on him by the prosecution. (One of the defence ballistics experts made an attempt to switch the barrel of Sacco's pistol on to another pistol.) Much of the other evidence, especially that of eye-witnesses on both sides, was so confused, contradictory and biased that it is almost valueless. What can be said is, as one historian demurely puts it, that Sacco's behaviour 'was not such as to compel the conclusion that he was incapable of crime to further what he so fervently believed to be a righteous cause.' On the evidence neither Sacco nor Vanzetti should have been convicted, but that is not at all the same thing as saying they were innocent.

Nicola Sacco *UPI*

Bartolomeo Vanzetti *UPI*

The lost generation

No doubt all generations are lost generations, but some are more lost than others. The short unhappy life of Starr Faithfull, and to a lesser degree the tragedy of Elvira Barney, do seem to typify the disastrous effects that the pressure of an era can have on the flawed and the weak. Yet it is true also that the dice were loaded against Starr Faithfull from the start. A background of family bickering succeeded by divorce, seduction in her early teens by a friend of the family, unimaginative and useless psychiatric treatment, her mother's remarriage to a man named Faithfull, a move from Boston to Greenwich Village – is it surprising that Starr Faithfull took to drink? Her sympathetic but uncomprehending stepfather, who was a chemist by occupation, used to make up flasks of gin for her because he was afraid that the liquor she got in speakeasies would contain wood alcohol.

But she drank speakeasy liquor too. There was a night when she was found in a hotel with a man, naked, drunk, and so badly beaten that she had to be taken to hospital. There were other drinking parties,

other men. There was a ship's surgeon for whom she nursed such a violent unrequited passion that she tried to stow away on his ship on a voyage to Europe. And then, in June 1931, her body was found on the water's edge in Long Beach, Long Island. Starr Faithfull was dead.

Had she killed herself or was she murdered? There was no apparent motive for murder, and the ship's surgeon produced a letter he had received from Starr in which she said that she was going to end her 'worthless disorderly bore of an existence', but the Faithfull family declared that these letters were forgeries, and certainly the writing does not much resemble her normal hand. Their theory was that Starr had been killed by thugs employed by her childhood seducer, who was named as a Boston politician with the initials A.J.P. There were details that supported the idea of murder. Dr Gettler, New York City toxicologist, said that she had taken veronal before she drowned – but then she was known to take drugs. Sand from the seashore was found in her trachea, and this might have

Starr Faithfull *UPI*

Starr's sister, Tucker Faithfull, holding extracts from the 'suicide letter' compared with Starr's ordinary writing *UPI*

meant that her head had been held under water. Nobody ever learned what really happened to Starr Faithfull, or how she spent the last hours of her life after leaving home early on a fine June morning.

Mrs Barney, who was acquitted of shooting her lover, a young man named Scott Stephen, is a far less sympathetic figure. She was the daughter of Sir John and Lady Mullens, and typical of what were called at the time the Bright Young Things. She and her friends were hard drinkers, practical jokers and reckless drivers. 'I'll teach you to put me in a cell, you foul swine', she said to a detective who had asked her to go with him to the station. She then spoke to her mother on the telephone, and went on haughtily: 'Now you know who my mother is, you will be more careful of what you say and do.' In fact it was three days before she was arrested, although the case seemed wholly straightforward. She had been alone with Stephen, a witness had heard her shrieking, 'Get out or I'll shoot you', there had been a shooting incident three weeks earlier. Sir Bernard Spilsbury, the pathologist, testified that there had been no smoke marks on Stephen's hands or clothes, and the celebrated gunsmith

Robert Churchill said that the revolver was a heavy one, with a pull of 14 lbs, and could not have been discharged accidentally.

Elvira Barney's acquittal was a triumph for her counsel, Patrick Hastings. It was his theory that she had been struggling to get the revolver away from Stephen, and that it had gone off by accident. To prove how easily this could happen Hastings pointed the revolver at the Court ceiling and pulled the trigger several times with apparent ease, although it is said that in fact the effort was so great that it gave him a sore finger. Mrs Barney, low-voiced, trembling, pitiful, made an excellent impression as she confirmed that this was just how it had happened. Hastings's final speech, which included a reference to Sir John and Lady Mullens ('Awful to see her parents tortured like this') was called by Mr Justice Humphreys one of the finest speeches he had heard at the Bar. The jury took an hour and fifty minutes to decide on their verdict.

A few weeks later Hastings was on holiday in France when a car driven by a woman passed him on the wrong side of the road, narrowly missing his car. It was Mrs Barney.

Elvira Barney   *RTHPL*

Sir Bernard Spilsbury leaving Mrs Barney's Knightsbridge mews cottage holding a magnifying glass in his hand   *RTHPL*

A confusion of alibis

The idea is sometimes advanced that English criminals are more sophisticated than their American counterparts. Certainly the attempts of the murderers to fake alibis in the famous Snyder-Gray case were both contradictory and deplorably crude.

Ruth Snyder, a Norwegian-born American in her early thirties, lived in Queen's Village, Long Island, with her art editor husband and her small daughter Lorraine. Early one March morning in 1927 Mrs Snyder pounded on her door to summon Lorraine, who found her mother tied up. She told the neighbours who were called that two men, one enormously tall, had hit her on the head and bound her, and that she was afraid they might have hurt her husband. The neighbours found that Snyder had been dead for hours. He had been tied up, hit over the head with some heavy instrument, strangled with picture wire, and made insensible by chloroform pressed against his nose and mouth.

Mrs Snyder told her story to the police, adding that the robbers had taken her jewellery and drawing attention to a sinister kerchief, of a kind worn by immigrants, found in the house. If the police ever believed her story they ceased to do so when they found the jewellery hidden under her mattress. Ruth Snyder was afterwards called in the press 'the Granite Woman', but she quickly gave way under police questioning, admitting that she and her lover Judd Gray had killed her husband for his sizeable $95,000

insurance policy. Gray had concocted an alibi as feeble as Ruth Snyder's, which placed him in a hotel in Syracuse at the time of the murder. Like hers it was easily broken and Gray, a neat quiet precise little corset salesman also confessed as soon as he was arrested.

In a way it was a commonplace murder, yet certain features of it are memorable in their cold-blooded viciousness. Ruth Snyder had tried several times to kill her husband, switching on the unlit gas in his room, trying to render him insensible with carbon monoxide, leaving bottles of poisoned and doped drink about the house. At last she called on Gray, and they devised their plan with its half-baked alibis. It was typical of them that Gray, hiding in the house for the Snyders to return home and for a matchbox to be put on the table as a signal for action, drank so much that he forgot what the matchbox was supposed to mean. In court Gray told how he had bought a heavy sashweight, clubbed Snyder with it when he lay asleep, and how during the attack Snyder had cried out, 'Help me, Mumsie, for God's sake help me'. He might as well have asked for help from a stone.

The jury took only two hours to find them guilty. It is hard to know which of two final touches in the case is the more macabre: the poem called 'My Baby' that Ruth Snyder wrote in prison, or the fact that a photographer snapped the moment of execution by means of a camera strapped to his leg.

Ruth Snyder *UPI*

Henry Judd Gray handcuffed to a detective *UPI*

One of several bottles of poisoned liquor in the Snyder home *NYPM*

Kerchief worn by immigrants, left on the scene to suggest that Snyder had been killed by a prowler *NYPM*

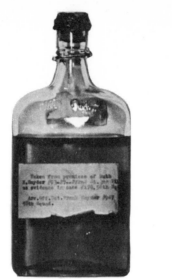

The rope, necktie and towel used to tie up Snyder *NYPM*

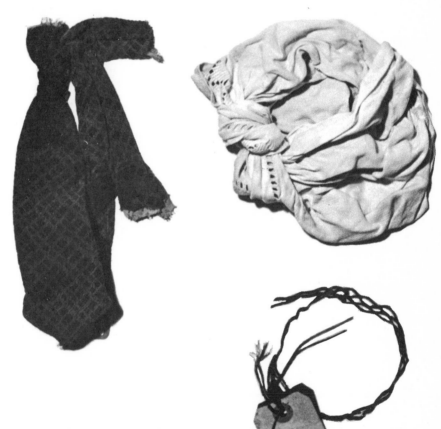

The murder tools, the sashweight and piano wire *NYPM*

An American era ends with Arnold Rothstein

Arnold Rothstein was shot in New York's Park Central Hotel in November 1928, and died within a few hours. An era died with him. Rothstein was connected with contemporary New York gangsters, bootleggers and dope peddlers like Dutch Schultz and Lucky Luciano, and he used 'Legs' Diamonds as a strong arm man, yet essentially he belonged to the crooked New York of an earlier time. He had been a friend of Herman Rosenthal and Charlie Becker (see page 98), and he was primarily a gambler, a crook who was not averse to violence but mostly operated on a basis of political fixing and as a financier of the underworld. It is almost certain that he was killed as the result of a private gambling quarrel, not of a gang war.

Of course this is not to say that gang killings were unknown or even uncommon in the twenties. One of the first was that of Big Jim Colosimo, who ruled crooked Chicago in the decade before Prohibition became law in 1920. Colosimo was known as Diamond Jim because of his passion for diamonds, which he placed on his fingers, carried in his pockets, and even wore on his suspenders. He signed his death warrant when he engaged as bodyguard a dapper New York gunman named Johnny Torrio. More intelligent and more ambitious than Colosimo, Torrio decided to take over his empire. In May 1920, Colosimo was shot down in his café, where he had gone to receive one of the first consignments of bootleg whisky. His extravagant funeral showed the links between gangsters and politicians in Chicago. His coffin was followed by three judges, two Congressmen, one Assistant State's Attorney, and eight Chicago aldermen. Five thousand mourners came after them. The band played 'Nearer My God To Thee'.

Colosimo died because he had become soft. That could never have been said of Arnold Rothstein. To the day of his death he was Mr Big or Mr Bankroll, a man who had the money to finance any crooked deal. He was prepared to bet on anything, and to lend money to anybody who might have a political or legal favour to give in return. But there were signs that Rothstein's mind had lost its cutting edge before his death. In September he became involved in a three day poker game with a bookie friend named Hump McManus, two gamblers from the West Coast, and several others. Such sessions were nothing new to him, but Rothstein played with uncharacteristic recklessness and left owing over $300,000, which he later refused to pay, saying that the game had been rigged. 'Nigger Nate' Raymond, one of the West Coast gamblers, was owed more than $200,000 of the money.

When Rothstein left for the Park Central Hotel on the night of his murder he said he was going to see McManus, and the bookie was arrested, but the case against him collapsed when a chambermaid changed her evidence about seeing him in the room where Rothstein was shot. Raymond was also quizzed without effect. The shooting remains an official mystery, but the explanation offered at the time that the winners had met and decided that they would take action if Mr Big refused to pay up is almost certainly the truth.

Big Jim Colosimo and his wife *UPI*

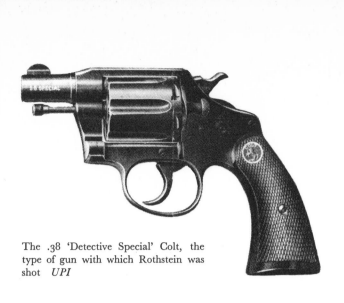

The .38 'Detective Special' Colt, the type of gun with which Rothstein was shot *UPI*

'Nigger Nate' Raymond, who won more than $200,000 from Rothstein in a poker game *UPI*

Arnold Rothstein at the beach with a good friend *UPI*

THE GANGS AND THE F.B.I.

A new era begins

Johnny Torrio, says one historian of the gangs, could have had a successful career as a business efficiency agent. He was certainly astute enough to see the opportunities for gangsterism offered by Prohibition, but gangland in Chicago during the nineteen-twenties resembled more than anything else a feudal society in which barbarous robber barons fought and killed each other for supremacy. Torrio and Capone may have possessed other talents, but the one they principally showed was for organizing murder and violence. It was by the threat of violence that the protection, prostitution and other rackets flourished. They operated also through the connivance of important sections of the judiciary, the law and the political machine.

In the early twenties more than a dozen gangs shared Chicago and its suburbs, among them Roger Touhy who ran a liquor business in Des Plaines, Terry Duggan and Frankie Lake who had a gang on the

Dion O'Banion. As Capone put it, in November 1924 'his head got away from his hat' *UPI*

Dion O'Banion's funeral *UPI*

After Big Jim Colosimo came Johnny Torrio *UPI*

And after Torrio came Al Capone *UPI*

West Side, the nine Aiello brothers, the North Side gang of Dion O'Banion, and the largest of them, the gang organized by Torrio with the assistance of a young New York gangster who had joined him in the lowly capacity of a chucker-out in a brothel, Al Capone. A number of gangs had links with the Italian Mafia, and when the Irish Dion O'Banion rashly said 'To hell with them Sicilians' after double-crossing Torrio and Capone over the sale of his share in a brewery, he made implacable enemies of several groups, including the six brothers known as the Terrible Gennas. The Gennas' bootleg operations, even more than those of other gangsters, were run openly under the eyes of the Chicago police. A number of policemen, and officials from the State Attorney's office, came round monthly for their payoff.

O'Banion had a perfectly respectable flower shop, and it was here that he was killed by one of the Gennas, together with two Sicilian killers named John Scalise and Albert Anselmi. One man shook his hand (O'Banion usually kept a hand in his pistol pocket) while another shot him. His funeral was much grander than Colosimo's. The ten thousand dollar coffin had carved solid silver corner posts and a satin couch for the gangster's body. Twenty thousand people followed the coffin through the streets, and there were twenty-six lorry loads of flowers. A basket of roses was labelled: 'From Al'.

His death began a holocaust. In the next year Hymie Weiss, who took over O'Banion's gang, killed three of the Gennas and had Torrio shot down. The gangster survived, but abdicated his Chicago territory in favour of Capone. 'It's all yours, Al', he said, when he left for convalescence in Italy.

The scene of the St Valentine's Day massacre, Chicago, 14 February 1929 *UPI*

Six of the seven dead men *UPI*

Adam Heyer

John May

Al Weinshank

The empire of Al Capone

It would be tedious to record in detail the Chicago gang killings of the twenties, in which Capone men killed Hymie Weiss outside the O'Banion flower shop and then were killed in their turn, and more killings followed on both sides with smaller groups taking sides with Weiss or Capone. The men involved were mere vicious thugs, altogether lacking the intelligence of Arnold Rothstein, and Capone stands out among them only because he had a certain drive for order. In 1926 he arranged a round table conference attended by the other gangs, at which a peace settlement was reached, with gang limits strictly laid down by Capone. At last he was the Big Fellow, accepted as the emperor of gangland Chicago.

But not for long. There were intransigent figures who did not accept the Capone rule, among them the Aiello brothers, who tried several times to have him killed, by shooting and by putting prussic acid into his soup at a restaurant. Capone disposed of the Aiellos, but then he was confronted with rebellion from George 'Bugs' Moran, who had inherited the O'Banion gang from Weiss. Capone decided to show his mastership once and for all. He tricked Moran's men into believing that a truckload of bootleg liquor would be delivered to their garage headquarters. Seven of them were there waiting to unload it, when a black Packard tourer of the kind used by detective bureau squads drew up and five men got out. Three of them wore police uniforms, the others were in plain clothes. They entered, told Moran's gangsters to turn round and face the wall, and the 'plain clothes men' mowed them down with machine guns. The 'policemen' then marched the 'plain clothes men' out of the garage, hustled them into the Packard and drove away. The whole affair was over in eight minutes. Moran's life was saved because he was late in reaching the garage and Al Weinshank, one of the men in the garage, resembled him in appearance.

George 'Bugs' Moran. His triumph: he survived *UPI*

Capone was wintering in Miami, and at the time of the massacre was talking to the local District Attorney. Nobody was arrested. Yet Capone had overreached himself in this 'triumph'. He felt the strain of living under constant threat of death, and deliberately arranged his own arrest in Philadelphia for carrying a gun. Sentenced to a year's imprisonment, he lived luxuriously in jail, and continued to supervise his empire over the Warden's telephone. When he came out in 1930, however, he found several Citizens' Committees organized against him, and also slowly realized that the Federal authorities were determined not to leave him free. He was finally trapped largely through the persistence of agents in the Chicago Internal Revenue office, who assembled material which procured his indictment on a tax evasions charge. An attempt to plead guilty in hope of a light sentence, and a further attempt to bribe the jury, failed. He was sentenced to 11 years' imprisonment.

Bugs Moran's only triumph was survival. He died a natural death of lung cancer in 1957, in Leavenworth Prison.

James Clark

Frank Gusenberg

Pete Gusenberg

The growth of the F.B.I.

The Federal Bureau of Investigation (originally the Bureau of Investigation) was inaugurated in 1908 through the determination of President Theodore Roosevelt that there should be a Federal instrument by which the government could enforce Federal law, and prevent criminals from escaping justice in one state simply by crossing a boundary into an area controlled by a different police force. The piecemeal way in which United States law enforcement came into being, and the rivalries between different states, counties and townships, have combined to create a haphazard development of law and order.

Roosevelt's idea took some time to get off the ground. The Bureau of Investigation, renamed the F.B.I. in 1935, was an uncertain infant during the years of the 1914-18 War, and its director, William J. Burns, who had been appointed through Warren Harding's crooked Attorney-General Harry Daughterty, was indirectly implicated in the Teapot Dome scandal. The Bureau did not become an effective instrument until in 1924 the 29-year old J. Edgar Hoover was made first Acting Director, and then Director. Hoover's reorganization of the Bureau into a powerful force for fighting crime was an extraordinary feat of administration and public relations. Agents were recruited with great care, preference being given to those with legal or accountant's training and to those with a solidly respectable background. For a long time Hoover was unable to convince the authorities – or other law agencies – that police agents should be trained. One chief of police said optimistically that all a policeman need know was the Ten Commandments. Not until 1935 was a class of 23 officers gathered for a twelve weeks' study course. The success of this and subsequent classes was so remarkable that they developed into the F.B.I. National Academy.

The most impressive of Hoover's achievements has been that of co-ordinating the technical and scientific services of the country's many law agencies. By 1910 most American police forces had changed from the Bertillon system to fingerprinting – the Warden at Leavenworth had received a shock when he discovered after taking the Bertillon measurements of a Negro named Will West that an unrelated Will West, with measurements that were identical within the Bertillon tolerance limits, was already in Leavenworth. The fingerprint records, however, were of very limited use because they were in so many different prisons. The 800,000 prints and 200,000 Bertillon files of which Hoover took charge in 1924 were co-ordinated within months into a valuable central register. After a long battle he obtained permission

The home of the Identification Division, Technical Laboratories and Crime Statistics section of the F.B.I. during part of the twenties and thirties *FBI*

The present U.S. Department of Justice building which houses the F.B.I. *FBI*

The F.B.I. pistol range at the U.S. Marine Corps Base, Quantico, Virginia. Point shooting at silhouette targets *FBI*

A special agent in the prone firing position on the Practical Pistol Course at Quantico *FBI*

in 1930 to form a 'Division of Identification and Information', and the F.B.I. fingerprint collection is now the largest in the world. A forensic science laboratory was set up in 1932, and the scope and intensity of police training through the National Academy, as suggested by the photographs, has increased year by year.

All this has not been accomplished without considerable criticism of Hoover and the organization he heads. He has been called authoritarian, and accused of being a headline hunter. It has been said that he would like to turn the United States into a police state, and that his hatred of Communists and Socialists is almost pathological. There is some truth in these criticisms – certainly Hoover's attitude towards Left–wing movements is such that he would find it difficult to co-operate with even a moderate Socialist regime, and the F.B.I. shaped by Hoover is a fanatical supporter of the American Way of Life. On the other hand even the F.B.I.'s opponents admit that the organization is free of the racketeering and personal venality that has marked so many United States police forces.

The F.B.I. played no part in the battle against Capone, because it was unable to act until the gangs violated a Federal law. It had a major role, however, in destroying Capone's successors, John Dillinger and 'Pretty Boy' Floyd.

John Dillinger, a modern Jesse James

The gangs who operated in the American Mid-West, in the states of Indiana, Illinois, Iowa, Minnesota, Ohio and Wisconsin, were of a different calibre and mentality from the city gangs of Chicago. They were outlaws in the Jesse James tradition. Bonnie Parker, who with Clyde Barrow led the Barrow gang, wrote:

You have read the story of Jesse James,
Of how he lived and died.
If you are still in need of something to read,
Here is the story of Bonnie and Clyde.

There was nothing especially memorable about the Barrows, a group of ruthless killers who were eventually tracked down by the F.B.I. in co-operation with the Sheriff of Arcadia, Texas, where they were ambushed and killed. Nor was there anything romantic or unusual about the Barker-Karpis Gang, headed by the formidable 'Ma' Barker, mother of Dock and Fred, except that they staged two kidnappings, one of a wealthy brewer and the other of a bank president, and let the men go free after obtaining $100,000 and $200,000 from them.

The Dillinger story is another matter. It is possible to feel some sympathy for this motherless son of a sternly religious Indianapolis grocer who tried to beat the vice out of a small boy. Dillinger was only 21 when he received a savage sentence of 10 to 20 years' imprisonment for a clumsy attempt at armed robbery. He came out of prison in May 1933, and was killed in July 1934. In a period of less than 14 months Dillinger and his associates carried out nearly a dozen bank robberies, were captured and made daring prison escapes, and half a dozen times wriggled out of the nets spread to catch them. The principal members of the first Dillinger Gang, whom he met in the Indiana State Prison at Michigan City, were all intelligent and one of them, Harry Pierpont, was a planner of considerable ability. They were violent only when it was necessary, and Dillinger himself rarely used his gun. A well organized prison break from Michigan City led to four months of robbery, and by the end of 1933 the Dillinger Gang were being hunted by the F.B.I., the Indiana State Police, and a special Dillinger Squad of forty picked men from Chicago. They were caught in Texas, but with the aid of a gun smuggled into the jail Dillinger made his escape from Crown Point, Indiana, forcing prison employees to open several barred doors, taking a Deputy Sheriff and a mechanic with him as hostages, and shaking hands with them both when he turned them out of his stolen car.

The second Dillinger Gang, formed after this escape, was far below the first in mental calibre. The

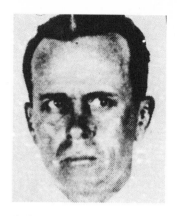

Arthur 'Dock' Barker. One of the Barker-Karpis Gang *UPI*
Alvin Karpis *UPI*

John Dillinger, 'Public Enemy No. 1 *UPI*
Charles 'Pretty Boy' Floyd. He took part in the Kansas City Massacre of 17 June 1933, when in an attempt to free a bank robber captured by the F.B.I., four police officers and the robber himself were killed. In October 1934, Floyd and an associate were found by the F.B.I. on an Ohio farm and killed in a gun fight *UPI*

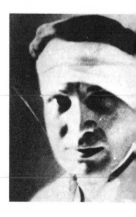

'Baby Face' Nelson. He and Homer Van Meter were leading members of the second Dillinger Gang *UPI*

Homer Van Meter *UPI*

WANTED

JOHN HERBERT
DILLINGER

On June 23, 1934, HOMER S. CUMMINGS, Attorney General of the United States, under the authority vested in him by an Act of Congress approved June 6, 1934, offered a reward of

$10,000.00

for the capture of John Herbert Dillinger or a reward of

$5,000.00

for information leading to the arrest of John Herbert Dillinger.

DESCRIPTION

Age, 32 years; Height, 5 feet 7-1/8 inches; Weight, 153 pounds; Build, medium; Hair, medium chestnut; Eyes, grey; Complexion, medium; Occupation, machinist; Marks and scars, 1/2 inch scar back left hand, scar middle upper lip, brown mole between eyebrows.

All claims to any of the aforesaid rewards and all questions and disputes that may arise as among claimants to the foregoing rewards shall be passed upon by the Attorney General and his decisions shall be final and conclusive. The right is reserved to divide and allocate portions of any of said rewards as between several claimants. No part of the aforesaid rewards shall be paid to any official or employee of the Department of Justice.

If you are in possession of any information concerning the whereabouts of John Herbert Dillinger, communicate immediately by telephone or telegraph collect to the nearest office of the Division of Investigation, United States Department of Justice, the local addresses of which are set forth on the reverse side of this notice.

JOHN EDGAR HOOVER, DIRECTOR,
DIVISION OF INVESTIGATION,
UNITED STATES DEPARTMENT OF JUSTICE,
WASHINGTON, D. C.

June 23, 1934

The F.B.I. reward notice for Dillinger
McDade Collection

22 July 1934. Dillinger's body in the patrol wagon   *UPI*

youthful Baby Face Nelson was a savage killer and Homer Van Meter, Dillinger's other chief aide, was erratic and liable to lose his nerve. The Dillinger hunt started again, and the lawmen involved became as quick on the trigger as the outlaws. When the F.B.I. trapped them at a lodge called Little Bohemia in Northern Wisconsin, innocent people were killed and wounded as the agents fired by mistake on a car containing a visiting salesman and men from a nearby camp. Dillinger went underground, had a clumsy plastic surgery job done on his face, and like other criminals tried to obliterate his fingerprints by cauterization. But the end was near. There was one more robbery at South Bend, Indiana, and then Dillinger holed up in Chicago. There he was found through a brothel madame who was tempted partly by the reward offered for him, but chiefly by the prospect that her deportation back to Rumania would be rescinded.

The F.B.I. men who set the trap for Dillinger outside the Biograph Cinema were told to take him alive if possible. (The Chicago Dillinger Squad were, remarkably enough, kept in ignorance of the operation.) As he came out of the cinema Dillinger realized that he was in danger, and drew his Colt automatic. He never fired it, for the agents shot and killed him.

Dillinger's exploits had a considerable effect on American attitudes towards the law. There was a

good deal of admiration for him and he undoubtedly had the qualities of courage and of loyalty to his associates. At the same time the hunt made both state and county police and the general public realize that the F.B.I. were not the 'College Cops' that they had contemptuously been called, but a formidable Federal police force which could be immensely helpful to local forces without violating their authority.

Dillinger's father and members of his family appeared on the stage at Indianapolis to recount 'Incidents in the Life of the Late John Dillinger, Jr'   *UPI*

143

A hole in the ground

By the end of 1935 the outlaw gangs of the mid-West had been destroyed. Pierpont and another member of the first Dillinger Gang, Charles Makley, tried to escape from the death house of Ohio State Prison with the help of pistols carved from soap. They bluffed and overpowered one guard, but a riot squad killed Makley and wounded Pierpont, who went to the electric chair a few weeks later. Homer Van Meter was shot in a gun battle with police at St Paul. Baby Face Nelson and an associate were caught by F.B.I. agents – or as they were now popularly called 'G' Man (for Government men). They fought a machine gun and pistol battle, and although Nelson got away he was mortally wounded. On the following day his body, stripped to delay identification, was found twenty miles away.

The Barkers did not long survive the Dillinger Gang. In January 1935, Dock Barker was caught in Chicago, one of the few outlaws to be captured without a struggle. As he remarked, 'This is a helluva time to be caught without a gun.' A circle drawn round Lake Weir, Florida, on a map in his effects led a charter plane containing a group of F.B.I. men to a luxury white house on the shore of the Lake. There Ma and her other son Freddie were installed, with an arsenal which included two machine guns, two shotguns, three automatic pistols and a rifle. Summoned to surrender by the inspector in charge, Ma Barker fired a burst at him from a machine gun. A battle lasting for half an hour followed, while the house was attacked with tear gas bombs, machine guns and rifles. At the end of it there was silence from within the house, and the two Barkers were found dead. Ma still clutched a machine gun. Alvin Karpis, the other leading member of the gang, was hunted for several months before a raiding party led by Hoover in person arrested 'Public Rat Number One' as the F.B.I. Director called him, in New Orleans. He received a life sentence for kidnapping, and was sent to Alcatraz.

The time of the outlaw and the gangster is short, and his end is a hole in the ground. For Capone, too, the days of power were gone. He was released from prison in 1939, suffering from syphilis which had already affected his brain. He lived on until 1948 in Miami, in doddering obscurity. Yet it is not the Capones but the outlaws who are more feared by the community, or the business community. The fact that no other crimes are regarded so seriously by them as crimes against property is testified by the offer made by the Texas Bankers Association (see notice opposite). 'The Association will not give one cent for live bank robbers. . .' The business world is not lacking in its own kind of ruthlessness.

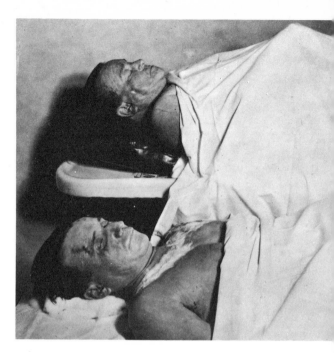

'Ma' and Fred Barker after they had been shot to death in the Florida gun battle   *McDade Collection*

February, 1947. Capone's grave is being dug in the family plot at Mount Olivet   *UPI*

$5,000 REWARD
For DEAD Bank Robbers

THE Texas Bankers Association, a corporation, offers a reward of $5,000 for each bank robber legally killed while robbing and holding up a reward-subscribing member bank in Texas during the daytime. Limits of the place and time of such killing are: in the banking house, or as the robbers leave the bank; while the holdup and threats are being committed within the bank; as the robbers flee from the bank with the property taken; or while the robbers are resisting legal pursuit and arrest, within five miles of the bank robbed and within one hour after the holdup.

❧ The amount of the reward for each dead robber will be $5,000.00.

❧ This reward does not apply where the bank is not a subscriber to the reward fund. This reward does not apply to night attacks on Texas banks.

❧ The Association will not give one cent for live bank robbers. They are rarely identified, more rarely convicted, and most rarely stay in the penitentiary when sent there - - - all of which operations are troublesome, burdensome and costly to our government.

❧ In order to protect the lives of people in such banks and to protect the property of such banks, the Association is prepared to pay for any number of such robbers so killed, while they are robbing and holding up its reward-subscribing member banks during the daytime.

❧ It is expressly provided that only the Texas Bankers Association shall determine whether or not payment of this reward shall be made hereunder, and to whom (if anyone) such payment shall be made, and such determination and judgment shall be final, conclusive and not reviewable.

❧ This reward is effective July 15th, 1946, and all other rewards, offers and statements are cancelled and superseded hereby.

TEXAS BANKERS ASSOCIATION

A $5,000 Reward will be paid for each Bank Robber legally killed while Robbing this bank

A notice offering a reward for 'DEAD Bank Robbers' issued by the Texas Bankers Association in 1946   *McDade Collection*

Diamond in hospital after the shooting of his colleague Little Augie in his presence. He put the sheet over his face so that he should not be able to identify the killers *UPI*

Jacob 'Little Augie' Orgen *UPI*

'Legs' Diamond – so called because of his speed in running away – in Court *UPI*

Rothstein's legacy

New York also had its gangster problems, although they never developed as bloodily as Chicago's. In a sense they were the legacy of Arnold Rothstein, who backed financially most of the men who came to power – Lepke Buchalter who controlled the garment industry, the miserly German Arthur Flegenheimer who was known as Dutch Schultz, and half a dozen others, including Legs Diamond. Photographs of Diamond do not suggest his slight frame and air of frailty. He was one of the few pathological killers among the city gangs. He killed for pleasure, and found compensation for his lack of physical courage in the possession of a shotgun. Rothstein set up Diamond as a professional bootlegger who hijacked the trucks of the many amateurs dealing in liquor, besides using him as a bodyguard. After the shooting of his friend Little Augie, probably by one of Buchalter's gunmen, and the death of Rothstein, Diamond aspired to become the boss of New York's underworld. He lacked the necessary toughness and astuteness, and was shot to death in 1931.

Dutch Schultz, who was responsible for Diamond's killing and became for a short time pre-eminent in New York's gangland looked, as one detective said, 'like a small businessman ready to announce his bankruptcy'. Like Diamond essentially cowardly, he had a considerable organization, based primarily on bootlegging but extending to fixed boxing matches and the numbers and policy rackets. The crusading young District Attorney Thomas E. Dewey had him arrested and charged with tax evasion, but Schultz bribed his way out of trouble. In 1935, however, he was shot down in Newark, New Jersey – very appropriately, while going over his policy receipts.

With Schultz gone, Dewey concentrated on James J. Hines, one of the Tammany district leaders. The struggle to involve Hines with the gangs became in effect a battle between Dewey and the politicians of Tammany, and it lasted for three years after Schultz's death. After two trials, Hines received a prison sentence. The cheque shown is typical of the evidence that helped to convict him. The sister of Schultz's lawyer Dixie Davis testified that she delivered it to Hines in person.

Dutch Schultz (left) handcuffed to deputy *UPI*

A cheque that played a part in linking Tammany leader James J. Hines to the Schultz policy racket *UPI*

147

GREAT CASES OF THE PERIOD

The Scottsboro boys

The Scottsboro case moved American liberal opinion more than any other except that of Sacco and Vanzetti in the years between the wars, and with better reason, for the affair of the Scottsboro boys exemplified all that was most prejudiced and illiberal in American society. No reasonable jury would ever have convicted them on the evidence, but in relation to crimes allegedly committed by Negroes against whites in Alabama, juries at that time were not by any means reasonable.

There were nine of them, the eldest twenty-one, the two youngest thirteen, and they were sad specimens of humanity. Four were almost mental defectives, one was nearly blind, one had venereal disease. Only three of the nine were literate. These nine boys had a fight with four white youths when they were all hitching a ride on a freight train. The white boys, and two girls with them, were thrown off the train, and one of them reported what had happened. At the next stop the sheriff was waiting with a posse. The boys were taken off the train and in Scottsboro, Alabama, they were jointly charged with raping the white girls, Victoria Price and Ruby Bates.

Doctors examined the girls, and could find no sign that they had been raped. There was no evidence against the Negroes except that of the girls and their companions, but none was needed. In an atmosphere of fury, with thousands of people surging about outside a courthouse ringed with National Guards, the jury found them guilty. All, except one of the thirteen-year old boys, were sentenced to death.

That was in April 1931. It was the beginning, not the end, of the Scottsboro case. Protest parades by Negro organizations and labour groups were followed by an order for new trials from the United States Supreme Court on the ground that they had not been adequately defended – six out of seven local lawyers had refused to take the case. Communist groups and periodicals made propaganda out of the affair. The new trial brought into the case the flamboyant New York counsel Samuel Leibowitz, who succeeded in winning a separate trial for Heywood Patterson, the most intelligent of the accused. Leibowitz, who was well known for his support of liberal ideas, used the case partly to expose the gerrymandering by which Negroes were kept off the jury rolls in the South. Patterson had his second trial in 1933, and a third in 1936, and at the third trial twelve Negroes were

Samuel Leibowitz, the defence attorney who took up the case, making a point during Patterson's trial   *UPI*

called as potential jurors although none actually served. Leibowitz had thus taken a step on the path towards obtaining jury rights for Negroes, but this did not help Patterson, who was found guilty on each occasion, even though at the second trial Ruby Bates dropped a bombshell by going back on her testimony.

She now said that neither she nor Victoria Price had been raped, and that the charge had been made to avoid their arrest for vagrancy. Shortly after changing her testimony she headed a deputation to the White House to appeal for the release of the nine Negroes. Infuriated Southerners concentrated their fury upon Leibowitz, and there were demands that the Jew from New York should be lynched. The appeal Judge had set aside the second conviction, saying that the evidence did not justify a verdict of 'Guilty', but the third trial was a farce.

The shabby tale has no happy ending, nor really any ending at all. An official attempt to do a deal by freeing some of the boys on condition that the others pleaded guilty was rejected, but as the years passed all but one were released on parole. They had gone into prison as boys, they came out as men in their thirties. Patterson only remained in jail, a revenge on him for having been the spearhead of the great agitation which by the end of the war had been forgotten. In 1948 Patterson, now violent and bitter, escaped from prison, killed a man in a fight and was caught and imprisoned again. He died of cancer in 1952.

Heywood Patterson (*right*) talking to the Sheriff in the jail at Decatur, Alabama *UPI*

Ruby Bates, wearing white coat, leaving the White House in May 1933, after heading a march of 2000 people appealing for the release of the nine Scottsboro boys *UPI*

Victims hard to kill

In June 1935, an odd job man named Charles Hope went into the Los Angeles barber shop of Robert James, said that he was broke and asked to have his hair cut on credit. James agreed, and said that if Hope knew anything about rattlesnakes he could earn a hundred bucks. 'I have a friend whose wife is bothering him, and he wants a couple of snakes used to bite her', he said.

Although Hope, as he said, did not take this extraordinary conversation seriously, he bought the snakes, delivered them to James's bungalow at La Canada, outside the city, and was paid his hundred dollars. The snakes, however, had come from a local sideshow and when they were put in a box with chickens, it was the snakes rather than the chickens who seemed disturbed by the encounter. James and Hope then bought a rattlesnake from another sideshow and put it into a box with a rabbit. On the following morning the rabbit was alive, but the snake had died. Undeterred, James bought for six dollars through his agent Hope two *Crotalus atrox* rattlesnakes guaranteed to be fresh from the Colorado desert. These killed chickens promptly enough. Could they be induced to bite a bothersome wife?

James's wife Mary – for, as Hope had realized,

Robert James. He had 'a friend whose wife was bothering him' *UPI*

The black widow spider found in the James garage *UPI*

The lily pond outside the James bungalow. Hope is on the extreme left. James stands in the middle *UPI*

150

there was no 'friend' – seems to have been remarkably credulous. She was pregnant, and had agreed to an abortion which she thought was to be performed by Hope. James persuaded her that it would be necessary to strap her on the kitchen table and seal her lips with adhesive tape, and that she must be blindfolded so that she could not testify against Hope afterwards. Her foot was stuck into the box with the snake and it struck. Hope took the snakes back to the dealer and resold them to him at half the purchase price.

The two men spent the rest of the day drinking in the garage, which housed some black widow spiders already bought by James in an unsuccessful attempt to kill Mary. In the house Mary's leg was swelling and she was in great pain, but she did not die. At last James said: 'Hell, the damned snake didn't work. I'm going in and drown her.' He drowned her in the bath, and then Hope helped him to drag her out. He put the body in the lily pond, head and shoulders in the water, face down.

The verdict of suicide was accepted at the time, and not until eight months later when James was imprisoned on a charge of having sexual relations with his niece, was his wife's body exhumed and found to contain rattlesnake venom. The full story came out when Hope confessed to his part in the crime. James killed his wife for the insurance policy taken out on her life, and he was almost certainly a multiple murderer. He had been married five times, and one of his other wives had drowned in her bath. He received the death sentence. Hope was sentenced to life imprisonment.

Mike Malloy, a cheerful alcoholic who was insured by his New York speakeasy friends in 1932 for nearly $2000, also proved a victim remarkably hard to kill. The men who formed what they called a 'Murder Trust' were the speakeasy proprietor Tony Marino, his bartender Joe Murphy, Dan Kreisberg, and very appropriately an undertaker named Frank Pasqua. Malloy, however, was evidently so soaked in alcohol that he had some degree of immunity. He absorbed almost pure wood alcohol and poisoned sardines without ill effects. Then Pasqua took him out into a severe sleet storm, but although Pasqua himself was ill afterwards Malloy suffered nothing worse than a head cold. They hired a taxi driver to run over Malloy when he was insensible through drink, but after a short stay in hospital he was back again in the speakeasy. Eventually they killed him by putting a rubber gas pipe in his mouth when he was in an alcoholic stupor. The crime was quickly discovered, and they were found guilty of first degree murder.

Killers of Mike Malloy in the dock. From left to right: Dan Kreisberg, Joseph Murphy, Anthony Marino, Frank Pasqua *UPI*

Paul Dwyer at his trial in 1937 on the charge of murdering Dr Littlefield and his wife. On the right, hat on his knee, is Sheriff Francis Carroll, the principal witness against Dwyer   *UPI*

Could the puny Dwyer have carried the heavy body of Dr Littlefield? Carroll (being carried) shows that it was possible *UPI*

Ex-Sheriff Francis Carroll, charged with the murder in 1938. Here he is seen at his trial, talking to his daughter Barbara   *UPI*

Bottom right: Carroll, released in 1950, in a happy reunion with his 82-year old mother. But what about Dwyer?   *UPI*

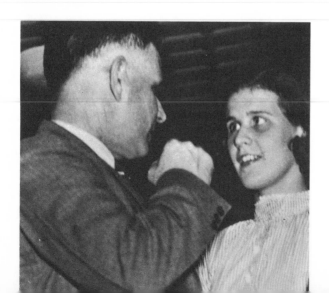

The case of the valiant sheriff

One of the most astonishing cases in recent American criminal history began in October 1937, when two policemen in New Jersey noticed a youth asleep in a car. His name was Paul Dwyer, and the policemen discovered that two dead bodies were in the car with him. They were Dr James Littlefield and his wife, and both had been battered and strangled. Dwyer was taken back to his home town of South Paris, Maine, and there confessed to quarrelling with the doctor, killing him with a hammer, and putting the body in his car boot. He had later killed Mrs Littlefield and put her in the car as well. He was sentenced to life imprisonment.

The chief witness against Dwyer had been the local sheriff, an alert and jovial officer named Francis M. Carroll. After the trial suspicions were aroused about Carroll's connection with the case, partly because of his subsequent wild behaviour and heavy drinking. His movements were checked, and witnesses were found who said that his car had been seen outside Dwyer's house on the night of the murder. His cigarette lighter was found in the drive. Dwyer, interrogated in prison, made a new confession in which he said that he had seduced Carroll's 17-year old daughter Barbara, and that Barbara had written letters to him saying that her father had had incestuous relations with her. Dwyer threatened Carroll with exposure. Carroll in turn said that Barbara was pregnant, and that Dwyer was the father. A showdown was arranged at Dwyer's house, at which Dr Littlefield would examine Barbara to determine if she was actually pregnant. According to Dwyer, Carroll came to the meeting alone, clubbed the doctor to death when he mentioned something about incest, forced Dwyer to hand back the letters from Barbara, killed Mrs Littlefield, and then ordered Dwyer to get rid of the bodies.

There was supporting evidence for some of Dwyer's story, including the telling negative evidence that Barbara was not put on the witness stand, although she talked and laughed with her father throughout the trial. The defence said that they wanted to shield her from publicity, but it was remembered that she set up a stall where she sold autographed photographs of herself. Carroll was found guilty, and sentenced to life imprisonment. He was released after 12 years on the ground that he had been convicted on 'false, perjured and manufactured evidence'. He died in 1956. But the most remarkable feature of the case is that Dwyer, who was presumably no more than an accessory to the crime, is at the time of writing still in prison.

The two murders committed by Kenneth Neu in 1933, when he killed men who had as he said pestered him with homosexual advances, were unremarkable, but he is an almost classic case of an obvious psychotic who was found to be sane. He had a history of mental illness, and there was a battle between State and defence psychiatrists in New Orleans, where the case was tried. In the end he was found sane and executed, even though one doctor testified that cerebral syphilis had already affected his brain. Neu was delighted by all the attention he received. He sang on the way to and from Court, tap danced in his cell, and composed several songs about his impending execution, one to his executioner which began 'Oh, you nasty man', and another with the refrain: 'I'm fit as a fiddle and ready to hang'.

Kenneth Neu in prison singing his song: 'I'm fit as a fiddle and ready to hang'. The suit belongs to his victim Sheffield Clark *UPI*

F. Donald Coster = Philip Musica

Richard Whitney's crime was not unusual. He stole securities entrusted to him, and in 1928 was given a sentence of five to ten years in Sing Sing. His embezzlement caused shocked amazement in the United States because of his name. Richard Whitney had Groton and Harvard as his background. He had five times been President of the New York Stock Exchange. He had been J. P. Morgan's broker. He lived at the rate of $250,000 a year, but his income was known to be treble that. The shock for other well-born Americans was that Richard Whitney should have turned out, when placed under financial pressure, to be a commonplace swindler.

In the year that Richard Whitney went to Sing Sing, a swindler who was far from commonplace put a revolver to his head in his house in Fairfield, Connecticut, and pulled the trigger. So ended one of the most brilliant business deceptions of the century. In 1913 Philip Musica, the eldest son of a barber on New York's East Side, had been given a suspended sentence when he pleaded 'Guilty' to a charge of obtaining loans from several banks amounting to about $500,000 on the security of what were said to be 216 cases of human hair, which proved when examined to be 'worthless hair and waste'. His brothers Antonio, Arthur and George and his sister Louise were all involved in the swindle. Musica's sentence was suspended when he turned informer, and he did so to good effect. During the 1914-18 War he seems to have done counter-espionage work for the U.S. Government, and after it emerged as F. Donald Coster, a member of a respected brokerage house. He started a drug firm which profitably sold alcohol to boot-leggers, and then bought the century-old famous drug house of McKesson and Robbins.

It was here that Musica's great swindle began. Under his direction the firm's profits increased tremendously, and the price of its stock went up and up. It did so because Coster himself handled the very profitable crude drug department. This department bought drugs in Canada which were invoiced to them through Manning's private bank in Montreal, and then sold them at a handsome profit through the Montreal office of the old-established W. W. Smith Company of Montreal, which as its letterhead showed had offices all over the world. The department then ordered more drugs and sold them just as easily, and so on *ad infinitum*. But the whole operation was a fiction. 'Manning's Bank' was a small office with one woman employee, 'W. W. Smith' just down the road was another single room with a typist in it. The drugs did not exist. The purpose of the scheme was to increase the value of McKesson and Robbins shares.

The fraud was carried on successfully for years, but Coster must have known that it could not go on forever, even though he and his brothers, now named Dietrich and Bernard, were the only people with access to the crude drug department records. During a recession in 1937 Coster was strongly urged to convert his stockpile of drugs into cash. His sharp refusal to do so made his friends suspicious. He might have been able to ride the storm, but the past of Philip Musica haunted F. Donald Coster, even though the Musica case records vanished from police files and Coster's birth certificate mysteriously appeared in the District of Columbia Health Records, and special typewriters

Richard Whitney presenting a cup at the Essex Fox Hounds race meeting, Far Hills, New Jersey *UPI*

Whitney leaving Court after being sentenced *UPI*

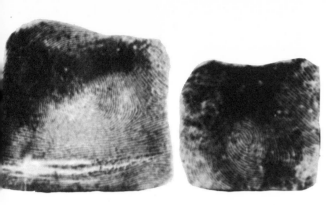

The deadly fingerprints. Philip Musica's left, F. Donald Coster's identical prints right *UPI*

Philip Musica in 1913 (*left*) and F. Donald Coster *UPI*

similar to those used by Dun and Bradstreet were bought to type favourable reports on his non-existent corporations. Too many people knew Philip Musica's secret, and by his own account he was paying an enormous amount in blackmail to prominent Republicans and New Deal Democrats. Musica's fingerprints had vanished with the rest of his file, but a detective found a set of his prints among some old case records and identified them with those of F. Donald Coster. When Musica learned this he must have known that it was the end.

One of the detectives working on the case was given by George Musica the names of a Senator, an official in the Attorney-General's office, a high Federal official and a lawyer who had all received substantial bribes. None of them was ever prosecuted.

The Musicas under arrest in New Orleans in 1913. Philip Musica has his hand over his face and is wearing a hat. Arthur, one of his brothers, is behind, hat in hand *UPI*

Frank Donald Coster's faked birth certificate *UPI*

155

Stavisky and Kreuger

The two great financial scandals of the nineteen-thirties involved the suicides of the central figures. Ivar Kreuger, faced by ruin, shot himself in a Paris hotel in 1932, and Alexander Stavisky put a bullet through his head in a villa near Chamonix in the winter of 1933. The two men were not, however, in any way comparable. Kreuger was a shy introvert – he greatly disliked being photographed – who turned to forgery only when the depression destroyed his credit. Stavisky was a professional swindler, whose exposure brought down the French Government and sparked off an almost revolutionary situation in Paris.

Kreuger had made a substantial fortune as an engineer in the United States when he returned to the country of his birth, Sweden, and founded the firm of Kreuger and Toll. He became known as the 'Swedish Match King' when, through the Swedish Match Company, he tried to obtain complete control of match manufacture throughout Europe. Sober in dress and behaviour and obviously dedicated to making money, Kreuger was the very model of the kind of man thought trustworthy by banks and other big businesses. How could you suspect a man who had lent nearly £100 millions to half a dozen European countries in return for a monopoly of their match

trade? When the depression came, however, Kreuger found all his assets frozen, while his expenses remained undiminished. He began to forge bonds, partly to back his loans, confident that the situation would improve so that he could call in the forgeries. But the economic situation deteriorated instead of improving. Before the discovery of what he had done, and while he was still thought to be one of the richest men in the world, Kreuger shot himself.

Not much is known with certainty about the background of the Stavisky affair. That Stavisky was born in 1888 in the Ukraine, that he was imprisoned more than once as a petty swindler and suddenly emerged running a night club – this is known, and it is known too that he operated various company swindles, ending with his control of the municipal finances of Bayonne, which netted him nearly £2 millions. The bubble burst and with associates informing on him and the police on his track, Stavisky shot himself.

What remains uncertain is who protected Stavisky, for he was certainly protected by politicians and the police. Because he had remained for so long immune from the consequences of his blatant swindles it was said, almost certainly without justification, that he

Alexander Stavisky *Keystone*

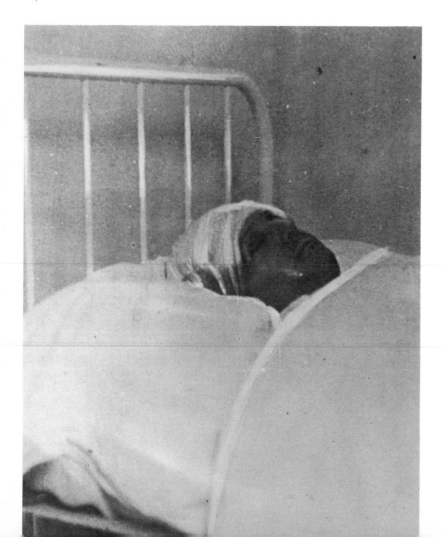

Stavisky's body after his death *Keystone*

Ivar Kreuger, the Swedish Match King

had been killed by the orders of the politicians to whom he had become an embarrassment. After his death the pro-Fascist Paris Prefect of Police, Jean Chiappe, was dismissed by the mildly Socialist government of Daladier. Riots followed in Paris, led by the Fascist *Croix de Feu*. The riots were suppressed, but they brought down Daladier, who was replaced by a Right-wing government headed by Henri Doumergue. An official enquiry followed, but the politicians who gave evidence shed no light on the men behind Stavisky. A High Court magistrate, M. Prince, was found dead on the railway line near Dijon, his body mangled and his head severed from his body by the train. Prince had been called to an interview to explain why he had not produced documents in his possession that would have led to Stavisky's exposure, and he was known to have said to friends that the responsibility lay with one of his colleagues who was the brother-in-law of an unnamed Left-wing politician. Had Prince committed suicide? The Right accused the Left of killing him, and the Left said that the Right was hushing up the facts. Four rival sets of investigators worked on the case, one headed by Inspector Bony from the Paris Prefecture, who was later involved in several scandals, and became an ardent collaborator with the Nazis. It is not surprising that no solution to the death of Judge Prince, or to the problems left by Stavisky's death, was ever found.

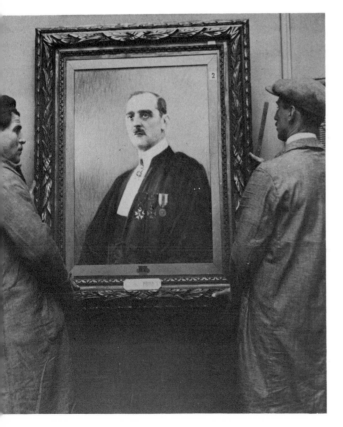

A portrait of Judge Prince, whose mysterious death gave new impetus to the Stavisky scandal   *Keystone*

Famous right-wing politician Camille Chautemps giving evidence at the 1934 Stavisky enquiry   *Keystone*

Death in Canada and Australia

In England it is customary if a jury is unable to agree on its verdict for the accused to be given the benefit of the doubt in the sense that a case stays on the file, but when in 1941 a Toronto jury split 10 to 2 in the case of young Aircraftman Bill Newall, ten believing that he had strangled his Finnish wife with a silk stocking and two holding out for acquittal, a second trial was ordered. At this second trial the jury again split 10 to 2 – but this time the other way, in favour of acquittal – and it was generally expected that Newall would now be freed. The jurors talked without restraint about the course of their 9 hour deliberations. 'When we first retired eight of us were straight for an acquittal', one of them said. 'Two men were undecided at first, but eventually voted with us. The two who wanted to convict Newall wouldn't budge.' The trials, which together lasted a total of forty-three days, set a record for the duration of a murder hearing in Canada, and they were marked by extraordinary happenings. During the first a juryman's mother died, in the course of the second a juryman's wife gave birth to a 7½ lb son. Newall's own behaviour also caused great attention. At one point he stuck out his tongue at a detective, and at another he broke away from his guards and ran down the aisle at the back of the public seats before being caught. When he learned after the second trial that the Attorney-General had refused to grant a stay of execution Newall tried to strangle himself by tying a handkerchief round his neck, knotting it to the grille work in front of his cell and turning round to tighten it. Sent to hospital he broke windows, barricaded himself in his room and started to smash the furniture. He was given six strokes of the strap and put into solitary confinement. The third trial lasted forty-two days, and the defence counsel broke all Canadian murder trial records by making a final speech lasting over 12 hours. Newall was found guilty. After spending well over a year in prison he was hanged, still protesting his innocence.

Was he guilty? Much of the evidence against him was given by forensic scientists, and was disputed by the defence. But the point that disturbed many Canadians was that a man who had been found innocent at one trial by ten jurors out of twelve should eventually have been hanged. In such a case, was there not a presumption of reasonable doubt?

It is a cliché of fiction that all criminals now wear gloves or wipe away their prints before leaving the scene. Fortunately for police investigation this is far from the truth. The case of Marie Anne Carrier, whose naked body was found in a shallow ditch near the town of Morrisburg in Dundas County, Ontario, is interesting because of the vital part played in it by fingerprints. There was little doubt of the murderer's identity, but it is doubtful whether it could have been proved to a jury's satisfaction without the fingerprint evidence.

The police quickly learned that the dead girl had had an affair with Lieutenant Peter Balcombe, who was attached to the 2nd Canadian Rifle Battalion stationed in Quebec, and that the affair had been broken off when she learned that Balcombe was a married man. Balcombe produced one of those vague alibis which is often difficult to break down. He had been on leave and his story was that he had driven from Quebec to his home near London, Ontario, pulling up the car beside the road at night and sleeping in it for several hours. When photographs of the car appeared in the press a motel proprietor thought that he recognized it as that of a man who had rented a cabin from him. In the cabin were found a pearl bracelet and some clothes belonging to Marie Anne, but the identification of the car and of the man with her were not positive. The case against Balcombe was clinched only by the fingerprints found on several enamelled chairs in the cabin which, in panic flight, he had neglected to wipe away.

Hugh Alexander Newall, the man three times tried *Toronto Star*

Ontario Provincial Police fingerprint specialists examining prints found in the cabin occupied by Marie Anne Carrier
Ontario Provincial Police

The Australian Pyjama Girl case became famous because of the preservation of the body found in a culvert near Albury in New South Wales. She was called the Pyjama Girl because she was wearing green and cream pyjamas with a dragon embroidered on them. Her body had been charred by burning. Descriptions of all her identifiable features were issued, but it proved impossible to identify her. A month after she was found in September 1934, the Pyjama Girl was taken to Sydney University Medical School, where she was kept in a formalin bath. There, as the years went by, she was produced and seen by dozens of people who thought they might identify her. Among the many who looked at her was a restaurant waiter named Antonio Agostini, who shudderingly said that she was not his wife Linda. In 1941 the body was claimed for burial by a woman who said it was her daughter, and the claim was backed by a doctor who made elaborate measurement comparisons of the Pyjama Girl with those of the missing daughter. The Police Commissioner, convinced that the claim was not well based and determined not to let the Pyjama Girl be buried, had her removed to police head-quarters. There she was given mortician's attention, the cheeks being rouged and the hair done in the style worn by Linda Agostini. She was now recognized by girls who had worked with her, and Agostini was brought in and confessed to killing her in the course of a struggle. He later retracted the confession, and although he was found guilty of manslaughter a good deal of doubt remains about several aspects of the case. The Pyjama Girl, after ten years above ground, was buried in July 1944, in the Preston Cemetery, Melbourne.

Tony Agostini with detectives

Detectives looking for clues at Albury, in the Pyjama Girl case

The torso and the mummy

Four people were arrested in connection with the murder of tram worker John Dick in Hamilton, Ontario, and in the end nobody was found guilty.

Evelyn Dick, the principal figure in the case, was on any count a remarkable woman. Her father Donald Maclean, like her husband, worked for the Hamilton Transit system, but he sent her to one of the best girls' schools in Toronto, financing her schooling by stealing tickets and change from the street car fare boxes, the tickets being later sold by Evelyn to immigrant steel workers who spoke very little English. She emerged from her schooldays lushly beautiful and completely promiscuous. Although she was not a prostitute she claimed to have had intercourse with more than two hundred men, many of them belonging to the 'best families' in the Hamilton area. She married John Dick in October 1945, but the couple quickly parted.

On 16 March 1946, some children found a man's torso, lacking head, arms and legs, near Albion Falls, south east of Hamilton, and it was quickly identified as that of John Dick, who had been missing for ten days. Police investigations showed that Dick had had an appointment with his wife on the evening of his disappearance, and several items of the equipment he used as a tram conductor were found in Evelyn Dick's house. This was not the only thing found there. Fragments of bone were discovered in the furnace mixed with ashes and clinker, and neighbours told of the horrible smell coming from the house chimney. Bloodstains were found on the wall of a nearby shed. Evelyn Dick had taken her car into the garage on 7 March and the mechanic who had handled it told the police that there was coagulated blood on the gear lever. When they examined the car Dick's sweater, with a bullet hole in it, was still in the back.

There was one more find, in an upstairs room of the house which contained trunks and suitcases. In one of these cases there was the body of a baby boy, cased in cement. A piece of coarse hempen string was tied round his neck. Inspector Charles Wood, who worked on the case, said that when Evelyn Dick was told of this discovery she listened with a deadpan expression and then leaned over, tugged at his coat, and said: 'Would you please get me a sandwich? I'm starving.'

She was arrested, together with her lover William Bohozuk (whom she named as the father of the child) and her father and mother. The police theory was that Dick's body had been dismembered in the shed, probably by Donald Maclean. Analysis of the bones found in the furnace showed that they were human, although they were too fragmentary for positive identification as those of John Dick.

Evelyn Dick *Toronto Star*

The evidence seems overwhelming, but in the end the prosecution case concentrated on Evelyn alone. Her mother was dismissed from the trial at an early stage, and the case against Bohozuk collapsed when Evelyn refused to give evidence against him. Donald Maclean pleaded guilty to being an accessory after the fact in John Dick's murder and received a sentence of 5 years' imprisonment. Evelyn Dick was found guilty, and sentenced to be hanged. At this point, however, a new defence lawyer named John Robinette, then little known but now famous, was appointed to the case. He fought it with passionate energy through an appeal and a second trial at which she was found not guilty. She received a sentence of life imprisonment for the manslaughter of her son.

The comment of Evelyn's mother on the murder charge verdict seems appropriate: 'We owe everything to Mr Robinette and prayer.'

The children who found John Dick's torso near Albion Falls
Hamilton Spectator

Section of wall in the shed, showing blood wiped from fingers on to the wall. *Ontario Provincial Police*

Evelyn Dick's car. There was coagulated blood on the gear lever
Ontario Provincial Police

The suitcase in which the baby's mummified body was found
Ontario Provincial Police

The war and afterwards

The 'Cleft Chin' murder caught the imagination of both the British and American public in the last months of the 1939-45 War, perhaps because the murderers, Karl Hulten and Elizabeth Maud Jones, lived out for six days in October 1944 a dream of violence which seemed somehow connected with the bombs falling in London. Hulten was a paratrooper who had deserted from the U.S. Army; eighteen and a half year old Betty Jones lived on the Army allowance made to her by a husband whom she had left the day after their marriage. When they met in a London café it was as Lieutenant Ricky Allen and Georgina Grayson. Georgina told Ricky that she was a striptease dancer, and would like to be a 'gun moll'. Ricky told Georgina that they were riding in a stolen truck (true), and that he was a Chicago gunman with a gang in London (false – he had lived a respectable life in Boston). Together they attacked and robbed a girl bicyclist near Reading, and then Hulten moved into her room. A couple of nights later they attacked another girl, Hulten hit her over the head with an iron bar, and they left her for dead. She had only a few shillings in her pockets. On the following night they got into a Ford car plying for hire, shot the driver, took the money out of his pockets, and then left him in a ditch. Hulten made no attempt to get rid of the car, and they were quickly arrested.

When asked by prosecuting counsel whether the taxi driver was dead or alive Hulten said he did not know.

'Did you care whether he was dead or alive?'

'I really don't know', Hulten said. 'I don't know what you mean by it.'

Hulten was hanged. Jones was sentenced to death but reprieved. She was released from prison in 1954.

Karl Gustav Hulten, the 'Cleft Chin' murderer *LEA*
Elizabeth Maud Jones, charged with Hulten *LEA*

Bernardi de Sigoyer was one of those curious figures who find the conditions of war especially suited to their talents. He had twice been in mental homes, he had run schools of black magic, and under his self-awarded title of the Marquis de Bernardy was wanted for fraud in Austria, Hungary and Rumania. During the war he collaborated actively with the German rulers of Paris. He married and had three children, two by his wife and one by the children's nursemaid, Irene Lebeau. After the war he was sent to prison for collaborating, and letters that he wrote to Irene and which she passed on to the police gave a clue to the situation of his wife, who had disappeared during the war. Her body was found in the wine cellar of his warehouse, and he expressed satisfaction at the news. 'One always wants to know where the dead are resting.' He was tried and found guilty. Irene Lebeau was acquitted. Bernardi de Sigoyer died on the guillotine in June 1947.

Bernardi de Sigoyer in the dock at the Seine Assizes. On the right of the other gendarme is Irene Lebeau *LEA*

The Hesse-Darmstadt Jewels case. Some of the jewels in the courtroom *Express Features*

Colonel Durant, with legal defenders *Express Features*

The theft of the Crown Jewels of Hesse-Darmstadt – and not only the jewels, which were worth perhaps £500,000, but also nine volumes of letters written by Queen Victoria to her eldest daughter – raised an ethical point that would never have been advanced except in the passion of anti-German feeling aroused by the War. The jewels were found when American soldiers occupied the castle of Kronberg, near Frankfurt-am-Main, in 1945, and Colonel Durant who was in command, Captain Kathleen Nash the woman's welfare officer, and Durant's aide-de-camp Major Watson, decided to keep them. When, early in the following year, Princess Sophie of Hesse was getting married, she asked the American authorities for her jewels, only to learn that nothing was known of them. The investigators' trail led back to Colonel Durant and his wife – who had been Captain Nash. The husband and wife, and Major Watson, were tried by a

military court at Frankfurt, with the jewels spread out on a table.

There was no question that the defendants had taken the jewels, but the point they raised was this. The Hesse family had been enthusiastic Nazis; all soldiers regard it as their right to loot from the enemy, and very high-ranking American soldiers had done so; the Nazis were the enemy: were not the jewels then legitimate loot? They discussed the matter, and decided that the former owners of the jewels were 'either dead, S.S. members or ardent Nazis, and as such the properties would never be returned to them'. Such thoughts could only have been entertained in the flush of victory, and the ingenious argument was not accepted. The jewels were returned to the Hesse family (although some were never found) and Watson, Nash and Durant received sentences of three, five and fourteen years' imprisonment.

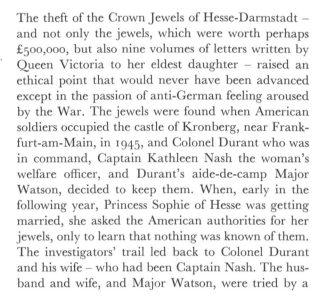

U.S. Army agents raid a Displaced Persons camp near Munich, and find the headquarters of a gang of counterfeiters. The paper used for the notes was smuggled in from Czechoslovakia *Keystone*

American currency was and remains highly prized. Inspector Benhamou of Interpol's Finance Squad holding rolls of false dollar bills, from 100 down to 5 dollars in value *Keystone*

'Christ at Emmaus' by Hans van Meegeren. This was his finest forgery, carefully composed with the help of the genuine Vermeer, 'Christ in the House of Martha and Mary'. It was bought as by Vermeer for a Rotterdam museum.   *A.C.L.*

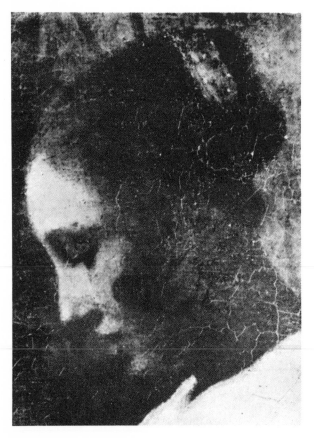

Detail of a genuine Vermeer, 'Woman in Blue' (left) compared with van Meegeren's 'Woman Reading Music'   *A.C.L.*

The greatest forger

After the end of the 1939–45 War the Field Security police started their hunt for collaborators in several countries. In Holland it was discovered that a Dutch banker had acted as go-between in the sale to Goering of a painting by Vermeer called 'The Woman Taken in Adultery'. Several people were found to be connected with the sale of this painting, among them a painter named Hans van Meegeren, who had left Holland in 1932, indignant at the failure of his countrymen to appreciate his work, and had returned on the outbreak of war. Van Meegeren was arrested on a charge of collaboration with the enemy.

After six weeks in prison he startled the world of art experts and art dealers by the claim that he had painted the 'Vermeer', and also five other presumed Vermeers and two de Hooghs. Nobody believed him – after all, experts had authenticated the paintings, and one had been bought by the Dutch Government and another by a Rotterdam museum – but when physical and chemical tests were carried out they proved that the paintings were undoubtedly modern. Under the eyes of the Dutch Field Security police van Meegeren began to paint 'Jesus Amongst the Doctors' to clinch

the matter, but when he learned that a charge of forgery had been substituted for the one of collaboration he refused to complete it. He was tried, sentenced to twelve months' imprisonment, and died in prison at the age of fifty eight.

Van Meegeren was almost undoubtedly the greatest art forger of all time, although it should not be forgotten that he operated in years when circumstances favoured him. His story that he was selling the pictures on a commission basis for a woman living in France, and that he would have difficulties with the French Vichy Government if they learned that such important paintings had left the country, would not have been accepted so easily in any other place and time. In another period, also, many experts from other countries would have had access to the paintings. He was certainly the best-paid forger who ever lived, making as he did nearly £750,000 out of a dozen pictures. Goering paid £165,000 for his 'Woman Taken in Adultery'. Art experts, wise after the event, now make many distinctions of merit between van Meegeren's various forgeries, but at the time few voices were raised to question them.

Van Meegeren in the dock at Amsterdam. In the background is one of the fake Vermeers   *AP*

'Age crackle' in paintings is the result of the natural ageing of paintings, due partly to variations of temperature. Spectroscopic and radiographic examination of van Meegeren's paintings showed that their 'age crackle' was false. The macrograph of his 'Disciples at Emmaus' (*top*) shows many more cracks than the radiograph of the same section (*below*), proving that it cannot be genuine.   *ACL*

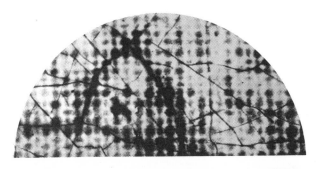

Question marks

There are many cases which, although they have been officially settled, leave question marks behind them. Two belonging to the nineteen-forties are those of Walter Graham Rowland and James Camb.

In 1946 the body of a prostitute named Olive Balchin was found on a Manchester bomb site. She had been battered to death with a leather-beater's hammer which was found nearby. Police investigations led them to question a taciturn lodger in a local hostel who was known to wander about at night, and they testified that when they saw him in his hostel cubicle he said at once: 'You don't want me for the murder of that woman, do you?' The police at first had little against the man, Walter Graham Rowland, except that he had been convicted years before of killing his young daughter. He had been sentenced to death for the murder, and then reprieved. When his clothes were examined in the laboratory, however, the evidence against him seemed overwhelming. Soil and brick dust like that on the bomb site were found in his trouser turn-ups, a bloodstain on his shoe was that of Olive Balchin's blood group, and he was identified as the purchaser of the hammer. He was condemned to death, and occupied the condemned cell at Strangeways Prison for the second time, but now there was no reprieve. On 27 February 1947 Walter Graham Rowland was hanged.

The question mark in his case appears because David John Ware, another prisoner in Walton Prison, Liverpool, confessed to the murder. Such confessions are not uncommon. Ware's did not correspond with the facts of the case in some details, and he later retracted it. But four years later Ware walked into a Bristol police station and said: 'I have killed a woman. I keep on having an urge to hit women on the head.' In fact the woman attacked by Ware survived. He was found 'Guilty but insane' and sent to Broadmoor. A later detailed examination of the case by Sydney Silverman, a leading opponent of capital punishment, led to the conclusion that some of the evidence against Rowland was not soundly based, and that Ware was at least possibly the killer of Olive Balchin.

James Camb got rid of a dead body by pushing it through a ship's porthole, and there is no doubt that he did so under the impression that in the absence of a body he was not likely to be convicted of any crime in relation to it. Whether he committed murder is another matter. Camb was a steward on the liner *Durban Castle*, and one of the passengers aboard was a neurotic young actress named Eileen Gibson, who called herself Gay Gibson. Up to a point there was no dispute about what happened. Camb entered Gay Gibson's cabin, No. 126, and tried to make love to her one night, by force according to the prosecution, with her consent according to Camb. She died – strangled by the prosecution's story, or as Camb said in a fit when they made love. He then pushed the body out of the porthole. Various facts pointed to Camb having

The bomb site in Manchester where Olive Balchin's body was found   *Mirrorpic*

Walter Graham Rowland. A murderer hanged for a crime he did not commit? *Mirrorpic*

166

James Camb. He pushed the body out of the porthole   *LEA*

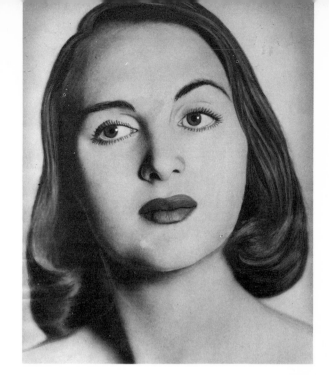

Gay Gibson. The girl in Cabin 126 on the *Durban Castle*   *LEA*

murdered the girl, and his callous composure in the witness box created a very bad impression. He was sentenced to death, but was reprieved because a clause for the abolition of capital punishment was then under discussion in Parliament. He was released from prison in 1959. Two points, one against him and one in his favour, were not brought out at the trial. Against him were the statements of two other women passengers who said that he had tried to strangle them, statements which could not be introduced at the trial because they did not concern the charge of murder made against him. In his favour, and never fully brought out by his counsel, were Gay Gibson's undoubted promiscuity, her strong inclination to masochism, and her history of illness and apparently neurotic fits.

The Joan Woodhouse case is an unsolved puzzle which has great legal interest. She was a London librarian, who was found strangled in August 1948, near her favourite beauty spot in the grounds of Arundel Castle. Two years later her father applied for a private warrant to arrest a man on a charge of murder, the second such application in British legal history. It was granted and Mr Woodhouse, accompanied by two police officers, arrested the man, a labourer who lived nearby. Since only the Director of Public Prosecutions is allowed to prosecute in England on a charge of murder, his representative outlined the case, and made it clear that he thought it a poor one. After a hearing lasting five days a Bench of magistrates decided that there was not sufficient evidence to justify sending the accused man for trial.

A policeman contemplates the scene of the Joan Woodhouse murder at Arundel   *Mirrorpic*

Dominici and Petiot

The tragic death of the Drummond family belongs by strict chronology in the next section, but certain aspects of it are connected in spirit with the secrets and hatreds of the immediate post-war period.

In August 1952, Sir Jack Drummond, a famous English bio-chemist, took a holiday in France with his wife and their 11-year old daughter, Elizabeth. They drove around in a shooting brake, and camped out every night. One morning their bodies were found by Gustave Dominici, the son of an old, taciturn Provençal peasant farmer named Gaston Dominici, at the edge of the land adjoining the Dominici family farmhouse. Drummond and his wife had been shot, and their daughter had been beaten to death. Commissionaire Edmond Sebeille, who came from Marseilles to take charge of the case, was convinced from the first that the truth of the murders was to be discovered in the Dominici family.

It was evident that the elder Drummonds had been killed first and Elizabeth afterwards, and by relentness questioning of Gustave, Sebeille obtained an admission that Elizabeth had been still alive when he found her. Suspicion hung over all of the Dominicis, who lived together on the farm, but there was no proof of individual guilt. For more than a year Sebeille paid them frequent and sometimes unexpected visits, and eventually Gustave, supported by his elder brother Clovis, broke down and accused their father of the crime. Confronted with these accusations old Gaston Dominici eventually confessed his guilt. He told a curious and in some respects unsatisfactory story of watching the Drummonds undress, shooting the father and mother when Sir Jack angrily accused him of being a Peeping Tom, and then feeling forced to kill their daughter. He was sentenced to death, but this sentence was commuted to life imprisonment, and in 1960 he was set free. It seems likely that the whole truth about what happened will never be known.

Dr Marcel Petiot was a wartime killer, although there are suspicions that he may have committed murder before then. Posing as a member of the French Resistance, he offered to help those who wished to escape from Paris. They came to his Parisian surgery in the Rue Lesueur, bringing all their possessions, were taken into a small roughly-cemented windowless room which had been specially built into the house, and were then killed by injections or by gas. The beauty of this method was that nobody would be surprised by the disappearance of the victims – were they not, after all, leaving France? After the fall of Paris in 1944 Petiot was caught, but his trial did not begin until almost two years later.

Petiot's defence was ingenious. It was true that twenty-seven bodies had been found in his cellar, but Petiot claimed that most of them were German soldiers, and that their deaths were a tribute to his patriotism. In the state of administrative confusion that prevailed after the war it was difficult to controvert such a defence, but members of the Resistance gave evidence that he was ignorant of many things he should have known. Perhaps the finally clinching piece of evidence against him was that the windowless room had a little trapdoor in it through which he could watch his victims die. Petiot was never able to explain satisfactorily the purpose for which he used this room. He was sentenced to death and guillotined. The pictures show interesting details of the process of the long and complicated investigation.

Elizabeth Drummond's body being carried across the road. The Drummond shooting brake is seen in the background *Mirrorpic*

Gaston Dominici in Court *Mirrorpic*

A view from above of the courtyard of Petiot's house in the Rue Lesueur. The lime was the remainder of that used in the cellar to help dispose of the bodies   *LEA*

Inspector Massu in Petiot's living room, examining the Doctor's gas mask   *LEA*

The hole leading from the basement down to the cellar where Petiot disposed of the bodies   *LEA*

Petiot after his arrest   *LEA*

In our time

THE MARCH OF SCIENCE

Cameras and teeth

Sophisticated use of scientific methods increased enormously during and immediately after the 1939-45 war. The use of cameras, closed circuit TV, and electronic devices in trapping criminals has expanded even during the past decade. The camera device rigged up by a Danish TV firm worked effectively, but it was a comparatively home-made affair, operated by a trip wire and a flashgun. The Montreal bank camera, however, installed under the direction of the local police, was operated by a switch which gave no hint to the robbers that their movements were being recorded. Similar cameras are used in many American banks, although they are still rarities in Europe.

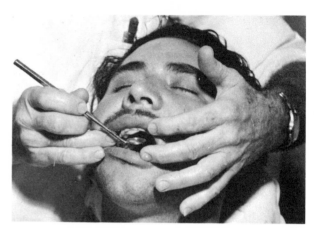

A dentist examines the teeth of a Mexican farm worker accused of raping and murdering a child. Teeth impressions were made to compare with the teeth marks on the child's body. *San Francisco Examiner/UPI*

A modern dental chart as supplied to police authorities *NYCMPB*

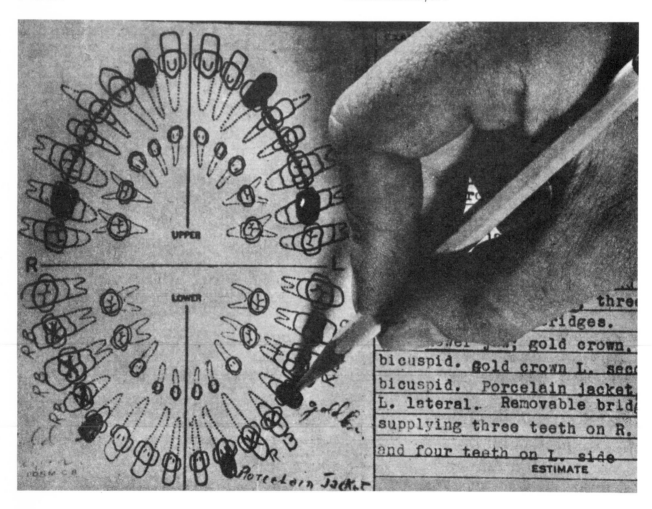

three
ridges.
gold crown.
bicuspid. gold crown L. sec
bicuspid. Porcelain jacket
L. lateral. Removable brid
supplying three teeth on R.
and four teeth on L. side
ESTIMATE

A hidden camera photographs a bank hold-up in Montreal. One of the robbers wore a mask and the other dark glasses, but the camera gave sufficient details to enable them to be identified in spite of these disguises *UPI*

A television firm in Copenhagen which had been frequently raided by thieves fixed up a camera and flashgun hidden inside a ledger (*right*). The thief escaped when the flashgun went off, but the picture taken (the face has been blacked out) identified him *Keystone*

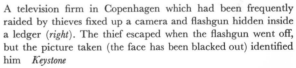

Bullets have fingerprints too

The discovery that bullets have fingerprints too – that every bullet fired from a rifled barrel (that is, a barrel grooved to increase range and accuracy) has its characteristic markings which are completely individual – belongs to the United States, which established a lead in ballistics investigation that has never been lost. The monumental task of attempting to catalogue all firearms likely to be used by criminals was undertaken by a lawyer in the New York Prosecutor's Office, Charles E. Waite. He set out to find 'Precise data on the construction, date of manufacture, calibre, twist and proportion of the grooves and lands, as well as type of ammunition of as many guns as possible.'

Waite's work was carried on after his death in the early nineteen-twenties by Calvin Goddard, a former medical specialist who was fascinated by firearms.

Goddard's first famous case was that involving Sacco and Vanzetti (see page 128), and the case was so clouded with errors and contradictions that it did not set the seal on his reputation as it might have done. His identification of the sub-machine guns used in the St Valentine's Day massacre, however, made him nationally famous. A Scientific Crime Detection Laboratory was established by wealthy Chicagoans, and Goddard was put in charge of it.

At the beginning his work on ballistics (the Laboratory dealt with almost every scientific aspect of crime) was made possible by Dr Philip Gravelle's invention of the comparison microscope. Before this invention scientists had looked at one bullet under a microscope, then looked at another under a second microscope. Did they match? It was always very difficult to say. The comparison microscope made it

Calvin Goddard's early comparison microscope

Goddard inspecting a pistol barrel

A modern comparison microscope in use *NYPD*

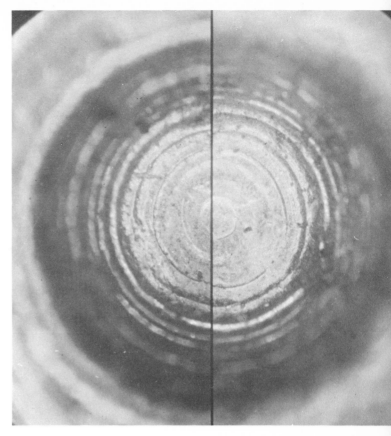

Comparing two bullets. The marks on them are brought into juxtaposition and photographed through a single eyepiece by the comparison microscope *FBI*

Comparing two shells. The black line through the centre is the line of separation of the shells. The comparison microscope shows that cuts made by the firing pin are so similar that they match. Some exterior differences are the results of dirt, or of changes in the firing pin between the firing of the two shells *FBI*

possible for the bullets to be looked at simultaneously, so that they could be compared exactly with each other. The photomicrograph reproduced on this page shows the dramatic result in one case. The bullets match perfectly. They were fired from the same barrel. There is no possibility of error.

Not all the credit of discovery goes to Waite and Goddard. In Cairo Sir Sydney Smith, adviser to the Egyptian Minister of Justice, had established a laboratory which was one of the finest in the world. A pathologist by training, Smith was interested in all forms of forensic science, and in the early nineteen-twenties he made his own comparison microscope. Its merit was proved in 1924 when Sir Lee Stack, the Sirdar of Egypt, was shot by Egyptian nationalists. Smith was able to say that the murder bullet had been fired from a Colt, and that 'the pistol was evidently in a bad state for the normal rifling grooves could hardly be seen, but on the bullet there was a clearly marked scratched groove, which betrayed a

fault in the muzzle end of the barrel'. He felt sure that he had seen identical bullets before, used in other political murder attempts, and the comparison microscope showed that he was right. When the suspects were caught, and the Colt was found on one of them, Smith fired test bullets and then compared bullets and cartridge cases with those left on the scene of Stack's murder. A cartridge case also shows special markings, and using twenty four other Colt revolvers as controls, Smith established that these particular cartridge cases had entirely individual markings.

The science of ballistics has limitations which do not apply to fingerprints. There is a good deal of room for human error (Goddard once made a wrong identification simply because he had been handed the wrong bullets), distorted and deformed bullets are not easy to match up, and of course it is generally necessary to have the gun from which bullets have been fired. Within these limits ballistics are immensely valuable.

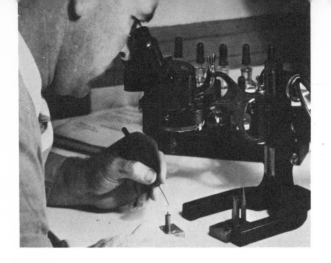

A minute specimen of paint is being mounted on a carbon electrode for analysis by the spectrograph *.FBI*

A microtome machine, used for the analysis of paint, tissue or hair *NZPD*

Hair, fibres, paint, blood

As one police scientist modestly says, science is only an adjunct to intelligent police investigation, not a substitute for it. Yet it is also true that in hundreds of laboratories in dozens of different countries, physicists, chemists, biologists and toxicologists are doing work which thirty years ago they would hardly have thought possible, with the aid of machines which help them to distinguish one kind of paint or hair or fibre or blood group from another.

Every laboratory is equipped with a spectrograph or a similar machine which makes it possible to analyse and permanently record through an electric arc and a photographic plate the tiniest fragments of material. A scrap of paint can be compared with another, the minutest traces of a drug can be discovered by the use of an X-ray Diffraction Unit. A hair can be analysed to tell what part of the body it came from, and to say whether it has been plucked or cut. Permanent waving is discernible from a single hair because it alters the nature of the hair structure.

Experiments are being conducted (see page 178) to prove that a single hair comes from a particular head.

In the field of serology – that is, the testing of blood groupings – immense advances have been made. It is now possible, under favourable circumstances, to determine the group of a bloodstain on any piece of material. If, therefore, a man says in explanation of the blood on his jacket that he cut himself and his blood is found to be Group O (the most common among white people) whereas the blood on his jacket is the rare AB, it is obvious to the serologist that he is lying. If he is accused of murder and the blood of his victim is AB, then the serologist would consider him a prime suspect. But the operations required for checking blood groups are delicate and need careful control and examination at every point. Scientists upon the whole deal in probabilities where juries ask for certainty, and it would be difficult to convince a jury of a bloodstain's conclusive importance without supporting evidence.

Science in action. The razor blade (*left*) was thought to have been used to cut through a wire screen in a burglary. The cutting edge (*above*) was found under the spectrograph to contain elements of the brass, copper and zinc from which the wire screen was made *FBI*

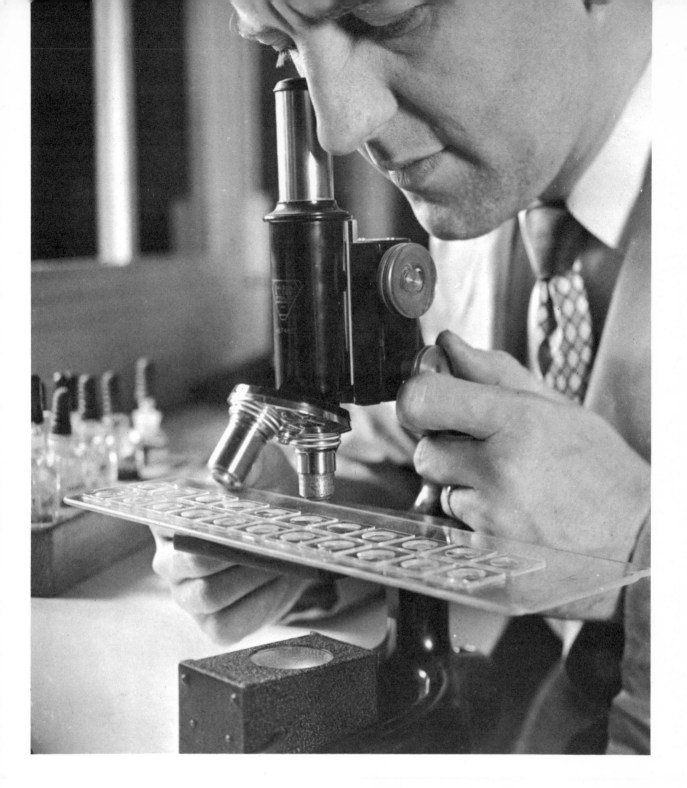

Testing blood groupings. The greatest recent advance in forensic science has been in ascertaining blood groups through stains
FBI

Fibre specimens under examination in the F.B.I. Laboratories
FBI

A single hair

For some years now scientists in several police laboratories have been trying to apply radioactive analysis to a variety of materials in a way that will be acceptable and comprehensible in criminal courts. In Canada Dr R. E. Jervis and A. K. Perkons of the University of Toronto and Francis M. Kerr, head of the Chemistry, Hair and Fibres Section of the R.C.M.P. have gone a long way towards what has been considered an impracticable ideal: the identification of a single human hair.

Components of eighteen trace elements including molybdenum, selenium, mercury and aluminium, as well as those mentioned in the diagrams, have been discovered in human hair. They vary between men and women, between young and old, between people of different races, nationalities and districts. They vary also at different times, as the graph of hair decay shows. Take hairs from two heads and it is quite likely that they may contain the same concentration of one or two of the elements, but if as many as nine components are found in comparable amounts the chances are as low as 3 in 100 million that they come from different heads. This kind of statistical assessment is still in its infancy because an insufficient number of hair samples has been examined, but non-destructive activation analysis has been applied in comparing single hairs in a murder case.

Recently in New Brunswick a single hair about 6 centimetres long and weighing less than 1 milligramme was found in the hand of a murdered woman. Samples of hair were taken from her head, and from the head of a male suspect for comparison. The significant similarities between the hair in the victim's hand and the hair specimen taken within two days from the suspect's head were presented in court.

The uses of such a specialized technique are obviously limited, although in the particular case mentioned other methods of analysis, including that made by spectrometer, were much less conclusive than that achieved by neutron activation. It also still remains a popular myth that scientists can say with certainty if a particular hair came from a particular head. The conclusions of Messrs Jervis and Perkons are that *provided* enough hair is available (their italics) and that analysis is done for at least ten of the trace elements, it is possible to compare specimens with a high degree of reliability. But they add:

'It is not yet reliable to extend the activation "matching" or "individualization" method to single hair evidence of the kind commonly encountered in crime investigation.'

A single hair. Dark hair contains more manganese and cobalt; grey hair has more nickel; the greatest iron content is found in red hair
Picturepoint

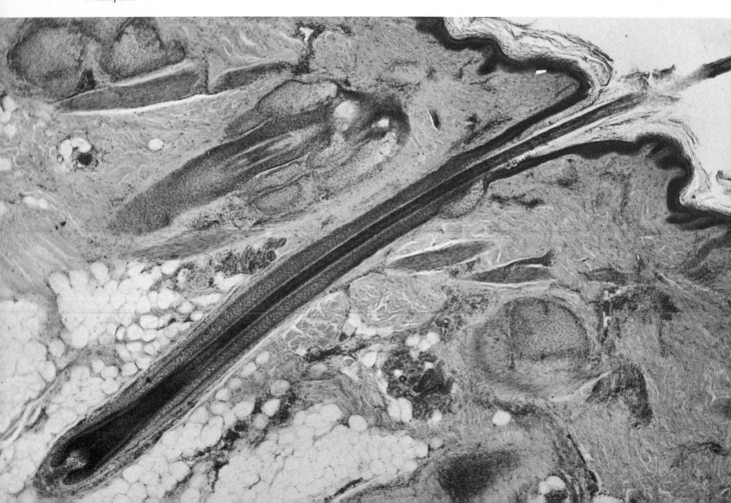

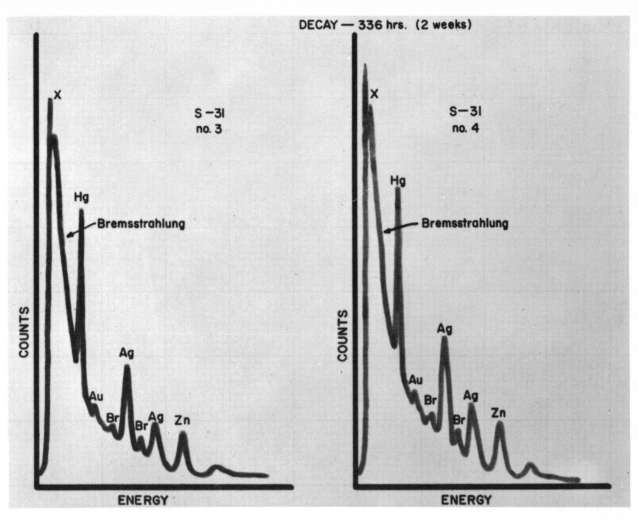

DECAY — 336 hrs. (2 weeks)

S—31
no. 3

S—31
no. 4

Gamma-ray spectra shows the decay in a hair sample after two weeks   *Attorney-General's Laboratory, Ontario*

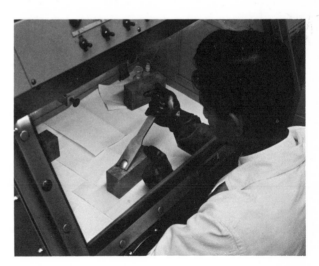

Close-up of the isolator box. Opening the capsule   *Attorney-General's Laboratory, Ontario*

On their return from the reactor radioactive samples are removed from their capsule in this isolator box   *Attorney-General's Laboratory, Ontario*

Heelprints, handwriting and the vacuum cleaner

The spectrophotometer provides an accurate colour comparison by a meter which records in the form of a graph the percentage of colour of any solution passed through the machine. It is used also for document examination, to compare passages of writing one of which is suspected of being more recent than the other, or to compare specimens of ink. Typewriting characteristics are checked by photographic enlargements of the typescripts, often with the overlaying of transparencies to show whether or not two specimens match exactly. Handwriting is now subjected to several different types of analysis, involving the writing itself, the ink and the paper. Actual handwriting comparisons are the least valuable of these, because it is now recognized that the same hand may change remarkably under different conditions, and that minute differences will always exist. The handwriting experts who gave evidence with such confidence in the cases of Beck and Dreyfus would be much less dogmatic to-day.

Comparing a suspect's shoe heel with a cast made on the scene of the crime. The casts are generally made with dental plaster of Paris   *FBI*

The use of ultra-violet light helped to solve a robbery at Lockheed Aircraft. One of the robbers used a Lockheed identification badge which was found afterwards, with a false number inserted in it. The original number had been filed away, and the badge seen in ordinary light showed nothing useful. An ultraviolet photograph showed up the number, which was that of a former employee involved in the robbery   *FBI*

Extracting dust from a suspect's trouser turn-ups with a vacuum cleaner. Pockets are also vacuumed carefully, and so in the case of women are their handbags. Afterwards any strands of hair, fibre, or any other suspect matter go under the spectrograph   *UPI*

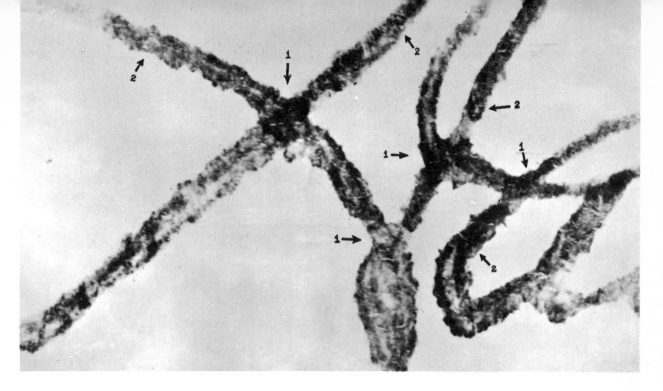

A much enlarged specimen of forged writing. The arrows marked '1' show which of two crossed lines was written under the other. Those marked '2' show the inevitable unevenness which comes when a signature is forged by tracing   *FBI*

A spectrophotometer in use in the New Zealand Police laboratory. It operates by means of an incandescent lamp directed to the face of a prism, which spreads out the light to form a continuous spectrum for very accurate colour comparison *NZPD*

Conducting ink research in the Document Section of the F.B.I. laboratory   *FBI*

Typewriting characteristics. The points of similarity of two of the samples establish that they were typed on the same machine. The right hand sample is from another machine of the same make   *FBI*

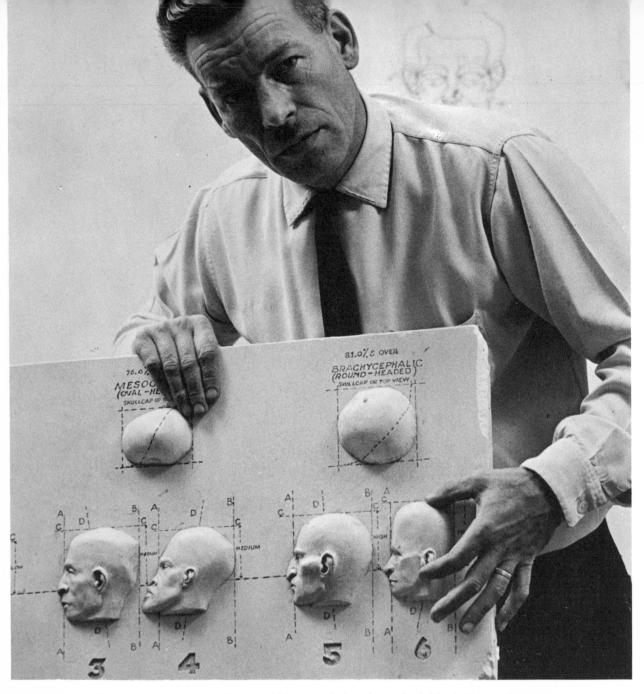

Charles Abbott, with a chart of various criminal types, which he uses in lecturing to the California Police   *Express Features*

A series of masks is shown to the eye witness, who says which one most resembles the suspect seen. Then Abbott slowly builds up a picture on his profile chart, supplementing it when possible by a chart showing the full face   *Express Features*
The completed mask of the suspect is cast in plaster. Abbott shows it to the eye witness, and asks if it is a good likeness.   *Express Features*

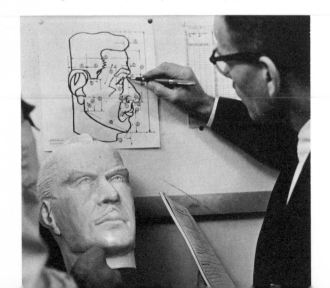

Identikits and lie detectors

The Identikit is a means of building up a picture of a suspect's face by making drawings, which may be done freehand or built up section by section. There has been a good deal of argument about the value of the composite picture evolved, and a Scotland Yard officer recently dismissed Identikits as useless. An ingenious variation, and probably improvement, of them has been developed in California, where Charles Abbott has a number of masks of what he calls characteristic criminal types. Using one of these as a basis he then makes changes in it, building a picture from what the witness tells him about the suspect, and finally producing his 'picture' in the form of a plaster cast which, if it does not seem right, can soon be altered again.

The value of the lie detector is also a matter of argument. Evidence obtained by it is accepted in some parts of the United States, but not in the United Kingdom nor in many other countries. Essentially it consists of a pneumograph, a cardiograph and an electrodermal appliance attached to the fingers. (The Japanese Deceptograph shown is only an electrodermal appliance.) Questions are asked of the suspect, and if the graphs attached to all three devices show marked changes on a particular question the subject is said to be lying. It seems doubtful if the lie detector has much value, except in a very limited number of cases, and it is certainly useless unless operated by a psychologist thoroughly trained in the study of criminal reactions.

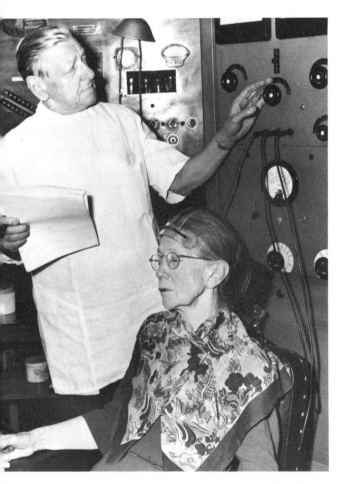

A lie detector in operation. The test made on this occasion indicated that Dr Alice Wynekoop, in the chair, had served 14 years in prison for a murder of which she was innocent. Was the lie detector right? Dr Wynekoop was paroled *UPI*

The Deceptograph, a midget lie detector made in Japan. Rather like the volumetric glove (see page 33), it is said to record emotional disturbance through two small plastic clips fitted to the first and third fingertips of the left hand. The makers advertised it as a 'Will She or Won't She?' indicator for men about women's feelings *Keystone*

183

And of course fingerprints

In spite of all other scientific advances, the discovery of the uniqueness of fingerprints made by Herschel and Faulds and developed by Galton, Vucetich and Henry, remains the chief weapon of the law man against the law breaker. It is true that all professional criminals nowadays wear gloves, but there are times when they relax, when they take off the gloves, when they leave a mark perhaps not on the scene of a crime but on an article connected with it. And if a print is left by a professional criminal in these days it is certain to be traced. The police of different countries now keep closely in touch with each other, and in the case of international criminals Interpol often provides vital information.

The function of Interpol is not understood by the general public. It rarely initiates the pursuit of criminals, but rather is a gigantic clearing house set up in Paris for the exchange of information. Violent criminals are surprisingly inclined to stick to their own country – or perhaps it is not surprising, for an American gunman in London or a Cockney razor boy in New York would be so conspicuous that they would be picked up within a few hours of doing a job. It is con men, thieves and drug traffickers who are international crooks, and it is in reaction to such men that Interpol, with its vast criminal habits index and its record of every known alias, performs its most valuable service. Obviously it has a lively individual existence, but it is primarily an example of international police co-operation.

No country has yet realized Vucetich's ideal of complete national fingerprinting, although the F.B.I. is said to have well over 100 million fingerprint sheets on record. But in the Lancashire town of Blackburn something like complete fingerprinting of men was achieved in 1948, in the search for a man who took a four-year old girl from her hospital ward, raped and murdered her, and left no clue except his prints on a bottle in the ward. Blackburn was then a town of 110,000 people, and thanks to the pertinacity of Chief Inspector Campbell, every male over sixteen years old was fingerprinted. The printing had no result until somebody realized that rationing, which still existed in England in 1948, could provide a further check. Fingerprint sheets were collated with ration cards, and it was found that nearly 800 men had not been fingerprinted. One of them was Peter Griffiths, whose father had been a mental patient in the hospital. His prints matched those on the bottle.

The whole fingerprinting exercise had been carried out on a voluntary basis, and the Mayor of Blackburn had also promised that there would be no comparison of the prints taken with those of any man on the police wanted register, except the murderer. After Griffiths had been caught the Mayor kept another promise. He burned all the fingerprint sheets.

A fingerprint expert of the Royal Canadian Mounted Police at work
National Film Board of Canada

An attempt to take prints off fingers preserved in jars *UPI*

Detective Matthew Bonora demonstrates the uses of an aerosol can that sprays fingerprint powder. The chart shows the superiority of his method over brush printing *UPI*

Some of the card indexes at Interpol, where fingerprint records are international *Interpol*

Examining the criminal habits index at Interpol *Interpol*

Lead dust and the electron autographic technique

What promises to be a breakthrough in fingerprint technique has recently been developed by two radiographers working at Glasgow Victoria Infirmary, Daniel Graham and Hugh Gray. The technique is that of electron autography, in which a high energy primary beam of X-rays, hardened by passing through copper, irradiates the emitting material and releases electrons to form an image. By this means remarkable results have been achieved in taking prints off skin and off such difficult backgrounds as the postage stamp and the copy of *Reader's Digest* shown in the illustrations.

The print taken from a female thigh is particularly notable. It has always been accepted that prints cannot be taken from skin, partly because of post-mortem bruising and partly because when the skin shrinks after death any prints that there may be tend to disappear. Messrs Graham and Gray, however, used for their experiments a lead powder instead of the customary black or grey. Black fingerprint powder consists mainly of carbon, and grey has a large percentage of mercuric oxide. The virtue of the lead powder, so far as autoradiography is concerned, lies in its high atomic number, which permits a large emission of electrons and produces an image on the film. The skin print shown was imposed on the thigh and dusted with 200 mesh lead. When the piece of skin was removed the skin shrank, and the print appeared to be lost. It reappeared when the skin was stretched on board, and the autoradiograph shows the final result.

The other prints shown are also very interesting. The fingerprint detail on the postage stamp is only partly visible, and would be difficult to show by photographic methods. The electron autograph reveals it perfectly by eliminating the stamp design.

The prints on *Reader's Digest* were fixed with shellac to protect them, and the X-ray emission was able to penetrate the shellac and show the prints clearly. Excellent results have been obtained from difficult surfaces, like rainwater pipes and other curved objects, by the use of lead dust and the same technique.

The originators of the electron autograph technique suggest that mobile units would be necessary for its use in general police work, and experimental tests suggest that they could work successfully. Obviously the technique is at an early stage, but the laboratory results already achieved suggest that its possibilities are immense.

Autoradiograph of a fingerprint obtained from a woman's thigh by electron autography. Skin has always been thought useless for taking prints *X-Ray Focus*

Photograph of a stamp with fingerprint on it   *X-Ray Focus*

Electron autograph of the same subject, which has eliminated the stamp to show the fingerprint in full detail   *X-Ray Focus*

Fingerprints on the front cover of a copy of *Reader's Digest*   *Graham and Gray*

Electron autograph showing the elimination of the design and revealing the prints clearly. A faint trace of 'January 1960' can be seen near the bottom of the print   *Graham and Gray*

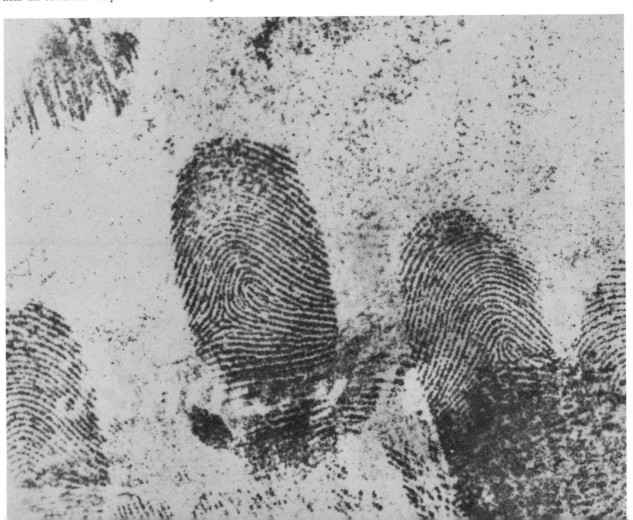

MODERN POLICE METHODS

The great machine

A modern police department is an enormous machine. Its smooth functioning depends on three factors, the ability and integrity of the police officers working in it, the effectiveness of their equipment, and their good relations with the public.

The police of the United Kingdom, West Germany and the Scandinavian countries have a high reputation for integrity. The scandal in Sheffield, when two detectives were found to have beaten suspects with a rhinoceros hide whip, and the occasion when a sergeant was found to have planted evidence on nuclear disarmament demonstrators, rightly caused indignation in Britain, but in other countries they would have been regarded as commonplace. The French and Italian police, to name no others, are rocked periodically by scandals which have no counterpart in the United Kingdom. The British police, however, are starved of modern equipment in a way that other countries would regard as incredible. It may be that the stories of detectives queuing up to use a police station's single typewriter are exaggerated, but Britain lags far behind other European countries, and much further behind the United States, in the use of personal two-way radios and electronic communications systems like that at Paris Police Headquarters. Nearly a hundred police forces in the United States use computers or data processing equipment, where at the time of writing not a single force in Britain has access to one. The New York police can identify a particular print in hours where it may take days in London.

The greatest advance in obtaining public co-operation has been made in Chicago. In 1961 a civilian Police Board of five unpaid members was appointed, and under their auspices the Police Department launched in 1964 'Operation Crime-Stop', a determined attempt to involve the citizens of Chicago in a self-help programme to check crime. The scheme, operated through firms and individuals, led to over 4000 arrests in the first year and, backed up by a campaign in which two hundred Police Department speakers addressed public meetings and by other forms of propaganda, has been highly successful. That other American cities are aware of the value of public co-operation is shown by, for example, the Police-Community Relations committees organized in San Francisco. The words of Thomas J. Cahill, Chief of the San Francisco Police Department, are relevant not only to the particular problems of San Francisco or even of the United States – their application is universal: 'The changing nature of our social controls makes it absolutely necessary for the *entire police department* to be trained in the understanding of ethnic groups, which will help them to overcome their own inclinations to participate in the cultural conflict by expressing in words or actions their contempt of the culturally different.'

One of Chicago's 'Operation Crime-Stop' Posters   *Chicago Police*

The Map Room at New Scotland Yard   *Metropolitan Police*

Right: Paris Police Headquarters at the time of the F.L.N. plastic bomb explosions. Each pin on the huge map shows an attack by the F.L.N. The lighted rectangles show police positions
Express Features

Nyasaland Police, masked against their own tear gas and carrying wicker protective shields, retire after dispersing rioters   *East Africa*

Israeli police on desert patrol   *Mirrorpic*

Danko, the first British helicopter dog. He travelled in a four foot long wooden kennel attached to the side of the helicopter, marked 'Fido Installation'   *Mirrorpic*

Ready for action

The city policeman still has his beat, which remains more or less unchanged by time. In wide open spaces things are different. The Israeli desert patrol often covers a hundred miles in its armoured car. An average Indian police station is about 100 square miles in area and has a population of 75,000 people. It may extend over twenty villages, each of which has a chowkidar (the name varies in different parts of the country), a kind of part-time rural policeman whose authority does not extend outside the village. Several countries use helicopter patrols and some, like the Royal Canadian Mounted Police, have an Air Division, used chiefly as a check on smuggling and for transport and rescue purposes. In 1963 the R.C.M.P. Air Division located a party of four Eskimos lost on Baffin Island.

One of the smallest police forces in the world. Members of the Liechtenstein Security Corps with their patrol van *NYPL*

Indian police on parade   *Indian Police*

The 'Flying Fortress' squads of Shanghai, armed with pistols, tommy guns and white clubs. The year is 1949, before the collapse of the Chiang Kai-Shek regime   *UPI*

All sorts of duties

The routine work done by the modern policeman covers anything from finding lost kittens to the activities shown here. One picture shows the end of a dramatic roof-top chase for PC Christopher Brett. Together with a colleague, PC Gale, Brett disturbed four men on the roof of a bank. The men ran away over the house roofs, pursued by Brett and Gale, and in making a 15 foot leap from one roof to another both men fell, although not to the ground. Brett broke both his legs and Gale suffered a broken ankle. The picture shows Brett grimacing with pain as he is lowered from the roof on which he fell. The four men, one of whom also fell and was injured, got away at the time but were caught later.

The loving couple (below) are part of a Liverpool undercover commando squad of both men and women, more than a hundred strong, equipped with short wave radios, and sent out in various disguises into the worst areas of the city. Results from this and a number of other measures like the installation of TV cameras at various hidden points may have brought down Liverpool's crime rate. The measures, in combination with the new equipment, have certainly improved police morale.

Three members of Chicago's Undercover Squad capture a mugger who has just attacked the team's decoy, second from right. The policemen's faces have been blocked out to preserve their anonymity *UPI*

For PC Brett, the end of a chase after an attempted bank robbery in Wembley, Middlesex *Mirrorpic*

Loving couple? *Mirrorpic*

C.I.D. officers search a flooded field with a mine detector during a murder case after a report that two schoolboys had thrown a weapon there. The result was negative   *Mirrorpic*

Palestine during the troubled nineteen-forties. A British and an Arab constable question a suspect   *Mirrorpic*

R.C.M.P. officer photographing a foot track which has been preserved by plaster of Paris   *Keystone*

F.B.I. agents firing tracer bullets from machine guns during training   *FBI*

New York police cadets firing on the Police Academy indoor range   *NYPD*

At England's Mounted Police Training College in Surrey, police horses are taught to step between fallen bodies, ignore revolver shots, and tolerate the playing of bagpipes close to their ears   *Mirrorpic*

Training, arms, defence

Police training in the United States is carried out at the F.B.I. Academy and in many cities with a comprehensiveness unapproached elsewhere. At New York's magnificent Police Academy grey-uniformed cadets get classroom instruction in the law and in criminal procedure, and physical training which resembles a commando course, including vaulting fences, shinning up bridge cables and learning unarmed combat. Firearms training with the standard .38 revolver is carried out at the indoor range, and at the outdoor range the cadets practise shooting from half a dozen positions and with both hands.

Most police training schools have a less elaborate programme, but are not necessarily less thorough. At India's central Police Training College cadets are trained for a year, emerging to become the officer's cadre of the whole Indian Police Force. In New Zealand a cadet is trained for nineteen months, and then works under supervision for almost another two years. In the United Kingdom there is a basic training period of three months with various refresher courses and a special course for particularly able men. This course, at a new Police College in Hampshire, has in some ways replaced the Hendon Police Training School for cadets which met with strong opposition because it was said to be organized on a class basis, and was discontinued in 1939.

In the United States training at all levels is concentrated more upon action and the likelihood of violence than it is elsewhere. Many Englishmen look with alarm upon the revolvers so zestfully carried by American and European police forces, and would be very suspicious of training which had any military or militant flavour. Some English police would like to carry revolvers. Others remember that four New York policemen are killed every year on average, while one London policeman is killed every four years.

American policeman taking it easy, but with revolver and nightstick handy   *Mirrorpic*

Formidable weapon for police pursuit cars in Texas. A gun is mounted on the hood of the car, with the trigger on the dashboard so that it can be pulled while driving   *UPI*

Italian Carabinieri are equipped with new quick-firing machine guns   *Express Features*

THE MARCH OF CRIME

Smuggling in the drugs

In the Far East the use of drugs has been common for hundreds of years. For the Western world drug-taking is a twentieth-century problem, an acute one for the United States and some South American countries, a minor but increasing problem in Europe. The traffic in morphine has several routes, one being Iran or the Lebanon to Egypt, Italy and France, and another from the same sources through Italy and France to the United States. The United States is a main objective of drug traffickers, because prices are extremely high. Official control in some countries is lax – in Italy, firms licensed to import drugs for medicinal purposes have often brought into the country far more than they needed and diverted a proportion to drug traffickers. American gangsters deported to Italy found that they could run an easy and profitable operation in sending drugs across the Atlantic. Opium in various forms has poured out of China, much of it destined for the United States.

The United States Bureau of Narcotics was established in 1930 to fight the drug traffic. It recruits by preference men with pharmaceutical training, is in constant touch with the International Bureau of Interpol, and has a very successful record in catching smugglers. But the profits are so enormous, and there are so many dozens of ways in which drugs can be brought into a country – consignments of oranges and other fruit are favoured hiding places, and individual seamen bring in drugs ingeniously concealed in cavities in their lockers or in the ship's fire extinguisher – that drug smuggling will only be held in check rather than cut off while the demand remains.

In a Turkish opium factory. Raw material is brought in by farmers, ground and mixed, and becomes processed opium

Max Mugnani, arrested in 1956 as boss of an Italian dope ring which included a Prince, a Duke, a Marquis and four doctors *UPI*

Improvised opium smoker's outfit. The pipe is made of rubber tubing connected to a small vase. The lamp beside it is a combination of a salt shaker and a tumbler

Drive against drugs in Egypt, 1961. Police in Cairo publicly burn papers and other containers used to smoke hashish *UPI*

San Francisco customs officials find a big haul of drugs in a house formerly owned by Judah Isaac Ezra, who served a prison term in 1933 for a drug traffic offence. He later operated in Hong Kong *UPI*

Heroin smuggled in through a ship's winch *NYPM*

Heroin was found pinned inside the knickers of this baby doll *UPI*

An Easter basket. The eggs were filled with heroin. The money was used by a Narcotics Bureau agent posing as a buyer. The coup led to the arrest of the biggest heroin supplier in Northern California *UPI*

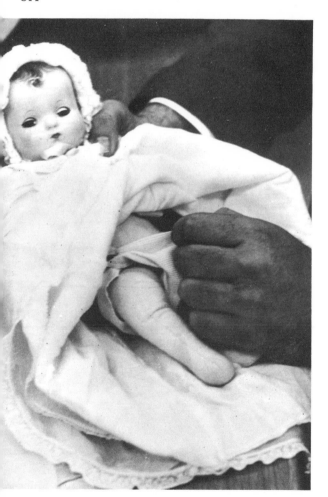

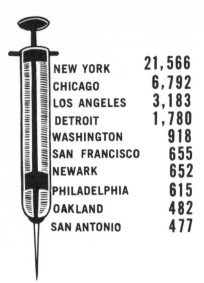

NEW YORK	21,566
CHICAGO	6,792
LOS ANGELES	3,183
DETROIT	1,780
WASHINGTON	918
SAN FRANCISCO	655
NEWARK	652
PHILADELPHIA	615
OAKLAND	482
SAN ANTONIO	477

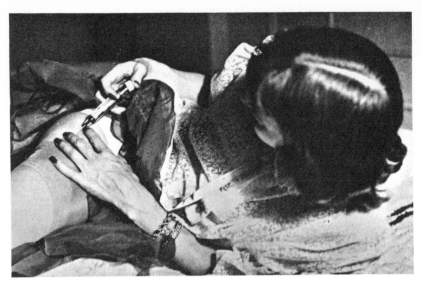

A chart showing the known addicts (only a small fraction of the users) in ten U.S. cities, as listed by the Federal Bureau of Narcotics in 1963   *UPI*

A girl giving herself a 'joy pop'. When this becomes ineffective addicts move on to 'main lining', injecting direct into an artery

Various methods of concealment. The heroin-saturated or 'satch' letter is used to send narcotics to prison inmates or addicts undergoing a cure. By chewing the letter the narcotic is extracted from the paper. It may also be concealed in a cigar   *NYPM*

Heroin addicts in a Hong Kong tenement   *UPI*

The users and the effects

It is a popular fallacy that all drug takers are drug addicts. There are degrees of drug taking, and many people manage to keep their usage within limits that may give sexual stimulation or produce erratic behaviour of various kinds, but do not lead to crime. Comparatively little is known about the exact properties of many drugs, and there is an increasing body of medical opinion which holds that the smoking of marijuana in 'reefer' form is non-addictive and no more harmful than the smoking of other cigarettes.

The real addict, however – and in particular the 'main liner' who injects heroin through an artery – ruins his health in a short time, and when in need of the drug becomes totally anti-social, prepared for any kind of degradation or crime. Violent crimes are generally committed by the addict desperate for a shot rather than the addict who is 'high'. A typical case was the murder of Janice Wylie and her friend Emily Hoffert by a young addict in need of money for heroin. Richard Robles struck them with such fury that two of the kitchen knives he used broke in half. Such cases come to public notice because the victims are pretty or well known, but there are dozens of other violent crimes where the addict, trying to support a heroin habit which costs him $40 a day, attacks with a gun or a knife the first well-dressed person he sees in the street.

Comedian Lenny Bruce clowns when on a narcotics possession charge in California in 1962   *UPI*

Janice Wylie, daughter of novelist Philip Wylie, and Emily Hoffert who shared an apartment with her. They were brutally stabbed to death in July 1963, by drug addict Richard Robles *UPI*

A clock radio in the apartment which timed the murder exactly. The plug was pulled from the socket when Janice Wylie's body fell across it   *UPI*

199

The boy who shouted

The Craig and Bentley case is of unique interest. Christopher Craig used his revolver to shoot a policeman. Derek Bentley, who carried a knife and a knuckleduster but did not use either, was found guilty of murder and hanged.

There was no dispute about what happened. Bentley was nineteen years old, Craig sixteen. Bentley was slow-witted although not sub-normal (he had ambitions to be a 'strong man'). Craig was intelligent but suffered from word-blindness, and his final school report was scathing. 'Chris makes no effort at all', one master wrote. 'I offered to teach him to read – at my home of an evening. This offer was rejected as he had more important things to do.' The boys tried to break into a confectioner's warehouse, were spotted on the roof, and Bentley was arrested. While being held by a policeman he shouted: 'Let him have it, Chris.' PC Miles moved to arrest Craig, and the boy shot him between the eyes with his revolver, killing him immediately. Craig then dived off the roof, injuring his spine. As he lay on the ground he said: 'I hope I've killed the bloody lot.' He had in fact wounded a Police Sergeant.

At the trial it was stressed that Craig was much attached to his elder brother Niven, who had just been sentenced to 12 years' imprisonment for armed robbery, and stressed also that his nature was or had been gentle, and that he had regularly attended Bible classes. Both boys were found guilty of murder, Bentley solely because he had shouted encouragement to Craig. Craig was too young to hang by English law, but Bentley was not.

The evident moral inequity of the situation caused a storm of protest, and almost up to the day of execution it was expected that Bentley would be reprieved. He was hanged at Wandsworth Prison on

The gun with which Craig shot P. C. Miles *Mirrorpic*

28 January 1953. Craig, whose character is said to have changed greatly in prison, was recently released.

Although the case is unique, the pattern of teenage violence for kicks is common to many countries. The Italian 'Gang of Calibre .22', which was led by the girl student Nadia Bebber, all came from perfectly respectable families, as did Craig and Bentley. In Holland recently three boys from Utrecht tried to poison a fourteen-year old playmate, and after finding that the pills they used were harmless, battered him to death and buried him in quicklime. Two of them were the sons of a rich insurance broker. In Buenos Aires a whole group of young girls from well-to-do families were found to be working as prostitutes and distributing opium and marijuana. The profound lack of adherence to the social standards of their society which horrified America in the case of Leopold and Loeb in the nineteen-twenties would be almost commonplace now.

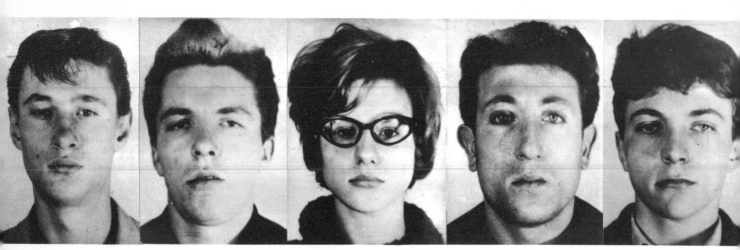

'The Gang of Calibre .22', with their leader Nadia Bebber *Keystone*

Derek Bentley *Mirrorpic*

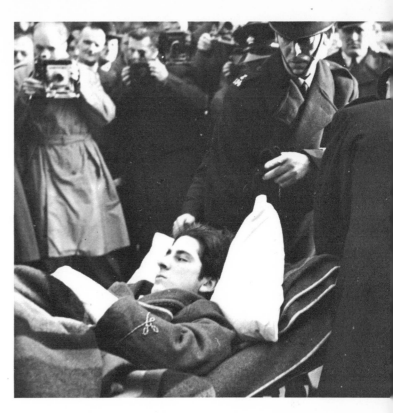

Christopher Craig being carried into Court *Mirrorpic*

Outside the prison after Bentley's execution. The crowd are trying to tear down the notice *RTHPL*

Not long ago the London *Daily Mirror* advertised for offensive weapons to be sent in to them. The weapons were sent on to Scotland Yard, and they were astonished by the variety and ferocity of those they received. Note at the left of this picture the chain with razor blade attached to it, and just right the spiked cogwheel. Almost every instrument has had a spike of some kind fixed to it. These are not weapons used by professional criminals, but the home-made concoctions of teenage gang. *Mirrorpic*

Weapons of terror

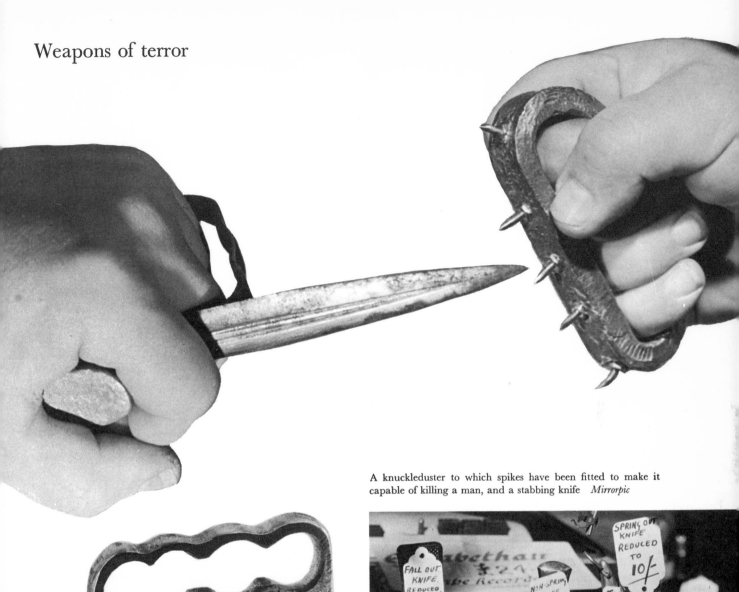

A knuckleduster to which spikes have been fitted to make it capable of killing a man, and a stabbing knife   *Mirrorpic*

The simple knuckleduster carried by Derek Bentley (see page 201)   *Mirrorpic*

Another item in the *Daily Mirror* collection. Closed up, it looks like a toy gun. Press the trigger, and it opens up to reveal a four inch blade tapered to a point. A mother in Manchester found it in the pocket of her 11-year old son   *Mirrorpic*

Sale of knives of this kind is now prohibited in Britain, although they are still obtainable. These knives were being sold off cheap in a shop just before the Bill banning them came into force   *Mirrorpic*

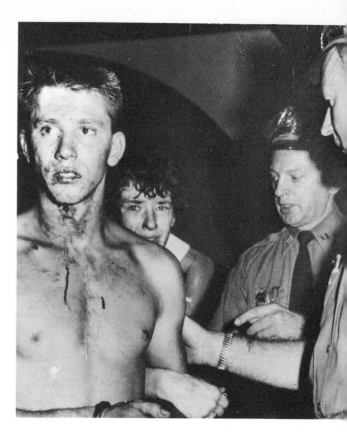

Two thousand motor cyclists rioted in Laconia, New Hampshire. One is led to a police truck   *UPI*

A boy being questioned after a riot on a Mississippi river steamer   *UPI*

These Puerto Rican boys stabbed two others to death in a New York school playground   *UPI*

One of two Dutch brothers, sons of a rich insurance broker, who battered a fourteen-year old boy to death and buried him in quicklime because they were afraid he would tell the police they had been stealing   *Keystone*

The increase of teenage violence

The last decade has seen an increase of teenage violence all over the world. In England the Mods and Rockers fight savage battles over imaginary differences on the beaches of seaside resorts, in the United States a trivial argument on a river boat quickly becomes a full scale riot, in France, Italy and West Germany crimes are committed casually as though they were jokes that might alleviate the boredom of everyday life, and even behind the Iron Curtain the *stilyagi* outrage sober Communists by violent protests against the dullness of their lives.

This wave of violence is traced by some to original sin, by others to lack of discipline, by others still to the threat of world destruction into which these children were born, and which they take for granted. No doubt the increase in the taking of pep pills and drugs by teenagers is partly responsible, but then why do they take them? Even where teenage crime has a rational basis, its ends are often absurd. The gang of boys shown here organized their liquor store raids intelligently, using a girl as lookout, but their objective of 'taking over New York City' was self-evidently ludicrous.

Arrest of a group who plotted to 'take over New York City', although they got no further than raiding fifteen liquor stores and restaurants *UPI*

The arsenal of the group included a high-powered rifle with telescopic sight, and a home-made machine gun *UPI*

Samples of prostitutes' postcard notices outside London newsagents and tobacconists   *Mirrorpic*

The notice boards remain

The story of the Messina brothers is typical of organized prostitution all over the world. The five Messinas were born at Linguaglossa, on the slopes of Mount Etna. They came to London in 1934 and quickly developed an empire of street girls, from France and Belgium. Carmelo arranged 'marriages of convenience' which gave them British nationality. They never saw the men again after arrival in England, but moved straight into one of the hundreds of flats leased by the Messinas, and went on the streets. Their earnings were colossal – one of Messina's girls wrote an autobiography in which she said that she once had forty-nine men in a day, and this was certainly by no means a record – but they were allowed to keep only a small fraction of the money. The rest usually went to their pimp, who acted as a Messina collector. Girls who tried to set up independently were threatened, and those who disregarded the threat were razor-slashed. For years the Messinas stayed one step ahead of the law, but in 1956 Eugenio and Carmelo were arrested in Belgium. Eugenio, who was the brains of the organization, received a seven-year sentence. Carmelo was given ten months for procuring girls. When he came out he returned to London, but he was jailed on the charge of failing to produce a passport, and then deported to Italy. With his occupation gone, Carmelo Messina returned to Linguaglossa and died there of a brain haemorrhage in a seedy boarding house at the age of forty-four.

Prostitution is international. In many countries it is linked with the drug traffic – when an Argentine vice ring was broken up recently quantitites of opium and marijuana were found – and American vice empires like those of Capone or Lucky Luciano are usually allied to bootlegging, gambling or drugs. Prostitution is also the most potent source of police corruption, especially where special 'vice squads' exist. The sums offered are so large, and the people involved often so important, that pressure to accept a bribe is very strong. Prostitution is, finally, ineradicable. The closing of licensed brothels in France drove thousands of prostitutes out of the houses on to the streets. In Britain the reverse process has operated. The Street Offences Act greatly increased the severity of punishments for accosting, and sent prostitutes off the streets. A rash of postcards on notice boards in big cities then appeared, advertising in a kind of code the services offered. 'Strict Governess' or 'Miss Birchy' is prepared to beat her client, 'Miss Kinky' practices unusual variations, and so on. It seems commonsense that since prostitution, like gambling and drinking, is a characteristic of human societies, it should be legalized. Even such phrases as 'vice rings', which one can hardly avoid using, are loaded with the implication that sexual intercourse is morally wrong. Until some commonsense is applied to prostitution the Messinas and their successors will flourish, and the notice boards remain.

Girls involved in a vice ring leaving Buenos Aires police station after interrogation *Keystone*

Left: Carmelo Messina. Death in a Sicilian boarding house in 1959. *Right*: Eugenio Messina *Mirrorpic*

Old games, new variations

In the wide green pastures of swindling there are no new tricks to be played, but the old ones have endless variations. One was played by Leonard Minchinton, who was called – nobody seems to have known why – Johnny the Bosch. He was extraordinarily skilful at making skeleton keys which, as he boasted, would open any lock. The original thing about Johnny the Bosch was that he made the keys as a business, criminals being his clients. He sold sets of keys like those illustrated at £30 a set, and like any good salesman threw in a fancy case. 'Undoubtedly you are a man of some misplaced ability', he was told at his trial, before being sentenced to 10 years' preventive detention.

The most notable cheque and passport forger of recent years is the Portuguese Candido Carinhas, who was arrested in October 1965. There are passport forgers in almost every country but Carinhas, feeling perhaps that other people were not to be trusted, forged his own. He was usually a South American diplomat – as an Argentinian José Humberto Perez, as a Paraguayan Leo Jimenez Stevens and so on – and he wisely elected himself a member of the Rotary Club, which led business men to welcome him with open arms. At the time of his arrest in Denmark, Carinhas was wanted in several countries, and Interpol's file on him listed 27 aliases.

An English detective called the equipment on this board the finest set of housebreaking tools he had ever seen. They were made by 'Johnny the Bosch' *Mirrorpic*

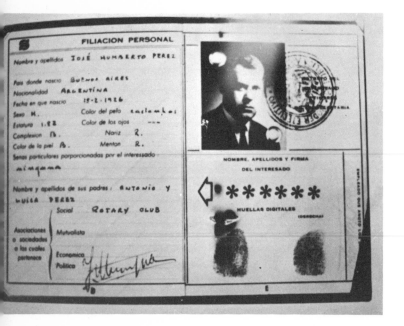

Carinhas's forged Argentinian passport. He had a dozen others
Keystone

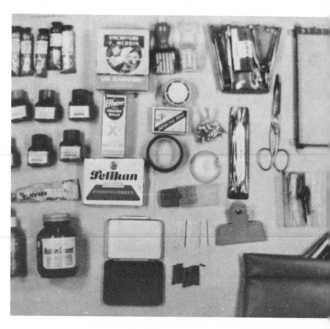

The equipment used by Candido Carinhas, champion cheque and passport forger *Keystone*

'Scotch whisky' sold in Japan. The bottles contained one-quarter genuine Scotch and three-quarters of a Japanese brew. The only obvious clue to the fake was that all the counterfeit labels bore the same registration number, 1271158 *Keystone*

An American fraud practised immediately after the war. Civilians who cashed these cheques for 'ex service men' found that the 'Disabled Veteran's Bureau' did not exist *UPI*

American mugger who preyed on couples, in a disguise which included blocks of wood wrapped in cloth round his shoes, to increase his height and to make his steps noiseless *NYPL*

Audacity is not enough

If a man's wife is killed and she is heavily insured the husband is the obvious suspect. When Maria, the wife of Giuseppe Fenaroli was murdered in her Rome apartment on 10 September 1958, he had an alibi which proved conclusively that he had been in Milan. It appeared, however, that Fenaroli had become strangely friendly with a man named Raul Ghiani. Maria's jewels were found by the police in Ghiani's office, and they suggested that Fenaroli had hired Ghiani as murderer, promising him a substantial share of the insurance proceeds. Ghiani also lived in Milan, and the police case was that the murder had been a masterpiece of intricate timing. They worked out that Ghiani could have left work on the evening of 10 September, been driven by Fenaroli to the airport, caught the plane to Rome, killed Maria, and then caught the night train back to Milan to be at work at his usual time on the following morning.

The trial of Fenaroli and Ghiani, together with Carlo Inzolia who was accused of aiding and abetting them, did not take place until February 1961, and it lasted until June. Public interest was kept at fever heat by the audacity of the alleged plot, in spite of the fact that many people felt that the issue had been prejudged by such incidents as a telegram of congratulation sent by the Minister of the Interior to the police after Fenaroli's arrest. Fenaroli did all that

man could do in his own defence. He wept in court, and both he and Ghiani offered to take lie detector tests to resolve contradictions in their evidence (the offer was refused), but in spite of the fact that identification of Ghiani on the airplane and the train was distinctly shaky, both were found guilty and received life sentences. Inzolia was acquitted.

Fenaroli (*left*) and Ghiani in the courtroom   *Mondadori*

Giuseppe Fenaroli bursts into tears during his interrogation by the judges   *Camera Press*

Jorgen Schmidt, who claimed to have inherited the title of Marquis de Sade and with it a fortune in Swiss francs, was generous with his inheritance. Although he continued to work at his poorly-paid job as cashier in Copenhagen, he bought a big house and gave elaborate parties to which guests – among them the company manager – were brought in hired cars. It was a sad day for the company when they learned that Schmidt had swindled them of nearly £50,000. Under arrest Schmidt loftily admitted the swindle, but maintained his right to the title of the divine Marquis.

Other crimes of the times showing that audacity alone is not enough for criminal success were those of Peippo Uolevi Helle, one-time director of the Finnish State Mint who turned to counterfeiting the country's coinage, and the exploits of the self-styled King of Car Thieves, Claus-Werner Frombeck, in Germany. Frombeck's method was simple. He obtained access to Volkswagen sales records, noted the names and addresses of new car purchasers, and stole the cars. They were driven away, quickly resprayed, and then – the supreme stroke of audacity – exported to the U.S. and to Russia. Between 1953 and 1957, when he was caught, Frombeck stole and exported, on his own admission, forty-four cars.

The Marquis de Sade: audacity in Denmark. Jorgen Schmidt, cashier in a Copenhagen firm, told other employees that he had inherited the title of Marquis de Sade and with it a fortune in a Swiss bank   *Keystone*

The King of Car Thieves: audacity in Berlin. Claus-Werner Frombeck. He not only stole the cars, he exported them *Keystone*

Counterfeiting: audacity in Finland. Peippo Uolevi Helle shown at the Finnish State Mint in 1954. He was director of the Mint from 1948 to 1958   *UPI*

Left: Some of the counterfeit Finnish coins   *UPI*

PUNISHMENT OR THERAPY?

The final punishment

Does the existence of capital punishment deter men and women from murder? Many policemen believe that it does, almost all modern criminologists that it does not. By the end of the nineteenth century Belgium, Holland, Portugal, Rumania and Italy had given up capital punishment, and during this century half a dozen other European countries have abandoned it, the United Kingdom being the most recent of them.

Criminologists and statisticians point out that the abolition of the death penalty has made no apparent lasting difference to the homicide rate in these countries, and that even in countries within which the situation varies from state to state differences are not apparent. In Queensland, Australia, there was a slight rise in the homicide rate when capital punishment was abolished in 1922, but so there was in neighbouring New South Wales which retained the death penalty. In subsequent years the Queensland homicide rate dropped, the New South Wales one did not. The same thing applies to the United States, where some states have abandoned the death penalty, while others use lethal gas, the electric chair or hanging. There is no discernible difference in the homicide rate. The two recent cases that have most stirred English opinion in favour of abolition are the Christie case, where Timothy Evans is thought to have been hanged for a crime he did not commit (see page 242), and the case of Ruth Ellis, a model who shot her lover as he got out of his car. Overwhelmed with remorse, she wanted to plead guilty, and refused to appeal. A fortnight before committing the murder she had had a miscarriage. Her execution caused widespread indignation.

It should be added that in many countries arguments from statistics do not have the slightest effect on the belief held by a large majority of people that capital punishment is a deterrent. The percentage favouring capital punishment when a poll was taken in France, West Germany and the United Kingdom was something like 80%. In the United States the percentage was much lower. Even if capital punishment is not a proved deterrent, many people feel that 'the country should be willing to avenge crime', in the words of Lord Goddard, and how can you avenge crime better than by killing the criminal?

The first man to be electrocuted in the United States was a murderer named Kemmler, in 1890. There was great doubt about the efficacy of the method, and a man wrote to the Governor of New York State offering to test the current by going to the chair himself, providing that $5000 was paid to his family if he died. The offer was not accepted. Kemmler was successfully electrocuted, and the procedure was thought to be painless. 'The several murderers in Sing Sing, Auburn and Dannemora prisons under sentence of death by electricity have every reason to rejoice', wrote a New York paper. But later cases showed that death was by no means always instantaneous and that it was never anything but agonisingly painful. Death by hanging is not immediate and its procedure can never be anything but disgusting, and French doctors have said that after the guillotine's knife has struck 'every vital element survives decapitation', making it 'a savage vivisection'. If society is to take its revenge in this way on those who have injured it, the most humane form of execution is undoubtedly by cyanide gas.

The crowd standing outside Holloway Prison on the morning of Ruth Ellis's execution. The figure in black is Violet Van der Elst, a prominent opponent of capital punishment. *LEA*

Ruth Ellis, hanged in 1955, the last woman to suffer the death penalty in England *LEA*

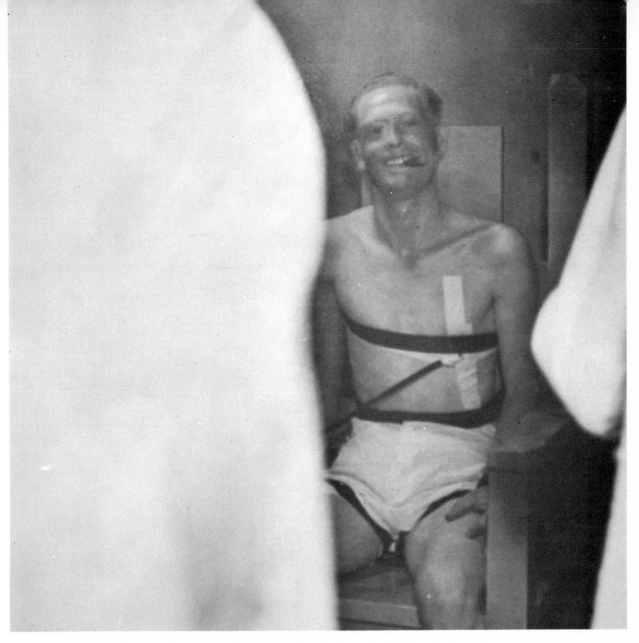

A remarkable picture of Jack Sullivan, a murderer sentenced to death, in the lethal gas chamber at Arizona State Prison. He went to his death grinning, and smoking a cigar. A stethoscope is taped over his heart. Prison physicians pronounced him dead less than two minutes after the cyanide gas swirled round his head *UPI*

Capital punishment was abolished in West Germany in 1949 This guillotine has been relegated to a jail basement *UPI*

The electric chair. It was in this chair that Julius and Ethel Rosenberg died *UPI*

When prisoners mutiny

A prison mutiny is not like an attempted escape. It has no chance of final success. The prisoners may, and often do, take hostages, and they try to use these hostages to make terms. But this is not a unions versus management struggle, although the prisoners may pretend to themselves that it is. In this fight the prisoners always lose, because no prison governor or warden is going to be bound by terms agreed through the use of force.

Why do men mutiny? Usually the immediate cause is something trivial like bad food, loss of a privilege, even the departure of a well-liked officer. From the outside it often looks bewilderingly trivial, but to the prisoner it seems vitally important. The tendency of most prison organizations is to try to turn men into obedient machines, because obedient machines are no trouble to handle. In prison as in the armed forces everything is done to rule, and everything has its particular place. The pictures of Alcatraz mess hall and of a Paris prison suggest the totally mechanical nature of prison life. This is something that most prisoners accept most of the time. Mutinies, hopeless and futile in themselves, are the moments when they wreck the neatness and order and engage in an orgy of futile destruction. Through such destruction they are, just for a moment, beating the system, and claiming that although they are prisoners they are also people.

Rioting prisoners at San Antonio, Texas. The main cause of the riot was inadequate food *UPI*

Utah State Prison. Prisoners tell their grievances in a live telecast *UPI*

The wrecked first floor of Rahway Prison after a riot *UPI*

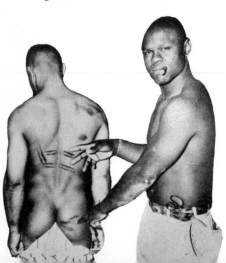

Rusk State Hospital, Texas. The leader of the rioters points to bruises on another prisoner which he says were the result of a beating by a guard *UPI*

Alcatraz. The mutiny from 2 to 4 May 1946. The circle shows a guard hugging the wall during a gun battle between prisoners and guards. Two platoons of U.S. Marines laid siege to Alcatraz with bazookas, machine guns and gas grenades before the convicts gave in. At the end of it two guards and three convicts were dead, fifteen men wounded   *UPI*

Warders making their rounds in a Paris prison   *Express Features*

The spotless mess hall at Alcatraz. Does such spotlessness breed mutinies?   *UPI*

Lincoln, Nebraska. Armed guards drive rioting inmates back to their cells with tear gas *UPI*

The bodies of sixteen Filipino convicts piled up after an attempted jail break near Manila *UPI*

End of a prison break from Brazil's 'Devil's Island', Anchieta. A soldier stands guard over the dead *UPI*

Riots and prison breaks

Prison breaks are rarer and usually bloodier than mutinies. In 1950 twenty three convicts at Muntislupa prison, near Manila, raided the arsenal, killed the guard and seized rifles. A four hour battle took place in which another guard was killed. The prisoners tried to escape through a hole blasted in one of the prison buildings, and sixteen of them were killed as they came through it one by one.

In 1952 two hundred and eighteen convicts rioted on Anchieta, where conditions were notoriously bad, and killed sixteen guards in their escape to the mainland. There they were hunted down by troops, who had orders to shoot on sight. Most of the convicts eventually barricaded themselves in the building shown in the picture, and many were killed when the soldiers charged it.

The warder being led out to safety in the illustration was lucky to escape with his life. He had been held hostage in a battle during which ten warders were killed. When the prison guards learned this after the battle they shot and killed fourteen of the prisoners.

Dazed prison warder held as hostage by prisoners in the Villa Devoto prison, Buenos Aires, comes out to freedom *Keystone*

Eastern Pennsylvania. A successful prison escape. A guard measures with his rule the seven inch opening through which five men slid through the sluice to the sewer *UPI*

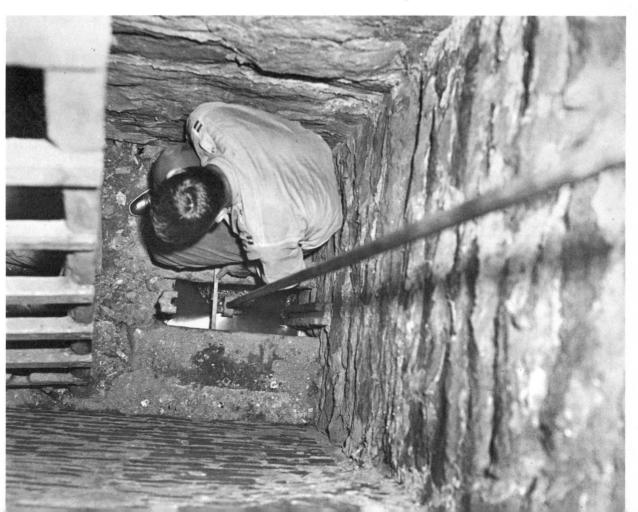

217

French lawyers and deputies inspecting Germany's most modern prison near Stuttgart *Keystone*

Rustic work by prisoners at New Hall open prison near Wakefield, Yorkshire *Mirrorpic*

Is rehabilitation possible?

'As in medicine it has been maintained that there are no diseases but only patients, so one is tempted to say that, strictly speaking, there are no crimes but only criminals.' This observation by the French criminologist Professor Saleilles, would gain much wider acceptance now than when it was made more than fifty years ago. It is becoming more and more generally recognized that society has two purposes in sending people to prison. The first is punishment, the second is reform, and the two are distinct.

Very few people who have seen anything of prison life now believe, as many believed a century ago, that you can reform people by punishing them. It is unlikely that a boy from a good home who has committed one offence will be reformed by putting him together with other young and already hardened criminals, and as one prison Governor has said, to put a homosexual into an ordinary prison is like trying to cure a dipsomaniac by locking him up in a brewery. It is sentimental not to admit that there are many confirmed criminals who cannot be reformed, and the pages of this book tell stories of sexual psychotics who are beyond the reach of

any help. But it is true also that many prisoners are capable of adjusting themselves to society and that, as Professor Saleilles said, the punishment should fit the criminal rather than the crime.

Some of the ways in which this can be done are by the use of more 'open' prisons like the one at Wakefield, where as much freedom as possible is given, by making the conditions inside ordinary prisons less mechanical and degrading, by trying to interest prisoners in useful occupations (in San Quentin most prisoners go to night school), by carefully segregating old lags so that they have as little contact as possible with young offenders. Homosexuality could be greatly lessened by organized colonies where prisoners live with their families such as exist in Brazil and the Soviet Union, and by permitting married prisoners to spend considerable time with their wives as is done in the Argentine. The likelihood of men coming out of prison returning to crime would be reduced if more effective help could be given them when they come out into a mostly hostile world. A calculated risk is involved in all reformative schemes, but by and large they have been shown to work.

Robert Stroud, the 'birdman of Alcatraz', famous for his books about bird life. Stroud has spent more than 50 years in prison for two murders, committed in his youth *UPI*

Sigmund Engel, frequently convicted swindler, teaches German to a convict class at the Illinois State Penitentiary in 1950. Nathan Leopold was a member of the class *UPI*

A cell at Holloway prison for women prisoners on preventive detention. They are kept away from short-term prisoners, but the room is bright and pleasant *Mirrorpic*

Women prisoners at Holloway working on murals for the common room *Mirrorpic*

THE MAFIA AND LABOUR RACKETS

The Camorra, the Black Hand and the Mafia

From the beginning of the nineteenth century secret societies flourished in Italy, the product possibly of the national temperament, certainly of the extreme poverty, feudalism and disregard for law which marked parts of Italy even after the unification of the country. The Camorra was a society for extortion and murder based on Naples, which was extremely powerful in the second half of the nineteenth century. Its members were sworn to total obedience. They murdered without compunction, and, as can be seen from the illustration, under licence. The Camorra's rule never extended far beyond Neapolitan limits, and by the end of the century it was waning.

The Mafia and the Black Hand were closely linked. The Black Hand was a terrorist group which operated primarily in the United States, where it specialized in the intimidation of Italian immigrants, whereas the Mafia had its roots firmly in Sicily and attempted, at least in part, to impose its own laws in place of the feeble local police organization. Strong Black Hand groups existed in several American cities, including St Louis, Kansas City, Detroit and New Orleans, and in New Orleans they were responsible in 1907 for the kidnapping and murder of Walter Lamana, the seven-year old son of an Italian undertaker. The discovery of his body and the subsequent arrest of the criminals caused such an outcry that the power of the Black Hand was broken in Louisiana.

The Mafia was and is an elaborate organization with separate branches for market gardens, fruit plantations, taxi drivers, undertakers, and so on. The 'Honoured Society' is a protection racket, yet it is something more than that. In a society where decent law enforcement existed the Mafia could have no place, but in Sicily its sway was so complete that landowners and civil servants became tribute payers. In return the Mafia kept its own kind of order. Its leader early in this century was Don Vito Cascio Ferro, whose fame was such that when he visited a town the mayor came to kiss his hand in homage.

Don Vito employed many murderers, but admitted to only one murder himself, a crime committed to maintain the prestige of the Honoured Society. This was the assassination of Lieutenant Joseph Petrosino of the New York police, who had realized that the Black Hand gangsters were all imported from Italy, and went to Palermo to investigate the situation. It is still not certain whether their importation was planned deliberately by Don Vito to obtain a Mafia foothold in the United States, although that was the result. The Mafia were warned of Petrosino's plan, and regarded his visit as a challenge. On the day of the detective's arrival Don Vito waited outside the Palazzo Steri, the seat of the Court of Justice, where Petrosino had an appointment, and killed him with a single shot. He was charged with the crime, but had provided himself with an alibi given by an influential local deputy. Nobody was punished for Petrosino's murder.

Filippi, one of the chiefs of the Camorra *CP*

A certificate of the order of the Decisi, a department of the Camorra, dated 1877 and granting a general licence to murder to the 'Registrar of the Dead' *NYPL*

Lieutenant Joseph Petrosino, the New York detective murdered by the Mafia in Palermo *NYPM*

The page from the New York Police Department journal for 13 March 1909, recording Petrosino's death. The entry reads: 'The Police Commissioner has this A.M. received a dispatch from the American Consul at Palermo, Sicily, Italy, announcing the assassination of Lieutenant Joseph Petrosino on the evening of March 12, 1909. It is with the utmost sadness and regret we receive this information. Let his death encourage us all to renewed efforts to stamp out the band of criminals now infesting our city, of which he was a deadly foe'. *NYPM*

The old and the new Mafias

Just as people used to praise Mussolini for making the trains run on time, so they praised him for wiping out the Mafia. Certainly it was repressed under Fascist rule by the most ruthless methods, and it is probably true also that many Sicilians were happy to abandon their civil liberties, which had mostly existed on paper, for the undoubted right to walk about the streets in safety. By a similar paradox the remnants of the Mafia co-operated with the Allies in the invasion of Italy during the 1939–45 war, and it is said that Lucky Luciano, among other American gangsters who were ex-Mafiosi, helped to pave the way for the Allied landings in Italy. It is certainly true that the Allies, and in particular the American Intelligence Service, were largely responsible for the revival of the Honoured Society by giving its members positions of power because they were anti-Fascist. A few years after the war was over, the Mafia's influence was as great as ever, and its links with American gangsters were extremely close.

There ensued a murderous struggle between the Old Mafia and the New Mafia, in which people were killed by the dozen. Essentially this was a struggle between the young men like Luciano Liggio, the most violent of the leaders to emerge after the war, and such comparatively respectable figures as Dr Navarra, head of the professional and white collar Mafia, but it also represented a difference between those who wished to keep the Mafia based as it had always been upon the countryside, and those who wanted to bring it into the towns and also to take part in the opportunities offered by the Honoured Society's links with American gangsters like Joe Profaci and Nicola Gentile to engage in the drug traffic. Between the Old and the New stood figures like the bandit Salvatore Giuliano, whose Robin

Left: Genco Russo, chief of the Sicilian Mafia from 1954 to 1964, in Lovera, Northern Italy, where he was exiled for five years *Keystone*

Right: Luciano Liggio of the 'New Mafia'   *Mondadori*

Hood qualities seem to have been much exaggerated. Genco Russo, chief of the Sicilian Mafia, stayed outside the struggle, in which the slaughter of Navarra by eight men armed with sub-machine guns was only an incident.

Recent years have seen the infiltration of the Mafia into the Christian Democrat party, but they have seen also a genuine attempt by the police to replace banditry by law. Russo is exiled from Sicily, Liggio is in prison, and so are many other important Mafiosi. Yet the Mafia is not defeated, merely in retreat. Its eventual fate is bound up with the political and civil development of Italy.

Women of the Riccobono family weep for 13-year old Paolino Riccobono, machine gunned during a feud between the family and the local Mafia which resulted in nine deaths   *Camera Press*

Giuseppe Zangara, a cemetery watchman in Palermo shot down near his home in 1961. Zangara was involved in the 'Requiem Mafia', the funeral racket, and left 3 houses, 2 cars and a large bank account *Camera Press*

Francesco Mineo, shot in front of Palermo Police Headquarters, 1962 *Camera Press*

The four Capuchin friars of Mazzarino in Court. Father Carmelo is the third from the left *Keystone*

L'Italia con S Francesco ha dato il più Santo dei Santi al Cristianesimo ed alla Umanità -   *Mussolini*

A sentence written by Mussolini on a wall of the Convent. 'Italy with St Francis has given the Saint of Saints to Christianity and to humanity' *Keystone*

The exterior of the Convent *Keystone*

The case of the Capuchin friars

The extent to which the Mafia, or at least banditry, is involved in every facet of Sicilian life was shown when the case of the four Capuchin friars was heard at Messina in 1962. The convent of the Capuchins was at Mazzarino, in the heart of the Mafia country, but also in the province where peasants after the war revolted against feudalism and the Mafia and occupied some of the feudal lands. In February 1957, the 82-year old Father Carmelo, who was well known in the village, went to see the pharmacist and demanded 2 million lire from him under the threat that a 'criminal gang' would kill his young son if payment were not made. Father Carmelo produced a typed threatening letter to prove his case. The pharmacist paid, and so did other villagers when Father Carmelo made his rounds, emphasizing always that he too was a victim, and that nobody knew better than he did how necessary it was to pay up.

After this blackmail by unseen bandits had gone on for months, Father Carmelo visited a rich farmer named Angelo Cannada, from whom he demanded ten million lire. Cannada refused to pay and in May 1958, three bandits came to the house where he was staying and shot him under the eyes of his wife and son. Signora Cannada now paid part of the blackmail to Father Carmelo, after being told that her son's life was in danger.

The local police arrested the four friars and their gardener, who after a few days killed himself in his cell. It was a convenient suicide, for the friars' defence was at first that they had been controlled by the gardener, who had threatened to set fire to the convent if they did not do precisely as he ordered. It was unfortunate for the friars that some of the blackmail letters still existed and were found to have been written on the convent typewriter. They were acquitted of causing the death of Cannada, but at their fourth trial two of them received prison sentences for blackmail and extortion.

Another case involving a Capuchin Convent at Velletri, near Rome, which was found to be a headquarters for smuggled cigarettes. One of the friars pleads in Court that they knew nothing about it *Keystone*

Joseph Barbara's house at Apalachin where the gang leaders met in 1957   *UPI*

The coming of the Syndicate

'Do you know what the Mafia is?'
'What?'
'The Mafia? M-a-f-i-a-?'
'I am sorry. I don't know what you are talking about.'

This exchange between counsel and racketeer Salvatore Moretti took place during the Kefauver
investigation in 1950, and there is a considerable
body of police opinion in the United States which
holds that the Mafia in America died in September
1931, on 'Purge Day'. On that day Salvatore Maranzano was killed in his office by unidentified men,
and during the next forty-eight hours thirty Mafia
executives all over the country were murdered. The
other Mafia leader, 'Joe the Boss' Masseria, had
already been killed on the orders of 'Lucky' Luciano
by a group said to have included Albert Anastasia
and Buggsy Siegel. The Mafia was replaced by the
Unione Siciliano. According to the theory, this is by
no means a distinction without a difference. The
Mafia was clannish, and confined exclusively to
Sicilians. Unione is a widespread organization in
which the mobs co-operate with each other to run
a nation-wide Crime Syndicate.

Whether or not the Syndicate is a single entity,
its influence over many aspects of American life is
immense. It controls, or has a share in, all forms of
gambling and prostitution, it has a hand in many
unions, it has penetrated deeply although indirectly
into politics. The crack made by Buggsy Siegel,
one of the more intelligent of the gangsters, 'We
don't run for office, we own the politicians', is often
bitterly true.

In November 1957, a group of sixty-three gang
leaders and racketeers met at the house of a man
named Joseph Barbara in New York State. They
had come, they said, to ask after his health – and in
fact he was ill, and died soon afterwards. Barbara

said he was surprised but pleased to see his friends,
and it was a fortunate coincidence that he happened
to have 200 lbs of steak in the kitchen. Most of the
gang bosses shown on the lower part of the chart
opposite were present. They may have met to split
up the empire of the recently-murdered Anastasia,
or to allocate spheres of influence throughout the
country – some had come from as far away as Arizona
and Florida. A number of them were arrested on
a conspiracy charge which came to nothing, and
the revelations made in 1963 by former gangster
Joseph Valachi have also produced few positive
results. Individuals may be sent to the electric chair
or imprisoned. The Syndicate goes on.

A foot stool used as a recording device, found in Barbara's house
UPI

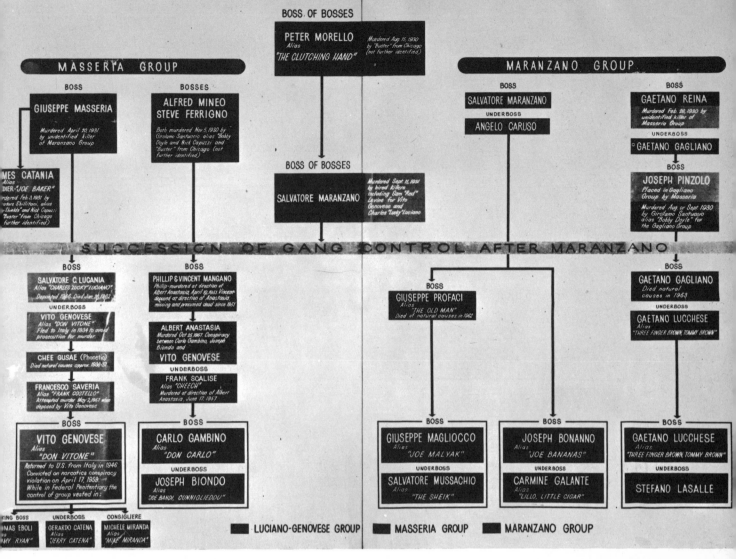

MASSERIA-MARANZANO WAR AND EVOLUTION OF GANG CONTROL-1930 TO PRESENT

BOSS OF BOSSES

PETER MORELLO
Alias
"THE CLUTCHING HAND"
Murdered Aug 15, 1930 by "Buster" from Chicago (not further identified)

MASSERIA GROUP

BOSS
GIUSEPPE MASSERIA
Murdered April 22, 1931 by unidentified killer of Maranzano Group

BOSSES
ALFRED MINEO
STEVE FERRIGNO
Both murdered Nov 5, 1930 by Girolamo Santuccio alias "Bobby Doyle and Nick Capuzzi and "Buster" from Chicago (not further identified)

JAMES CATANIA
Alias
DIER-"JOE BAKER"
Murdered Feb 3, 1931 by ...ature Shillitani, alias ...Shields" and Nick Capuz.. "Buster" from Chicago ... further identified)

BOSS OF BOSSES
SALVATORE MARANZANO
Murdered Sept. 11, 1931 by hired killers including Sam "Red" Levine for Vito Genovese and Charles "Lucky" Luciano

MARANZANO GROUP

BOSS
SALVATORE MARANZANO
UNDERBOSS
ANGELO CARUSO

BOSS
GAETANO REINA
Murdered Feb. 26, 1930 by unidentified killer of Masseria Group
UNDERBOSS
GAETANO GAGLIANO
BOSS
JOSEPH PINZOLO
Placed in Gagliano Group by Masseria Murdered Aug. or Sept. 1930 by Girolamo Santuccio alias "Bobby Doyle" for the Gagliano Group

SUCCESSION OF GANG CONTROL AFTER MARANZANO

BOSS
SALVATORE C. LUCANIA
Alias "CHARLES 'LUCKY' LUCIANO"
Deported 1946. Died Jan. 26, 1962
UNDERBOSS
VITO GENOVESE
Alias "DON VITONE"
Fled to Italy in 1934 to avoid prosecution for murder.
CHEE GUSAE (Phonetic)
Died natural causes approx. 1936-37
FRANCESCO SAVERIA
Alias "FRANK COSTELLO"
Attempted murder May 2, 1957 when deposed by Vito Genovese
BOSS
VITO GENOVESE
Alias "DON VITONE"
Returned to U.S. from Italy in 1946 Convicted on narcotics conspiracy violation on April 17, 1959. While in Federal Penitentiary the control of group vested in:

ACTING BOSS
THOMAS EBOLI
Alias
TOMMY RYAN
UNDERBOSS
GERARDO CATENA
Alias
"JERRY CATENA"
CONSIGLIERE
MICHELE MIRANDA
Alias
"MIKE MIRANDA"

BOSS
PHILLIP & VINCENT MANGANO
Phillip-murdered at direction of Albert Anastasia, April 19, 1951 Vincent deposed at direction of Anastasia, missing and presumed dead since 1951
ALBERT ANASTASIA
Murdered Oct 25, 1957. Conspiracy between Carlo Gambino, Joseph Biondo and
VITO GENOVESE
UNDERBOSS
FRANK SCALISE
Alias "CHEECH"
Murdered at direction of Albert Anastasia, June 17, 1957
BOSS
CARLO GAMBINO
Alias "DON CARLO"
UNDERBOSS
JOSEPH BIONDO
Alias
"JOE BANDI, CUNNIGLIEDDU"

BOSS
GIUSEPPE PROFACI
Alias "THE OLD MAN"
Died of natural causes in 1962

BOSS
GAETANO GAGLIANO
Died natural causes in 1953
UNDERBOSS
GAETANO LUCCHESE
Alias
"THREE FINGER BROWN, TOMMY BROWN"

BOSS
GIUSEPPE MAGLIOCCO
Alias "JOE MALYAK"
UNDERBOSS
SALVATORE MUSSACHIO
Alias "THE SHEIK"

BOSS
JOSEPH BONANNO
Alias "JOE BANANAS"
UNDERBOSS
CARMINE GALANTE
Alias "LILLO, LITTLE CIGAR"

BOSS
GAETANO LUCCHESE
Alias "THREE FINGER BROWN, TOMMY BROWN"
UNDERBOSS
STEFANO LASALLE

■ LUCIANO-GENOVESE GROUP   ■ MASSERIA GROUP   ■ MARANZANO GROUP

The master chart of power among gang bosses revealed by informer Joseph Valachi to the Senate investigations sub-committee in 1963
UPI

Albert Anastasia. One of the Syndicate's most ruthless killers. Murdered himself in 1957   *UPI*

Michael Miranda, one of the sixty three who attended the Apalachin meeting
UPI

Joe Bonnano, also present at Apalachin
UPI

The end of Buggsy Siegel. A gun through a window in Beverly Hills *UPI*

Bug and Meyer and 'el loco'

The precise range of Murder Inc. is still uncertain. Certainly most of its members came from Brooklyn, but according to Burton Turkus, the Assistant District Attorney who prosecuted several Murder Inc. men with the help of a gangland informer named Abe ('Kid Twist') Reles, it was an execution squad used by the Syndicate on a nation-wide scale. When a man had been marked for execution, after a Syndicate meeting where a 'defence counsel' was allowed to speak up for him, the job was allocated to one or another killer. It is a mark of the Syndicate's broad-mindedness that a Jewish gang like that of Siegel and Meyer was accepted within the fold. A Siegel and Meyer man was present at Maranzano's killing, and Buggsy Siegel himself, according to rumour, at that of Masseria.

Body of a Murder Inc. victim being excavated from quicklime, identity uncertain *CP*

Buggsy was an ambitious and unusually intelligent and personable gangster, who was sent out to the West Coast in 1937 to organize Southern California. He established himself in a 35 room house with swimming pool and maroon marble bath. He blackmailed film stars on the threat of arranging strikes by extras if they did not pay protection money, moved in on bookmaking and Las Vegas gambling houses, and had a hand in the drug trade. He was remarkably popular with the very film stars he was blackmailing. His end came when he unwisely tried to buck the Syndicate by retaining his California empire as a personal possession. He was a powerful and respected figure and it was not until 1947, it is said after a special gathering of gangsters in Cuba, that he was sentenced. Two weeks later he was sitting in the living room of the Beverly Hills apartment he had set up for a film and television star named Virginia Hill when somebody put a gun through the window and riddled him with bullets.

The nearest recent approach to American style gang warfare in another country has been in Buenos Aires. The capital of the Argentine is a fairly wide open city, but the authorities regard themselves as having organized crime under reasonable control. Early in 1964, however, it seemed that a ferocious gang war was developing. Within a few weeks a number of criminals were killed, some in old time Chicago style like Raoul Luis Diaz who was machine gunned on the street by men who sped away in a black car, others with refined cruelty. One man's body was placed in the cemetery on his wife's grave, two others were tied hand and foot and it was thought that they had then been burned alive. In several cases the men killed were suspects about to be taken in for police questioning. One or two criminals were killed by the police, who in Buenos Aires are quick to use their guns.

The police received tip-offs that the man behind the killings was Miguel Angel Prieto, known as 'el loco', the nut. Soon afterwards an off duty policeman proudly brought in Prieto, who had been arrested while making a clumsy attempt to rob a truck. The circumstances made it seem likely that Prieto had staged a fake hold-up in order to get himself arrested, having created a gang war which had moved beyond his control. At his trial it was learned that he had infiltrated the police department so thoroughly that he was told when any of his men were likely to be picked up, and killed them off in case they were tempted to talk under interrogation. As a result of his admissions six important police officials were arrested and received prison terms. There is no death penalty in the Argentine, and Prieto himself got a twenty-year sentence.

'El loco' Prieto under arrest *Keystone*

Luis Bello and Adolfo Ocampo. These two young boxers were both part of the Prieto gang. They were killed because of their failure to turn over the complete proceeds from robberies *Keystone*

The gangs and the unions

More than a third of the gangsters who met at Apalachin were involved in labour rackets, several of them in the garment industry, which was first penetrated by Lepke Buchalter in the nineteen thirties. The procedure was simple and effective. Votes for the election of officers were controlled through threats and bribery, and once office had been obtained it was easy to blackmail the employers and bleed the workers at the same time. A standard operation would be the threat of a strike and the acceptance of a bribe for calling it off on one side, and the collection of dues for imaginary benefits on the other. The procedure for inducing employers to give union recognition was first to declare the employer's goods 'black', and if he was still obdurate to beat up his staff and damage his plant. Johnny DioGuardi, known as Johnny Dio, who operates chiefly in the garment industry, is one of the best known strong-arm men.

Not all American unions are controlled by racketeers, nor is the control always complete. The Teamsters Union, however, has become notorious in recent years. A determined effort was made to rid it of gangsterism from the top down when a Senate Committee showed publicly that the President, Dave Beck, had built his house with union funds and then sold it back to the union for $163,000. Beck was finally convicted of grand larceny and sent to prison, but he was succeeded by the tougher, shrewder Jimmy Hoffa, who has been accused of milking the union of hundreds of thousands of dollars, of using gun-carrying toughs to enforce his laws, and of sanctioning any kind of violence to retain power. Robert Kennedy said that Hoffa ran a hoodlum empire, and he may not be able to survive as ruler of it, but who will replace Hoffa? When the New Jersey building racketeer Joe Fay was sent to prison in 1943 on extortion charges, after a long investigation hampered by the disappearance of some witnesses and the refusal of many more to testify, it was learned that a procession of politicians and labour leaders were visiting him in prison. Leading them was Lieutenant-Governor Arthur H. Wicks. He explained that there were labour troubles in upstate New York, and that after all Joe Fay was still the boss of the construction industry.

Gangster Johnny Dio throwing a punch at a press photographer after being ordered from a Senate Rackets Committee hearing in 1951 *UPI*

Teamster President Dave Beck explaining in 1957 that he is innocent of the tax evasion charges against him *UPI*

Robert Kennedy uses a blackboard to demonstrate how Beck siphoned money from the Teamsters for his personal use   *UPI*

Jimmy Hoffa, Beck's successor, holds up a paper minutes after the counting of the votes, saying that he has won election to the Presidency by a landslide, in a shot distinctly reminiscent of *Citizen Kane*   *UPI*

New York truck drivers get the news that Hoffa has been found guilty of fixing a jury   *UPI*

231

SEX CRIMINALS AND KIDNAPPERS

The Superman and the Slave

The relationship between eighteen-year old Richard Loeb and Nathan Leopold, who was a year his senior, was not basically a very unusual one. Loeb was elegantly handsome, Leopold short and near-sighted. Leopold adored Loeb, and was his devoted slave – the word was one he used himself. Both had read Nietzsche, and Leopold respected Loeb as a superman, not to be bound by ordinary morality. But at this point the conventional pattern is broken, for although Loeb was intelligent Leopold, the youngest student ever to graduate from the University of Chicago, was undoubtedly his intellectual superior. Both came from wealthy German-Jewish homes in Chicago (Loeb's father was a Vice-President of Sears, Roebuck), yet their actions may be traced to the feeling of many Jews that they are unacceptable to the society in which they live. The sado-masochistic feelings so marked in German life and thought may be found as well in German Jews, and with them may go the desire to commit an action which outrages and shows contempt for the society that tolerates rather than welcomes or admires.

Such thoughts were not consciously in the minds of Loeb and Leopold. Loeb stole things as a proof of his superiority to other people and to conventional morality. Undetected, he proposed to Leopold that they should commit a murder – a murder without motive would be a further proof of their superiority to their surroundings – and then pretend that the crime was a kidnapping and collect ransom for it.

On 21 May 1924, they hired a car and waited for the schoolboy they had chosen as victim. When they found that he had gone home early and a distant cousin of Loeb's, fourteen-year old Bobby Franks, came along, they invited him to come for a ride. Leopold drove the car and Loeb, sitting in the back with Bobby Franks, hit him four times with a cold chisel and stuffed a gag into his mouth. He went on hitting the boy until he was dead. They took the body to a culvert near the Pennsylvania railway, stripped it, poured acid over the face, and pushed it into a drainpipe. Some of the clothes were buried, others burned in the furnace of Loeb's house. They washed the hired car, telephoned Mrs Franks to say that her son had been kidnapped, and sent the ransom note.

It was far from the Perfect Crime of their imagination. A bare foot was seen sticking out of the drain-pipe the next morning, and in spite of the disfiguration caused by the acid, the body was quickly identified. Nevertheless, Loeb felt confident of their safety, and in his role of superman was almost pushing in his attempts to help the police. But they had made another mistake. Leopold's spectacles were found near the drain where he had dropped them, and they were traced to him within a few days through some very alert police work. His explanation that he had dropped them when out bird-watching some time before the murder was disproved by the fact that the spectacles bore no weather marks. Then

Leopold and Loeb (*left*) with their counsel Clarence Darrow between them, listen to Judge Caverly pronouncing sentence *UPI*

specimens of Leopold's typing were found to match the typing of the ransom note. Under constant police interrogation Loeb broke down. Later Leopold also admitted his part in the crime.

They were defended by America's most famous criminal lawyer, Clarence Darrow. Celebrated as a defender of labour leaders, he had been disillusioned by the nature of some of the cases he handled, and turned to the defence of accused criminals. Darrow was passionately opposed to capital punishment, and no prisoner he defended had suffered the death penalty. He saved Loeb and Leopold, although this

may have been because they were under age rather than because of the emotional two day speech in which he quoted both A. E. Housman and Omar Khayyam and referred to a mother looking into the blue eyes of her little baby and wondering whether he would meet death upon the scaffold. Judge Caverly, who heard the case without a jury, passed a sentence of life imprisonment for murder plus 99 years for kidnapping.

Loeb was stabbed to death in a homosexual prison brawl in 1936. Leopold was paroled in 1958, and lives in Puerto Rico.

Left: Leopold's spectacles, which he dropped near the point where the body of Bobby Franks was found. This was the first clue that led to Leopold and Loeb *UPI*

The ransom note, written when Bobby Franks was already dead *UPI*

Dear Sir:

Proceed immediately to the back platform of the train. Watch the east side of the track. Have your package ready. Look for the first LARGE, RED, BRICK factory situated immediately adjoining the tracks on the east. On top of this factory is a large, black watertower with the word CHAMPION written on it. Wait until you have COMPLETELY passed the south end of the factory - count five very rapidly and then IMMEDIATELY throw the package as far east as you can.

Remember that this is your only chance to recover your son.

Yours truly,

GEORGE JOHNSON

Hickman and Heirens

There are few more horrifying cases than that of the murder committed by William Herbert Hickman, who in his deliberately semi-literate ransom notes called himself 'The Fox'. Hickman was a young clerk working in the Los Angeles bank where Perry Parker was an important executive, when he was arrested for forgery and sent to prison. There was no doubt of his guilt, but he blamed Parker for the prosecution. This was the ostensible motive for what followed, although the real motive lies obviously in Hickman's personality.

One day in October 1928, Parker's twelve-year old daughter Marion was taken from her school by a

stranger, and ransom notes signed 'Mr. Fox' and 'Fox-Fate' followed. The sum demanded was small, and a rendezvous was arranged. Parker had told the police, and they were nearby when he went to the place. The kidnapper did not appear, but wrote a threatening note saying that he knew the police had been present. Another meeting was arranged in a Los Angeles car park. The money was handed over and the kidnapper said he would leave Marion in the car, just down the street. She was found to be dead. Her hands and legs had been hacked off, and wire had been used to prop open her eyelids. No other kidnapper has shown the refinement of cruelty involved

The first letter sent by Hickman to banker Perry Parker *UPI*

William Hickman in his cell *UPI*

in presenting the father with the mutilated corpse of his child. Hickman was caught after a chase through several states, and was eventually hanged at St Quentin prison.

William Heirens's history is an almost classical case of schizophrenia and fetishism. He had been a constant burglar from the age of twelve, often throwing away the things he stole. Sent to a school of correction for a year he immediately began to steal again when he came out, was discovered and sent to another similar school for eighteen months. On being released at the age of seventeen he began to attack women, as well as continuing to burgle apartments. He killed at least one woman, severely injured another, and raped and murdered a small child. At the time he did these things he was attending classes at the University of Chicago. His marks were not high.

When Heirens was caught nearly forty pairs of women's knickers were found in the attic of his home, and a good deal of burglary loot in his room at the University. He said that the act of entering a house illegally induced an orgasm, and so did wearing the knickers. He told of throwing away his clothes and the key of his room to stop himself going out at night, but said that eventually he had to go out and get the key. He said that the crimes were committed by another part of himself named George, who was 'just a realization of mine, but he seemed real to me'.

Heirens was tried in 1946, in Chicago. A psychiatrist said that he could find no sign of any psychotic disturbance. He was sentenced to life imprisonment.

Some of the loot found in Heirens' room at the University of Chicago   *UPI*

William Heirens in a police line up *UPI*

Victims, Accusers Ring Heirens— Odds 20-1 in Courtroom Drama

The odds against William Heirens are 20 to 1 and more as he stands before Chief Justice Ward in Criminal Court for his arraignment—postponed by agreement for 30 days.

Surrounding him are the people whose homes he robbed; a woman he shot—fortunately only slightly wounded —the policemen whom he battled like a wild man before he was captured, to reveal his dual character of brilliant student by day, dangerous bandit by night.

There is Tiffin Constant, the policeman whom he battled on the porch at 1320 Farwell av. before he was captured —a man left with a permanent injury, but whose life perhaps was saved when Heirens' revolver failed.

In the crowd is Policeman Abner Cunningham, who perhaps saved Constant's life by knocking Heirens cold with a heavy flower pot.

Spotted through the courtroom are victims of burglaries—many of whom never saw the agile young bandit.

There is Mrs. Marion Caldwell, who never saw the youth who fired through the window of her home, to wound her in the face

There are the many others who didn't see the looter, but who identified the valuables, found in the youth's room.

They are Abe Rehm, William Fauntz, Michael Jennings, David Vosburgh, Joseph Landsman, Mrs. Alda Greenwald, Mr. and Mrs. Richard O'Gorman, E. E. Clark, Leonard Petra.

There, too, are Nat Golds, Francis Hahley, S. R. Wells, William Owens, Harry Gold, and Mrs. Ruth Hager, from whose basement locker was stolen the sack in which part of the body of little Suzanne Degnan was placed after it was dismembered in the washtubs of the apartment at 5901 Winthrop av.

And there are Jack McAlpine and Ernest C. Banks, beaten by the young bandit now identified as Heirens.

Who wins in the end? The odds are 20 and more to 1 against William Heirens.

An American news story on the Heirens case, of a kind which would be rejected in England as involving contempt of court   *UPI*

Tragedy and farce

The tendency of American tragedy to be blended with grotesque, distasteful farce is shown by the Lindbergh kidnapping. On 1 March 1932 the twenty-month old son of Charles and Anne Morrow Lindbergh was kidnapped from his nursery in their house at Hopewell, New Jersey. Two months later, after $50,000 had been paid in ransom, the body of the baby was found. He had been killed by a blow on the head very soon after the kidnapping. In September 1934, Bruno Richard Hauptmann, an American of German origin who lived in New York, was arrested. Some of the ransom money was found in his apartment, handwriting specimens proved beyond doubt that he had written the thirteen ransom notes, and there was evidence linking him with the ladder used to get into the child's nursery. He was convicted and went to the electric chair.

Those were the tragic facts. But because Lindbergh was an idol, young, modest, naive, a great airman who represented in himself many American dreams, the case was surrounded from the start by honest simpletons, crooks and con men. In the first class came Dr 'Jafsie' Condon, a retired educationist who put an advertisement in a New York paper offering his services as a go-between. This offer was accepted, and it was through Condon that, after prolonged negotiations, the ransom money was eventually paid. Condon was an honest blunderer, but the ex-detective Gaston B. Means received a fifteen-year prison sentence when he used the occasion of the kidnapping to con a rich woman named Evelyn Walsh Maclean out of $104,000. Even from prison the unabashable Means tried to halt Hauptmann's execution, offering to reveal the true story of the crime if he were released. The Lindberghs themselves, desperate for news of their child, were deceived by the president of a boat-building corporation named John Hughes Curtis, who told an immensely circumstantial but wholly untrue story about his contacts with the kidnappers, and led both the Lindberghs and the police on a chase after an imaginary schooner. He received a twelve months' sentence. Cranks in dozens pestered the police and the Lindberghs, and several underworld characters popped in and out of the story. Until the discovery of the child's body Lindbergh was naturally ready to listen to any of them.

It was not until October 1933, when the F.B.I. was given exclusive jurisdiction over the investigation, that a careful analysis of all the known aspects of the case was made, and in particular of the ransom notes, which were numerous enough to give a real guide to their writer's identity. The conclusion had been reached before Hauptmann's arrest that he was of German origin. The most damning piece of evidence at the trial was the discovery by wood technologist Arthur Koehler that one rail of the home made ladder left outside the house matched perfectly a piece of floor board in Hauptmann's attic.

Dr 'Jafsie' Condon. He acted as go-between and paid the ransom money *UPI*

Hauptmann in the line up. Condon identified him, but refused to say so at the time *AP*

236

Lindbergh on the witness stand giving evidence about the ransom notes *AP*

Extracts from one of the ransom notes (*right*) with (*left*) extracts from words appearing on his car licence and in a letter *AP*

Arthur Koehler, the wood technologist from the Forest Products Laboratory, examining the ladder used in kidnapping the baby *AP*

Albert Fish, murderer and cannibal *UPI*

Wisteria Cottage, where Fish killed Grace Budd *UPI*

The telegram which played a part in the arrest of Fish. Hand-writing experts compared the writing with that on an envelope written by Fish six years later, and decided that they came from the same hand. *NYPD*

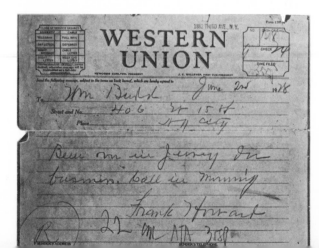

Killers of children

The violation and murder of children are the crimes that, more than any other, stir demands for the return of the death penalty where it has been abolished. 'Even accepting that the man who does these things is insane and cannot help himself, what possible place can he ever have in society, and why should he be allowed to live?' is perhaps the most difficult argument that abolitionists have to answer. It is particularly potent in such cases as that of Albert Fish, a painter and decorator in his late fifties (the picture shown was taken six years later), who got in touch with the Budd family using the name of Frank Howard, said that he had seen Budd's advertisement for a job, and offered him work. Fish was a meek, pleasant little man, and the Budds allowed their ten-year old daughter to go off with him, as he said to a children's party which was being given by his sister. Fish took the girl to an empty house called Wisteria Cottage, killed her, and then cooked parts of her body and ate them with carrots and onions. He was not arrested until six years later when he wrote a letter to the Budds in an envelope that was traced to him, and that was in the same writing as that of the telegram sent the day before the girl's murder by 'Frank Howard'.

The psychiatrist Frederic Wertham, who interrogated Fish, said that he was one of the most extraordinary cases in the history of abnormal psychology. He confessed to sadistic and masochistic practices which were almost incredible – one of the milder examples was sticking needles beneath his testicles. It may be that some of the stories were fantasies, but X-rays which showed twenty-seven of the needles inside him make his stories of tortures inflicted on himself and on children seem plausible. He is thought

Alfred Kaser, murderer of nine-year old Arthur Konig. Sentenced to life imprisonment in Munich in 1965   *Keystone*

to have been involved in killing at least fifteen children.

Fish was sentenced to death. What can be said about people like him or like Fred Thompson, who felt an 'irresistible urge' to kill a small girl, or about Alfred Kaser who drank his victim's blood? In some countries, and particularly in Scandinavia, it is said that some extreme sexual aberrants have been cured, and there are Dutch, Swedish and Danish clinics where they are voluntarily castrated. But is there any point in keeping castrated sex murderers alive? That depends on your view of the sanctity of human life. Such arguments will seem irrelevant to those who have suffered through sexual maniacs. 'We want him to be killed piece by piece', said Edith Kiecorius's cousin about Fred Thompson. The sentiment is not admirable, but it can be understood.

'Electric Chair for the Killer is what we want.' Members of the Kiecorius family demonstrate outside a New York police station   *UPI*

Fred Thompson, who killed four year old Edith Kiecorius, waves as he is taken to Bellevue Hospital for psychiatric observation   *UPI*

Sex murderers: Germany

It is tempting to believe that there is something in the German temperament tending towards the production of more perverted sex murderers than may be found in other countries. A Christie, a Heath or an Albert Fish are comparatively minor figures beside Peter Kürten, the 'Monster of Düsseldorf', who admitted to dozens of attacks on men, women and children, many of them ending in murder. Some victims were battered with a hammer, a small child was stabbed thirty-six times, others had their throats cut. Some, but not all, of them were raped. Kürten was excited by many different kinds of sadistic activities. He was an arsonist from his early youth, and practised bestiality with sheep, pigs and goats while in his teens. He found that he obtained great sexual pleasure from having intercourse with a sheep at the same time that he stabbed it.

The background of Kürten's childhood was an appalling texture of rape, incest and cruelty. At the age of eight he was taught by a dog-catcher to masturbate dogs, and also watched the man torturing them. But children in other countries have suffered such things without being turned into Peter Kürtens .

Kürten was born in 1883, and nobody knows how many people he attacked between 1913 (when by his own account he committed his first sexual murder, although he was already a criminal) and 1929, when he gave himself up. In person he was mild, pleasant, soft-spoken. He was guillotined on 2 July 1931.

Kürten was only the most notable among German sex murderers – a word he would have appreciated, for at the age of 16 he said while looking at waxworks figures of murderers that one day his fame would equal theirs. Contemporary with him was Karl Denke, the landlord of a house in Silesia where he gave lodging to the poor, killed them, ate some of their flesh and pickled the rest, keeping the records carefully in a ledger. Denke was a religious man, who worked the organ at the local church. He hanged himself before coming to trial. Another contemporary was George Karl Grossmann, who picked up girls, slept with them, killed them, cut up the bodies and sold them for meat.

The homosexual Fritz Haarmann also cut up and sold the bodies of his victims – it should be remembered that after the First World War many German people existed on a level of near-starvation, and did not worry much about where their meat came from. Haarmann's photograph shows a cast of features curiously similar to Kürten's. He lived in Hanover, in a house on the river Leine. His activities as a meat-smuggler were looked upon indulgently by the police, because he was also a petty police spy. He killed only boys, and by his own account only good-looking ones. At his trial he insisted that he was innocent of the death of an ugly boy. The police work in his case seems to have been extremely poor. He was known to be homosexual and had a long prison record, there were suspicions that the meat he sold was human flesh, and bones were found near his house, yet he was not arrested until the evidence against him was overwhelming. In December 1924, he was sentenced to death and was beheaded.

The picture of Hans Pommerenke shows a feeble, weakly sensitive face, and it is likely that Pommerenke's crimes sprang from a simple awareness of sexual inadequacy. He was arrested in 1960, charged with ten murders involving rape, twenty other cases of rape, and a number of other crimes, and was sentenced to life imprisonment. Like many sex murderers, Pommerenke felt the need for boastful confession, and like them admitted many things that seem improbable. Yet confronted with the realities, who can say that these improbabilities were not the truth?

And remembering the concentration camps, who can say either how far the idea of 'normality' can be stretched, so that any bestiality may be perpetrated without a sense of outrage to human dignity? At the beginning of the war W. H. Auden wrote:

Accurate scholarship can
Unearth the whole offence
From Luther until now
That has driven a culture mad,
Find what occurred at Linz,
What huge imago made
A psychopathic god.

The psychopathic god was worshipped in the concentration camps, by Irma Grese for example, who used her power over thousands of women to whip, club and shoot them to death. Those she killed were creatures for whom no human feeling was possible in her psychology. It is not surprising that the Nazis did their best to hush up sex criminals under their regime, for it was a frightening conclusion, pushing logic over the brink of nightmare, that the murders which had to be punished when committed by private individuals were officially approved when carried out under the authority of the Nazi state.

Hans Pommerenke

lfd. Nr.	Name des Opfers	Anklagebehörde / Straftat		Beantragte Strafe	Anträge des Verteidigers	Urteil des Schwurgerichts	Gesamturteil
1	Kind Christine Klein	Mord	Die unzüchtigen Handlungen sind verjährt	Todesstrafe	Totschlag daher bereits verjährt	Todesstrafe	
	Frau Berta Kühn	Mordversuch in Tateinheit mit versuchter Vornahme unzüchtiger Handlungen		10 Jahre Zuchthaus	gefährliche Körperverletzung	10 Jahre Zuchthaus	
	Kind Rosa Ohliger	Mord in Tateinheit mit gewaltsamer Vornahme unzüchtiger Handlungen		Todesstrafe	Totschlag	Todesstrafe	
	Maschinist Rudolf Scheer	Mord		Todesstrafe	Totschlag keine Ueberlegung	Todesstrafe	
	Hausangestellte Maria Hahn	Mord in Tateinheit mit gewaltsamer Vornahme unzüchtiger Handlungen		Todesstrafe	Totschlag keine Ueberlegung	Todesstrafe	
	Fräulein Anne Goldhausen	Mordversuch		10 Jahre Zuchthaus	gefährliche Körperverle...		Urteil:
	Frau Mantel	Mordversuch		5 Jahre Zuchthaus	gefährliche Körperver...		9 × zum Tode,
	Arbeiter Kornblum	Mordversuch		5 Jahre Zuchthaus	gefährliche Körperverl...		15 Jahre Zuchthaus,
	Kind Hamacher	Mord in Tateinheit mit gewaltsamer Vornahme unzüchtiger Handlungen		Todesstrafe	keine Ueberl... Totschla...		...tellung unter Polizei...
	Kind Luise Lenzen	Mord in Tateinheit mit gewaltsamer Vornahme unzüchtiger Handlungen		Todesstrafe	keine Ueberl... Totschl...		...fsicht und
	Gertrud Schulte	Mordversuch in Tateinheit mit versuchter Notzucht		15 Jahre Zuchthaus	gefährlic... Körperverle...		...berkennung der bür...
	Hausangestellte Ida Reuter	Mord in Tateinheit mit vollendeter Notzucht		Todesstrafe	keine Ueberl... Totschl...		...rlichen Ehrenrecht...
	Hausangestellte Elisabeth Dörrier	Mord in Tateinheit mit gewaltsamer Vornahme unzüchtiger Handlungen		Todesstrafe	keine Ueberl... Totschl...		...f Lebzeit.

Peter Kürten, the 'Monster of Dusseldorf'   *Express Features*

A chart of some of Kürten's murders and attempted murders
Express Features

Fritz Haarmann, homosexual mass murderer   *Express Features*

Haarmann's house (left of picture) on the river Leine in Hanover

10 Rillington Place, the dismal house in which Christie and Evans lived   *LEA*

Left: Digging in the garden of 10 Rillington Place. On the extreme left is a pathologist. C.I.D. men are digging. The men bending over the table on the right are forensic scientists.   *LEA*

Below left: Christie and his wife
Mirrorpic

Below: Evans, his wife and baby
Mirrorpic

Sex murderers: England and France

In murder motivated by sexual frustration, as distinct from sexual love, Germany holds the unwanted palm. Yet England has its share of undoubted sex murderers. It is not always easy to decide whether frustration or monetary gain is the prime motive in such cases, for example, as that of John George Haigh, who said that he killed people because he wished to drink their blood, but who certainly profited considerably from the deaths of the several people whom he killed and disposed of by tipping their bodies into drums filled with sulphuric acid.

There is no doubt about the primacy of the sexual motive in the case of Neville Heath, whose passion for whipping women reminds us that flogging is still regarded as the characteristic English vice by the rest of Europe. The case of Heath became particularly notorious because after he had killed and sexually mutilated a woman named Margery Gardner no photograph of him was issued to the press, and before his arrest he killed and mutilated another girl. Yet there are good reasons for the reluctance of the British police to issue press photographs of suspects, the prime one being that they tend to nullify identification by witnesses at a later stage.

Was Heath insane? A jury decided that he was not, and he was hanged at Pentonville in October 1946. Was John Reginald Halliday Christie insane? Again a jury rejected the plea, and Christie also was hanged in 1953. Almost ever since that time a controversy has continued about the guilt of Timothy Evans, who lived in the same wretched house as Christie, and who had been convicted in 1949 of strangling his wife and baby daughter. Christie admitted to four murders, including that of Mrs Evans, although not of the baby. He was a typically aberrant sex murderer, in the sense that his sex instinct could be stimulated only by intercourse with his victims while they were unconscious, or perhaps already dead.

Were two murderers really resident in the same house, or had Evans been hanged for a murder that he did not commit? One official enquiry came to the conclusion that he was guilty, but thanks in part to the efforts of Mr Ludovic Kennedy, whose *Ten Rillington Place* presents strongly and logically the case for Evans's innocence, another enquiry was held in 1965. The result of it is not yet known. The passion of Evans's defenders can, of course, be devoted only to the task of clearing his name.

The *Police Gazette* photograph of Heath, not reproduced in the press *Mirrorpic*

Lucien Léger, 'the Strangler of Paris', had like Jack the Ripper a passion for writing letters to the newspapers. He wrote in all thirty-three letters, signed 'the Strangler', boasting of killing a small boy in the forest at Verrières and of other crimes. Images of excretion abound in these letters which justify his crimes as attempts 'to put pressure on society and make it vomit its bloody pus and money'. When arrested, Léger proved to be a harmless-looking young man. Taken back to the forest to reconstruct the crime he broke down, wept, and asked to be returned to his prison cell.

Lucien Léger, 'the Strangler of Paris' *Express Features*

Lonely hearts and lesbians

The case of Fernandez and Beck is the most famous Lonely Hearts murder case, but it is also psychologically interesting, because the effect of these two people on each other was so disastrous. 'Some strange and inexplicable alchemy', as one writer has put it, was set in motion by their meeting, an alchemy that led to multiple murder.

In November 1947, Martha Beck received a letter from a Lonely Hearts club to which a friend had sent her name as a joke. She was an intelligent trained nurse, head of a school for crippled children in Florida. She had been a very fat girl and remained a fat woman, with sexual urges for which she rarely found an outlet, but she had never been in trouble with the law. Raymond Fernandez, a Hawaiian-born Spanish American, was a seaman who had worked for British Intelligence during the war. He seems to have suffered a personality change when he was hit on the head by a falling hatch in 1945. It was later learned that the blow had left a scar on his brain tissue, and after it he engaged in a headlong career of seduction and swindling. He operated through Lonely Hearts clubs, and claimed to have seduced a hundred women in two years. When he met Martha he realized that she had no money, and escaped from her after two days. She then attempted to commit suicide, and her suicide note was sent on to him. Trapped – for he could not contemplate the publicity that would be involved in her suicide – he invited her to New York.

This was the beginning of a relationship that lasted a little over a year. When she knew of Fernandez's swindles Martha enthusiastically co-operated in them as his sister. She was, however, frantically jealous and when Fernandez 'married' his victims did her best to prevent consummation of the affairs by sharing the bride's bed. They drugged a woman in Arkansas who later died, murdered a sixty-six year old widow

Raymond Fernandez and Martha Beck. A night out at the Bowery Follies in New York *UPI*

Juliet Hulme (*left*) and Pauline Parker *RTHPL*

This looks like a standard 'bondage' picture of the kind sold in bookshops specialising in erotica. In fact it is the prelude to murder. Harvey Glatman of San Diego advertised for girls who would pose for glamour photographs, tied them up (whether with their consent or not is uncertain), took his photograph, and then untied, raped and killed them. He killed three girls in this way, and was arrested while attempting a fourth murder *UPI*

in Albany, and then got in touch with Delphine Downing, also a widow, who lived in Grand Rapids, Michigan, with her small child. When the couple went up to see her Delphine was charmed by Raymond and thought Martha 'loads of fun'. Marriage was quickly arranged, but there was trouble because Raymond broke the promise he had given Martha that he would not have sex relations with any other woman. One night after Delphine threatened to withdraw from the marriage arrangements (she had been shocked by seeing Fernandez without his toupee and realizing that he was bald) Fernandez shot her. A day or two later Martha killed the child. They buried the bodies in the cellar, where the police found them after neighbours became curious about the whereabouts of Mrs Downing.

There is no death penalty in Michigan and the trial was transferred to New York, where the couple were charged with the murder of the widow in Albany. In August 1949, they were sentenced to death, and two years later they went to the electric chair.

There is something pathetic about the relationship of Juliet Hulme, a fifteen-year old schoolgirl living in New Zealand who was well known for her meekness and politeness, and sixteen-year old Pauline Parker.

They lived in a fantasy world not unusual among the young, in which they wrote letters to each other assuming different imaginary identities. They had an erotic relationship, and 'enacted how the saints would make love in bed', as Pauline Parker put it in her journal, but this was not the primary force leading them to the murder which they seem to have carried out in a spirit of make-believe.

Pauline hated her mother, and wished that she would die. She discussed ideas for killing her with Juliet, but the discussions had always a kind of never-never-land quality, and the pleasure derived from them seems to have been in discussion rather than in genuine planning. On 20 June 1954, Pauline wrote in her journal that they had talked about 'our plans for moidering mother and made them a little clearer', adding casually, 'I want it to appear either a natural or an accidental death'. When it occurred three days later it was quite obviously neither, for a stocking-wrapped brick was found beside the body as it lay in a park, and the girls' tale that Mrs Parker had slipped and banged her head was plainly untrue. It seems likely that Pauline turned fantasy into reality in an explosion of unreasoning hatred when she struck her mother on the head with the brick. At their trial they were found to be sane, and sentenced to detention for an indefinite period. They were both released in 1958.

Kidnapping as threat

The threat of kidnapping, if it is made to timid people, offers the chance of making a fortune without the risks attendant on the actual snatch operation. There is no problem about finding a safe place in which to keep the kidnapee, no argument about whether he must be killed or shall be allowed to go free. On the other hand, the extortionist who works by threat of kidnapping alone must be prepared for the threatened man to go to the police.

This was done by Lloyd R. Smith, President of the A. G. Smith Corporation, when he received a letter in April 1933, telling him that he would be kidnapped if he did not pay $20,000. Since no instructions were given for delivering the money, the police advised Smith to await further developments. They came in the form of weekly threatening letters, designed purely as part of a softening-up process, which still did not mention any meeting place. Unsuccessful attempts were made to trace the typewriter on which the letters had been written. At last the fifth letter arrived (reproduced opposite), appointing a place and time to leave the money. A detective resembling Smith obeyed the instructions. He left the money in marked bills in a can under the highway signpost and then drove away. The watching detectives posted nearby saw the can slowly begin to move, apparently of its

own volition, into a nearby field. When it had gone far enough for them to be certain that it was being pulled away by a wire previously attached to it, the police acted. As the man collected the money from the can and ran, they shot and killed him. He was Frank H. Jess, who with his partner Oscar Mueller, ran an unsuccessful garage business in Wauwatoso, Wisconsin. Mueller, arrested later, made a complete confession.

A more vicious and ingenious extortion threat was made twenty-one years later against the whole Jewish community of Dallas. An oil dealer named James Hollis Jones, together with his brother Ralph, singled out Julius Schwepps, a civic leader in Dallas, as the principal target and as collector. Twenty families received letters threatening them with death by dynamite, gunfire and acid if they did not pay extortion money through Schwepps. The pressure on Schwepps and his relatives was intense.

Schwepps was in touch with the F.B.I. from the beginning, and a package was made up and left at the suggested spot, near a muddy railway embankment. James Hollis Jones collected it and, when challenged by F.B.I. men, fought a gun battle with them which ended in his arrest. He and his brother both received long prison terms.

Louis Schwepps (*left*), one of the victims of the 1954 extortion scheme against Jewish families in Dallas, Texas, and (*right*) James Hollis Jones *UPI*

Dear Sir ;-
Mr. L.R.Smith
2220 N. Terrace Ave.
Milwaukee Wis.

to ask you for the $25,000.00 This is the very last time we are goin,
it will be to bad for you we got you do not come across wit
ute .If the cash is delived with no interfers of the law or
police you will be 100% safe.
######

Go west on Wisconsin Ave. out on highways. 18 19 and30
as far as the Sunnyslope Road turn left on the Sunnyslope
Road about two hunderd feet is a highway sign on the left
hand side of the road by the sign is a box you place the
money in the box and close it and go on your way.

#######

The time for you to be there is sharp ten oclock at
night the day of May 1933. Your last chance Mr.Smith
to obey the orders we hope you good luck.
If the money is in the box you will be safe if on
one interfers with it in the next twenty four hours.

YOUR LAST CHANCE CASH OR YOUR LIFE.

Truly Yours
Gang Of CLDNSF.

The fifth and last letter demanding
money sent to Lloyd R. Smith, and the
first one which told him where to leave
the cash   UPI

Oscar Mueller under interrogation by
Milwaukee's Chief of Detectives, Frank
J. Probaska, after his capture   UPI

GREAT MODERN CASES

The Rosenbergs

Julius and Ethel Rosenberg leaving court after the rejection of their clemency appeal by the President in February 1953 *UPI*

Rosenberg's engineering shop at his firm, Pitt Engine Products, shortly after his arrest *UPI*

There are two important questions in relation to the Rosenberg case. The first is whether they were correctly found guilty of selling atomic secrets to the Soviet Union, and the second is whether, assuming the verdict to have been the right one, they should have been executed.

For most people, and certainly many Americans, the Rosenbergs' guilt is obvious. They were accused

by Ethel's brother David Greenglass when he confessed to stealing atomic secrets, by his wife Ruth, and by half a dozen other people involved in the 'atom spy' case. Yet certain doubts do exist, based partly on the fact that almost all the evidence against the Rosenbergs was of the 'guilt by association' kind, and partly on the unlikelihood of Greenglass having the knowledge to obtain the information he is said

18 June, 1953. A special session of the United States Supreme Court meets to decide whether a surprise stay of execution for the Rosenbergs granted by Justice William O. Douglas (*front row, extreme right*) shall be vacated. They decided that the execution should not be stayed *UPI*

19 June, 1953. The man who threw the switch that ended the Rosenbergs' lives was Joseph Francel, State executioner for the previous fourteen years. His fee was $150 for each execution *UPI*

18 June 1953. Demonstrators gather at Pennsylvania Station, New York, en route to Washington to plead for clemency *UPI*

Afterwards, flowers in Paris. They were placed at the foot of the Tuileries Gardens wall where Nazis shot members of the French Resistance in 1944 *UPI*

to have passed on in 1944 and 1945. The doubt may be small, in view of the immense amount of testimony against the Rosenbergs, but it is often voiced outside the United States.

About the proper answer to the second question there is less doubt. Assuming the Rosenbergs' guilt, the death penalty in American law was applicable only to spying in wartime, and no civil court had previously imposed it. Some of the secrets had been passed on during the war, but from 1941 to 1945 the Soviet Union had been an American ally. Was the Espionage Act (1917) meant to apply to the sale of secrets to an ally? Supposing the secrets had been passed to France in 1945, would the Rosenbergs have been executed? Few people would say so. The truth is that the trial took place when the Korean war was being fought, when McCarthy was at the height of his power, when war with Russia was expected within a year or two, when American Radicalism was everywhere in retreat. These were the basic reasons why the sentence was passed and carried out. It was natural that the clemency pleas which came in millions from all over the world should have infuriated many Americans at the time, but it is likely that many of those directly involved in making the decision now regret what was done.

The crime that was not

In April 1953, the body of a girl was found on the beach about fifteen miles south of Rome. Her name was Wilma Montesi, she was the daughter of a carpenter, and she had died of drowning. A few weeks later rumours were spread both by the Communist and neo-Fascist press that they could say something more about her death if they wished. If the girl had been paddling and had fainted, as was said, where was her suspender belt? There was a joke that carrier pigeons had brought it into police headquarters and that there it had been destroyed. Pigeon in Italian is *piccioni*, and Attilio Piccioni was the Foreign Minister. In January of the following year Silvano Muto, the editor of a Right-wing weekly, published an article pointing out that the body had been found near a hunting resort and hunting lodge run by a syndicate of which the secretary was a Sicilian named Ugo Montagna. At the lodge, the article said, there were parties, drugs, orgies. At one of these parties Wilma Montesi had died . . .

Muto was put on trial for publishing falsehoods. The source of his information proved to be a girl named Anna Maria Caglio, who was found living in a Florentine convent. From the convent she emerged to give evidence which became steadily more lurid. She had been Montagna's mistress, she had heard Montagna receive a curious telephone call from Piero Piccioni the Foreign Minister's son, she thought she had once seen Montesi. Orgies? She had not taken part in them, but she had heard that things were done 'which cannot be described'. Drugs? Well, Montagna had a cupboard with a special lock on it, and she had always thought that the source of his enormous earnings was a dirty one. She believed that he had once tried to poison her at dinner. She had been with Montagna to see a flat which he was giving to the Italian Chief of Police, Tommaso Pavone. And she could say more. At length she did say more, in a 'testament' which was found in the Post Office, and was dramatically read by the Judge. 'I know the character of Ugo Montagna and Piero Piccioni', she wrote. 'I am afraid of disappearing and leaving no trace behind. Alas, I know that the head of the gang of drug-traffickers is Ugo Montagna . . . He is responsible for the disappearance of many women. He is the brain of the gang while Piero Piccioni is the murderer.'

Caglio had been called 'the Black Swan' from the beginning of the case, but now a grateful press and nation acclaimed her courage in speaking out and renamed her Italy's Joan of Arc. Piccioni was arrested and charged with 'culpable homicide', in English terms criminal negligence, leading to Wilma Mon-

Piero Piccioni, waiting for a vaporetto after the day's hearing at the Venice court   *Keystone*

Anna Maria Caglio, the 'Black Swan'   *Keystone*

Ugo Montagna, Marquis of San Bartolomeo *Keystone*

Ezio de Sanctis, the clairvoyant
Keystone

Cinema actress Alida Valli, who confirmed Piccioni's alibi *Keystone*

tesi's death. Montagna and the head of the Roman
police, Saverio Polito, were charged with complicity.
Pavone resigned. Piccioni the Foreign Minister offered
his resignation, which was refused.

Their trial took place three years later in Venice.
They were all acquitted. It is amazing that they
should ever have been charged. There was no evidence at all to show that Montesi had ever met Piccioni or Montagna. If she had engaged in orgies
they were strange ones, for she was still a virgin.
Piccioni had an unbreakable alibi, supported by film
actress Alida Valli among others, showing that he
had been in Amalfi when Montesi drowned. There
was nothing to link Montagna with drugs, although
it was true that Caglio had been his mistress. Among
the more farcical aspects of the Venice trial was the
appearance of two professional clairvoyants who
supported Caglio's story. One of them, Ezio de
Sanctis, who practised under the name of 'il Mago
Orio', said that Montesi had visited him with Piccioni
in Milan, at a time when she was certainly in Rome.
Sentenced to eighteen months' imprisonment for
perjury he promptly retracted his evidence and was
released.

And Caglio? She repeated and considerably ela-
borated her previous evidence. 'If you'd seen the
filthy things they did in that house', she said. But

people no longer thought of her as Italy's Joan of
Arc, and the Court's verdict on the case implied
what had always been plain: Wilma Montesi had
died of natural causes. And her missing suspender
belt? Perhaps, as one of the witnesses timidly suggested, she wasn't wearing one.

The spot at Tor Vaianica where Wilma
Montesi's body was found *Mondadori*

A criminal dies

There is undoubtedly something tiresome about those who demonstrate in support of what they think are good causes. Their protests often have a 'holier-than-thou' element about them, the person or object for which they demonstrate becomes automatically virtuous in their eyes, and many of them give point to the old joke: 'What are we protesting against this week?' Most of them assumed that Caryl Chessman, who went to the gas chamber in May 1960, was innocent, missing the point that the death sentence was an outrageous punishment even if he was guilty.

Caryl Chessman, born in 1921, was a habitual criminal who had served several prison sentences. He was accused, in January 1948, of twice in three days stopping young women who were riding in cars, leading them at gun point over to his car, and there forcing them to perform oral copulation. He then released them, without injuring them in any other way. What, then, was the 'Red Light Bandit', as he was calling from the flashing red light on his car, accused of? Indecent assault? Rape? Not at all. He was accused of kidnapping the two women with intent to rob with bodily harm, and in the State of California kidnapping is punishable by death. The charge of kidnapping seemed ludicrous to every other country in the world, and no doubt to many other Americans outside California. That the death sentence should have been passed and carried out for this offence still seems hardly credible. It should be added that there is considerable doubt about whether Chessman was the 'Red Light Bandit', and that he himself in his last statement said: 'In my lifetime I was guilty of many crimes, but not those for which my life was taken.'

That is the Chessman case. What chiefly shocked world opinion was the cat-and-mouse legal game played with Chessman for more than eleven years. He was sentenced to die in July 1948, and he then survived seven execution dates by making various appeals. Dozens of different organizations, thousands of individuals, expressed their horror at the idea of a man waiting eleven years between life and death, and many of them could not be dismissed with the label 'progressive'. The Vatican paper, *L'Osservatore Romano*, called the waiting an 'excruciatingly slow agony' and suggested that 'he has expiated his guilt, however grave, because a more severe penalty than this does not reasonably exist'. During his eleven and a half years in Death Row Chessman became famous. A forty-five minute film, *Justice and Caryl Chessman*, was made about him, and a recording of 'The Ballad of Caryl Chessman' became immensely popular on juke boxes. He wrote three books about his life in prison and his attitude towards it, and the first of them, *Cell 2455 Death Row*, was a best seller. He painstakingly educated himself through the prison library, and impressed people who met him as humane, reasonable and intelligent.

Part of Chessman's plea for life was that during his years in prison he had become a different and better man, and there seems no reason to doubt that he had. The change in him is a tribute to the prison authorities. Just before his execution he wrote: 'Now that the state has had its vengeance, I should like the world to consider what has been gained.' The world did consider, and decided that Chessman's execution was the worst blot for years on the forms of American justice and legal procedure.

March 1960. Caryl Chessman makes the cover of *Time*   UPI

Chessman confers with two of his attorneys, George Davis and Rosalie Asher   *UPI*

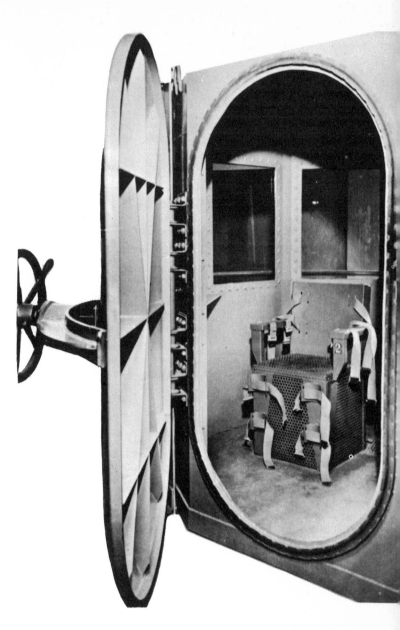

The gas chamber at San Quentin in which Chessman died   *UPI*

Demonstrators both against capital punishment and against Chessman's execution gathered outside San Quentin prison. Some wept when they learned of his death.   *UPI*

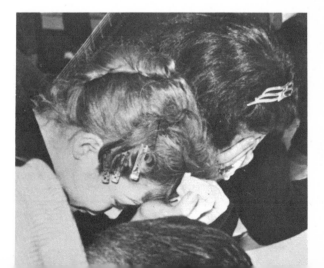

2 May 1960. Attorney Dayton M. Harrington leaving the U.S. Supreme Court after filing a last-ditch appeal for a stay of execution. Justice William O. Douglas rejected it.   *UPI*

253

Mandy Rice-Davies *Keystone*

Christine Keeler *Keystone*

Matters of scandal and concern

Stephen Ward was a successful society osteopath. He also organized communal sex parties and had a string of young attractive girls whom he introduced to well-known men. One of the girls was Christine Keeler, who was very fond of West Indians, and another was 18-year old Mandy Rice-Davies. One of the men who had sex relations with Christine Keeler for a short time was the War Minister in Macmillan's Government, John Profumo.

These unremarkable facts were the basis for an extraordinary outburst of British hypocrisy when the case came into the headlines after one of Christine's West Indian friends fired shots at her home and another, 'Lucky' Gordon, made a scene outside the Old Bailey. Profumo first lied about his association with her, which had ended months earlier, and was then forced to resign when the lie became known. Christine had also had sex relations with Captain

Aloysius 'Lucky' Gordon under police restraint outside the Old Bailey after trying to approach Christine Keeler, April 1963
Keystone

Stephen Ward (*on left*) arriving at the Old Bailey, July 1963
Keystone

Ivanov, a Russian attaché, and it was suggested that the affair might have endangered national security. Ward was placed on trial for living on immoral earnings. A parade of prostitutes entered the witness box at the Old Bailey, some apparently enjoying themselves like Mandy, others uneasy or indignant. Before the trial ended Ward, deserted by the influential friends for whom he had provided girls, committed suicide by taking an overdose of drugs. A Royal Commission presided over by Lord Denning buried the whole affair in a Blue Book, in true British fashion.

The salad oil and liquid fertilizer scandals in the United States were of great financial importance. Tony de Angelis, who set out to make almost a corner in soybean oil, had a shady background. He paid top prices for his oil, but was able to sell it extraordinarily cheaply. The miracle was managed by loans from many of America's biggest finance houses, loans on which Tony gave part of his salad oil stocks in the enormous tanks at Bayonne, New Jersey, as collateral. Not until he had taken the financial establishment for nearly $200 million did Wall Street learn that they had lent money on the basis of faked warehouse receipts saying that the Bayonne tanks contained oil, whereas many of them were simply filled with water. De Angelis received a 5 year sentence.

In March 1963, almost a year before the salad oil scandal broke, Billie Sol Estes had received a 15 year sentence for fraud in relation to his liquid fertilizer empire. In Billie Sol's case public indignation was all

Senator John McClellan, chairman of the Senate Investigation Committee into the Estes case, demonstrates the improbability of the accepted version of Henry H. Marshall's death *UPI*

the greater because he was such an apparent model of the American success story, and also a paragon of civic and domestic virtue. His frauds could only have been carried out with complicity by some Government officials, and there was a strong suspicion of foul play about the death of Henry H. Marshall, the Department of Agriculture official who, in May 1961, had been the first person to sniff something wrong about Billie Sol. Early in June Marshall was said to have shot himself with a bolt action rifle, but it was demonstrated that this was almost impossible. His death, like other aspects of the case, remains unexplained.

Tony de Angelis, President of the Allied Crude Vegetable Oil Refining Company *UPI*

The tanks at Bayonne. Where was the salad oil? *UPI*

Billie Sol Estes, a model of civic virtue *UPI*

Some of Billie Sol's liquid fertilizer tanks at Peco, Texas *UPI*

Calculation and passion

There are few stranger cases of murder prompted by consuming passion than the killing in 1951 of a medical student named Felix Bailly by his former mistress and fellow-student at Lille, Pauline Dubuisson. The case is remarkable because their love affair had been over for eighteen months when they met again in Paris in March 1951, and during that time (and indeed before it, and in the course of their relationship) she had had many other lovers, including two of her professors at Lille University. Nevertheless, when they met again and she learned that he was engaged to be married to another girl, she decided to kill him and then herself, and rather oddly announced this intention to her landlady in Lille who in turn warned Bailly. He wisely took the threat seriously enough to ask some student friends to act as bodyguards, but less wisely let Pauline into his flat one afternoon when he found her waiting on the stairs. She shot him, and tried but failed to commit suicide by gassing herself. Later she cut her wrists in another suicide attempt. Her demeanour at her trial was one of contemptuous calm, although she wept when the counsel for Bailly's parents said: 'You make a mess of your suicides, but you succeed all right with your murders.' One of her tutors at Lille had remarked on her haughtiness, and she showed no emotion when, in front of a crowd which she said reminded her of 'the raving mobs of the Revolution', she was found guilty of what in America would be called second degree murder, and received a life sentence. It upsets preconceived ideas about nymphomaniacs – and Pauline Dubuisson undoubt-edly was one – that she should have had such strong feelings about a particular individual.

Lorraine Clark's murder of her husband was, like Pauline Dubuisson's, a mixture of calculation and passion. To all appearances she was the contented wife and mother (she had three children) of an electronics engineer. The degree of her discontent is shown by the fact that, when Melvin Clark was away from home, she attended parties in her Boston suburb where wife-swapping went on in the form of a game at which husbands threw down door keys for women to pick up. On 10 April 1954 Melvin Clark returned home unexpectedly, and found his wife with a man. In the quarrel that followed after the man had left she stabbed him with a darning needle and then killed him with two shots from a revolver. She trussed the body with wire, drove to a bridge that crossed a nearby river, attached weights to the legs (see picture) and heaved the body into the river. Six weeks later it was found and identified, and under interrogation she confessed to the murder. Her 'Guilty' plea to a charge of second degree murder was, a little surprisingly, accepted, and she was sentenced to life imprisonment.

The passion of Pierre Jaccoud overbore the sense of calculation that might have been expected of a man who was the senior lawyer in Geneva and the leader of the local Radical party. He must have been almost out of his mind with jealousy when, on learning that his mistress was having an affair with a man much

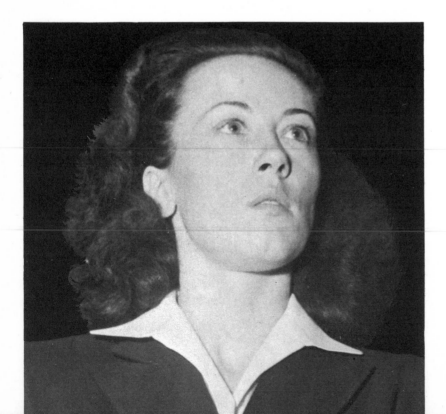

Pauline Dubuisson, who shot her former lover Felix Bailly. 'I wanted to force myself to love other people, in order to persuade myself I was capable of having lasting sentiment for him', she said *Keystone*

Right: The lawyer Pierre Jaccoud, head of the Swiss Bar Association, looks thoughtful while he listens to an expert witness *Keystone*

A demonstration of the way in which Lorraine Clark disposed of her husband's body
UPI

Lorraine Clark   *UPI*

younger than himself, he wrote the man a series of abusive and obscene anonymous letters. The man, a radio technician named André Zumbach, guessed that Jaccoud was the letter writer, and threatened to expose him. Jaccoud was a bungling killer. He went to Zumbach's house intending to kill him and to get back the letters, but when surprised by the young man's father was forced to kill the old man instead. Jaccoud was convicted at his trial in 1960 largely on the testimony of medical experts about a blood-stained dagger which was found in his home. He received what seems the light sentence of only seven years' imprisonment, and even this was reduced at a later date to three years.

'I was never quite sure about Dr Sam'

The Sheppard case roused more controversy than any other murder trial in the decade of the fifties. Dr Sam, as he was generally called, still has many passionate adherents who believe that the greatest possible injustice was done to him. Others are content to accept the jury's verdict that, on 3 July 1954, Sam Sheppard killed his wife Marilyn during a quarrel, a crime which in Ohio is second degree murder, 'intentional slaying without premeditation'.

Sam and Marilyn Sheppard had been married for nine years. They lived in a pleasant white house on the shore of Lake Erie in Bay Village, a suburb of Cleveland. They had a son, and there was another child coming. Sam Sheppard, an osteopath, and his two doctor brothers, practically ran the Bay View hospital as a family possession. The Sheppards look at first glance like the perfect American couple.

What happened on the night of 3 July? Some friends came in, and left at about 12.30 a.m. Then, by Sheppard's own account, his wife went upstairs, and he fell asleep on the sofa. He was wakened by a scream, rushed upstairs, saw misty figures grappling together, and was knocked out. He recovered sufficiently to stagger into the garden and down to the beach house, where he was knocked out again. When he came to (he was very vague about times) he went back to the house. Marilyn was dead. There were thirty-five wounds on her body, made by some instrument which was never found. Sheppard, with a puffed cheek, a swollen eye, and a hair-line fracture of a vertebra, was taken to hospital by his brother.

The whole of this story was disbelieved by the

Sam and Marilyn Sheppard water skiing *UPI*

A view of the Sheppard estate. 1 is the house where Marilyn Sheppard died. The arrows to 2 show the route Dr Sheppard says he took to the beach house 3, where he was knocked out. The jurors can be seen looking over the summer house 4. The garage is at 5, and the swing used by the Sheppard's son is 6 *UPI*

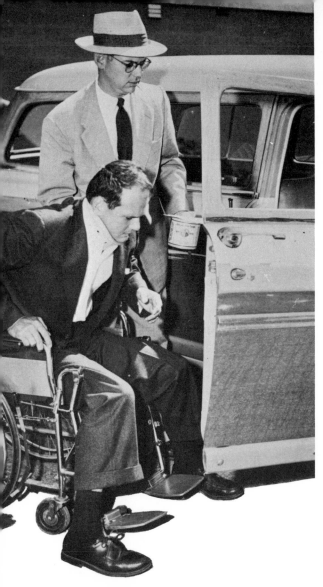

Sheppard leaving hospital. The prosecution said his injuries were self-inflicted *UPI*

police. Their case, as presented at the trial, was that the attack was a fabrication, that Sheppard's injuries were self-inflicted, and that his vertebra was not fractured. (Two X-ray plates told different tales, and surprisingly enough the point was never finally resolved.) The motive? He had been carrying on an affair with an attractive laboratory technician for two years, he had kissed at least one other patient, he had complained of his wife's 'lack of sexual aggression', and had talked of a divorce. There are other minor aspects of the case – a perfunctory attempt at burglary had been made, and the prosecution ascribed this to Sheppard – but those are the essentials. Was Sheppard telling the truth? The jury decided against him. He was paroled in 1964 and settled down with his second wife, who had written to him in prison expressing her passionate belief in his innocence.

The controversy has died down, although it was revived briefly in 1957 when a convict serving a ten-year sentence confessed to the murder. It was the twenty-sixth such confession, but this one was more convincing than most, although it left out certain vital details.

The Supreme Court in 1966 overturned the verdict because too much publicity influenced the outcome of the case. The prosecution has not yet decided whether to try Dr Sam again.

Was Sam Sheppard just a little too good to be true? This is certainly the feeling one has in reading accounts of the case, a feeling well expressed by Mrs Ahern, who with her husband visited the Sheppards on the night of the murder. There was no doubt of Marilyn's affection, she said, but 'I was never quite sure about Dr Sam'.

Sheppard on the witness stand, with a special orthopaedic collar round his neck *UPI*
Susan Hayes after she gave evidence *UPI*

Ten years later. Dr Sheppard, released on parole, and his second wife Ariane *UPI*

The Black Widow and Ronald Chesney

Marie Besnard was a little woman with a pasty face and thick glasses, and she dressed almost always in black. The result of her trial in 1952, in the Palais de Justice at Poitiers, seemed at first to be a foregone conclusion. Its dramatic ending fascinated the whole of France. She was accused of poisoning no less than eleven people in the little town of Loudun where she lived. They included her father, her husband's father, mother and sister, and eventually her husband too. Most of the victims were in their sixties and seventies, or even older. The motive was said to be personal gain – when her husband died the whole of his considerable family property came to her. The method was arsenic, which was said to have been found in all of the bodies.

The prosecution built up what looked like a formidable case. Marie Besnard, known alternatively as the 'Black Widow' or the 'Good Lady' of Loudun was a bad, vague witness on many important points. Had she put something in her husband's soup? She could not remember. Had she tried to bribe a witness to change her story? Again she said: 'I don't remember.' The prosecution case went swimmingly until Dr Beroud, the Marseilles police toxicologist who had made the arsenic analyses, took the stand. Then, under merciless examination by Maître Gautrat for Marie Besnard, it was revealed that the boxes of remains sent for analysis to Marseilles had been hopelessly mixed up. In one case eight boxes had been sent and ten arrived, one of them containing an eye which could not possibly have belonged to its attributed body. A bad day for Dr Beroud ended when he identified the contents of three glass tubes as containing arsenic, only to be told that there was arsenic in none of them. Dr Beroud retired discomfited, and did not appear on the following day. He had had an accident going home in the fog and moreover, he said, 'I did not come to the Assizes to have arguments with the defence experts, nor to pass examinations'. When Maître Gautrat went on to assert that the prosecution had become utterly confused about the amounts of arsenic in the bodies the case was hurriedly adjourned, and four French medico-legal experts went to work on the specimens with the help of an atomic pile and a Geiger counter.

Dr Beroud dubiously examines the glass tubes *Central Press*

The 'Black Widow', Marie Besnard, in court *LEA*

At the resumed trial the charges were reduced in number so that they involved only six persons, and the method used led to a battle of the experts to end all such battles. Was the nuclear physical test a useful and accurate one? British atomic experts offered their opinion that it was not. The French experts were indignant – national honour was at stake. Maître Gautrat suggested that arsenic might have got into the bodies through the arsenic-laden water in the cemetery, and then – the final stroke – a prosecution expert was called who said that some of his colleagues were old fashioned and that they had been using very dubious methods.

At this point the prosecution gave up. The case was officially adjourned while yet more medical experts pronounced on it, but they have never done so. Marie Besnard was freed. She had been in prison for nearly five years.

In February 1954, a man who called himself Ronald Chesney ended his life by shooting himself through the head in a wood near Cologne. Before he died he confessed to his German girl friend that in 1926, when he was a boy of seventeen, he had murdered his mother. He had been tried for the crime, and acquitted.

Young Donald Merrett, already a heavy-featured boy six feet tall who looked like a man in his twenties, was a student at Edinburgh University and lived in the city with his mother, who had parted from her husband. 'Donald is doing well at the University and is quite settled down to the life here', she wrote to a friend, but Donald was far from settled. He was cutting his classes, going on the town secretly, and forging his mother's name on cheques. He was very eager to get a new motorbike which cost nearly £140, but had no money to buy it. One day Mrs Merrett was found shot behind the ear, and although Donald immediately said that she had shot herself, the gun belonged to him. During the fifteen days that she lingered between life and death demanding to know what had happened to her, Donald forged and cashed several cheques and paid £70 off the motorbike. After his mother's death he was charged both with murder and with forgery.

He would almost certainly have been convicted but for the dogmatism of Sir Bernard Spilsbury, who appeared for the first time in his life as a defence witness, about powder blackening round the wound. There was no sign of blackening, and the prosecution said that this proved Mrs Merrett had not committed suicide, because traces of powder must have been left. Spilsbury denied this, and said that bleeding and washing of the wound would have eliminated them. The jury believed the man who had a reputation for infallibility. Donald Merrett went to prison

for twelve months on the forgery charge. He never got the motor bike.

During the next quarter of a century Ronald Chesney, once Donald Merrett, squandered a fortune of £50,000 and lived by theft and blackmail, interspersed with spells in prison. During the war he became commander of a small ship and used it for smuggling. He was a roaringly genial man, an enormous eater, drinker and spender. In 1954 he determined to get back some £8000 which had been settled on the wife he married when first released from prison. She had left him shortly afterwards, but they still met occasionally. He shaved off his beard, took off his piratical gold earring, put on horn-rimmed spectacles, and flew over from Germany to England with a false passport. He then went to see his wife, who ran with her mother an old people's home in Ealing, stupefied her with drink and drowned her in the bath. As he was leaving the house he was seen by his wife's mother, and had to kill her also. Then he flew back to Germany. But he had been seen leaving the house, and Scotland Yard put out a 'Wanted' notice for him and got in touch with Interpol. For the boy who had wanted a motor bike and the man who had lived so riotously, it was the end of the trail.

Ronald Chesney, shortly before his death *Mirrorpic*

The case of Wilbert Coffin

In June 1953, Eugene Lindsay, his seventeen-year old son Richard and a friend of Richard's named Frederic Claar left their Pennsylvania home on a bear-hunting trip in the wild Gaspe part of Quebec province. Rather more than a month later, when they had failed to return, a search was made for them and their dead bodies were found. The elder Lindsay's wallet was intact, but he had been carrying nearly $1000 which had disappeared. The three hunters had been dead for some time, their bodies had been reduced to skeletons, and it was at first thought that they had been killed by bears, but young Lindsay's sweat shirt and windbreaker had bullet-holes in them, and round the hole in the sweatshirt was a large spot of blood. Their abandoned truck was found some distance away.

The police quickly arrested a mining prospector living in the district named Wilbert Coffin, who admitted that he had seen the Americans on 10 June, when their truck had broken down. Coffin said he had helped them to get it going, and that they had given him $40. As his movements were built up in detail, the evidence against Coffin seemed very strong. A man had seen a rifle sticking out of the back of his truck, and after the murder he had driven to Montreal paying for things along the road – and paying off old debts – with a trail of U.S. $20 bills, leaving extravagantly large tips. In Montreal he had deposited with his mother-in-law what proved to be Claar's suitcase with some of his clothes in it, a pair of binoculars and a new gasoline pump. Coffin's trial at Gaspe, conducted in both French

and English, with six French-speaking and six English-speaking jurors, lasted seventeen days. The jurors took only three-quarters of an hour to find him guilty. In February 1956, after the failure of several appeals, he was hanged.

The rights and wrongs of this apparently straight-forward case are still furiously debated. Papers publish cartoons like one showing a worried-looking bear saying to its hibernating mate: 'In your place I would not sleep calmly – they are talking about the Coffin case again.' A book published two years ago, *J'Accuse les Assassins de Coffin*, brought its author a month in jail and a $3000 fine, a sentence which was reversed on appeal.

Coffin's defenders believe that he was judicially murdered because a culprit for the killings was urgently needed to save the tourist trade. His defence was conducted with such ineptness that no witnesses were called on his behalf, and he did not take the stand. Hearsay evidence favouring the prosecution was admitted, but a good deal of rather vague evidence favouring Coffin was never called. A jeep was said to have been seen near the truck after Coffin had left it, a note is said to have been written by one of the murdered hunters after Coffin had left the Gaspe area on his way to Montreal. The note (if it ever existed) mysteriously disappeared, and so did the so-called murder weapon.

What about the money and Claar's suitcase? Coffin's story, not told at the trial but submitted in appeal briefs, was that he had not told the whole truth at his original interrogation. He had found

The cabins used by the murdered bear hunters   *Toronto Star*

Police search for weapons in one of the cabins   *Toronto Star*

The abandoned truck. The pictures gives an idea of the wildness of the country.   *Toronto Star*

the unattended truck, had come across a bottle of whisky in it which he drank while waiting for somebody to turn up, and as he grew drunker had decided to take some of the equipment. He supplemented his original explanation about the money by saying that some Gaspe people for whom he worked had paid him in U.S. dollars. The thinness of this story may partly explain the reluctance of Coffin's lawyers to put him on the stand. There is no doubt that the investigation and trial left something to be desired, but that is not the same thing as saying that he was innocent.

Mining prospector Wilbert Coffin   *Toronto Star*

Eugene Lindsay and his son Richard, two of the hunters   *Toronto Star*

Taking up the cabin floor

In August 1952, Arthur James Kendall, a labourer working in a wild area of Ontario infested by bears and rattlesnakes, took his five children away from the small wooden cabin in which he had been living with them and his wife and went to stay with a woman named Mrs Hogue. He explained the move by saying that he and his wife had had a row, and that after hitting him with a teacup she had walked out. Mrs Kendall was known to be much attached to the children and her friends and relatives did not believe this story. They reported her disappearance to the police.

A thorough investigation and a search of the surrounding district revealed nothing to contradict Kendall's tale. The three eldest children were interviewed, and although their manner was evasive they confirmed that their parents had quarrelled, that their father had driven away in the car (as he said 'to cool off') and that their mother had then packed her things in a shopping bag and walked out. Police enquiries continued, but without result. In 1959 Kendall swore an affidavit that he had not seen or heard of his wife for seven years. A Judge agreed that she should be presumed dead, and he married Mrs Hogue.

When his children Margaret and Ann Kendall married and left home, however, they made statements to the police saying that their father had killed their mother and dragged her body out of the house. He had later wiped the floor clean of blood. They had been eleven and nine years old at the time, and ever since had gone in terror of their lives. Could these statements be supported? Mrs Kendall's body was never found, but by the considerable feat of taking up the whole cabin floor in sub-zero temperature and transporting it undamaged to Toronto, the girls' story was confirmed. The wiping marks were plainly visible, and scrapings from the floor were identified as blood. In October 1961, more than nine years after the crime, Kendall received a death sentence which was later commuted to life imprisonment.

A small section of the cabin floor in the Kendall case, much enlarged. It shows marks of having been wiped, and the stains were identified as blood. The whole floor was removed and transported in sub-zero weather   *Attorney-General's Laboratory, Ontario*

Meryem Simsek, a thirteen-year old girl living in Izmir, Turkey, was jealous of her half-sisters, five-year old Nergul and two-year old Ayten. She said that her stepfather treated his own children kindly but often beat her, and did not allow her to sit at table with the rest of the family. When first Ayten and then Nergul died, certificates were given that the deaths were from natural causes, but a local midwife noticed marks on Nergul's neck, and it was found that she had been strangled.

Under interrogation Meryem admitted killing both the girls. She had given Ayten a peach soaked with D.D.T. and had strangled Nergul with a necklace. (She is holding the bottle and necklace in the picture.) When arrested Meryem shrugged her shoulders. 'What can be done now?' she asked. 'I am sorry that I killed them.'

Right: Meryem Simsek holds up the tools of murder   *Express Features*

Cafer Guler and Zeki Ozalp, two Turkish villagers. In October 1963, they attacked two young German tourists camping out in a tent, shot the man and raped and then shot the girl. Other villagers tried by lynch them   *Express Features*

The Public Prosecutor stands at the spot where the murderers buried the German girl, Renate Colschen, hurriedly covering her grave with stones   *Express Features*

Right: Egyptian murderer Aly Hammoude calmly illustrates his method of strangulation. This 17-year old Cairo wall painter had killed four children and was arrested while attacking a fifth
Express Features

An Australian mystery

One of the most interesting unexplained crimes of recent years began when, about 9 o'clock in the morning of 2 January 1963, some schoolboys found two dead bodies near a river bank just outside Sydney. They proved to be those of Gilbert Bogle, a former Rhodes scholar and expert in physics who held an important post in the Commonwealth Scientific and industrial Research Office, and Margaret Chandler, the wife of an official in the C.S.I.R.O.'s Division of Radiophysics. Bogle and Mrs Chandler had both been at a New Year party which they left at about 3.45 a.m., and it must have seemed at first a simple case to the police investigators, a matter probably of a love affair and a suicide pact.

It proved to be not at all simple. Bogle was happily married, with four children. He was about to take up a new job in the United States. Margaret Chandler was also happily married, with two children. Bogle and Mrs Chandler did not know each other particularly well, it was pure chance that he had driven her home that night, and sexual intercourse had not taken place between them. Mysteries piled up. Both victims had been violently sick, and it was thought that Bogle had stopped the car because they felt ill. But then why was he wearing only shoes, shirt and socks, with the rest of his clothes neatly rolled up beside him? Why was she wearing brassiere and slip, with her skirt rolled up to the waist? Why was her body fifty feet away from his? And why were both bodies covered, his with an old carpet thought to have come from the car boot and hers with cardboard from beer cartons? It seemed

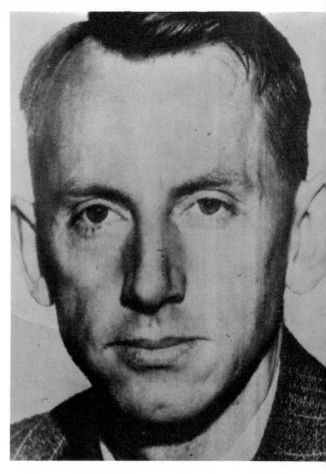

Dr Gilbert S. Bogle. How and why did he die? *Keystone*

A remarkable picture taken a few seconds before Little's death. The police fired over the chicken house in which Little and his foster-daughter Susan Lyon were hiding. Little shot the girl and then killed himself *Keystone*

that a third person must have been on the scene at some time, and the official view veered from suicide to murder. Bogle and Mrs Chandler had obviously been poisoned, and no doubt the poison would soon be discovered.

The poison was not discovered. After weeks of analysis the Police Laboratory accepted the offer of help already made by R. H. Thorp, Professor of Pharmacology at Sydney. But the professor was baffled too. He came to the conclusion that both victims had been poisoned, and that the poisoner was 'virtually a biological genius'. There the case rests. Nobody knows whether Bogle and Mrs Chandler took poison by accident or whether it was administered to them deliberately. Nobody knows whether it was a plant poison or a synthetic compound. Such a case as this shatters the comfortable illusion that all poisons leave unmistakable traces, an idea which forensic scientists know to be erroneous, and it prompts the thought that some of the new techniques now developed might have produced results in this case.

The caravan in which William Stanley Little killed Reginald Hunter   *Keystone*

There was nothing mysterious about the case of William Stanley Little, which provided a spectacular end to the year in Australia which had begun with Bogle's death. Little was a quiet, unobtrusive bush worker in the back country of New South Wales, 450 miles from Sydney. On 19 December he shot dead both Reginald Hunter, a building contractor in Oaklands where he lived, and P. C. Howe, Oakland's only policeman. The cause of the shootings remains uncertain.

Little then fled with his foster-daughter, 14-year old Susan Lyon, and became the object of a search of all the back country stations, made by aircraft, police and armed civilians. He was eventually found in his home area, hiding in a chicken shed with the girl. Shots were exchanged, but although Little shot at his pursuers they fired over the roof of the shed in the hope that Susan would remain unhurt. More shots were fired, and then Sergeant Shearer gallantly crawled to the chicken shed in an attempt to catch Little by surprise. He found that the hunted man had shot his foster-daughter and had then put a bullet through his own head.

The end of the hunt. Ambulance men remove the body of Susan Lyon from the chicken house. Armed policemen look on   *Keystone*

The bombs in the planes

That a man should blow up an airplane, killing innocent people to get rid of his wife seems unlikely; that he should find two accomplices who casually agreed to help him is almost beyond belief, yet this happened in Canada in September 1949. A Canadian Pacific Airlines DC 3 on a local flight from Quebec to a point three hundred miles away was ripped by an explosion twenty minutes after it left the airport, and crashed into the side of a steep hill. The passengers, sixteen adults and three children, and the crew of four were killed instantly. One of the passengers was Rita Guay, who had been sent by her husband, a jewellery salesman, to pick up two suitcases containing rings and watches which he had left at a place named Baie Comeau. The crime had been arranged in order to dispose of her, so that he could marry the former waitress with whom he was having an affair.

Since his unfaithfulness was well known, Guay wanted his wife to die in a way that would bring no suspicion on him. He had at one time offered a friend five hundred dollars to kill Mrs Guay by putting poison into a bottle of cherry wine, but the man thought he was joking. He found a more receptive listener in Marguerite Pitre, a neighbour of his in Quebec's Lower Town. Herself a petty criminal and abortionist, she responded to his request as though it were the most natural thing in the world to help a man to kill his wife. When Guay decided that a bomb in a plane was a safe murder method they consulted her brother, a crippled jeweller and watchmaker named Généreaux Ruest.

Their proceedings were amazingly careless. Ruest found difficulty in putting the dynamite into the alarm clock he was rigging up, and when a miner came into his shop said exultantly, 'Here's a man who can tell us about dynamite!' Mrs Pitre on another occasion proposed to a taxi driver she knew that he should take the Guays plus bomb for a ride in the country. At a certain point he and Guay would make an excuse to get out, and the bomb would go off. The man refused, not on moral grounds but because he did not want to lose his taxi. In the end Ruest made the bomb and parcelled it up, Mrs Pitre took it to the airport in a taxi, and shipped it on the plane, and it exploded.

Guay had calculated that the plane would be over water when the bomb went off, and had the flight from Quebec not started late there might have been no useful clues. He was traced because the airline, a subsidiary of the Canadian Pacific Railway, were determined to find out why the plane had exploded. Working closely with the Mounted Police they found through the cargo manifest that one parcel had been shipped to what proved a non-existent adress. The background of every passenger was carefully checked, and Guay's affair with his waitress was discovered. The taxi driver described the dark woman he had taken to the airport, and the description tallied with that given by the waitress of Mrs Pitre. When the driver saw and identified Mrs Pitre, the arrests were only a matter of time. All three of them were hanged.

There have since been several other attempts to

Albert Guay *Toronto Star*

Généreaux Ruest, the jeweller who made the bomb *Toronto Star*

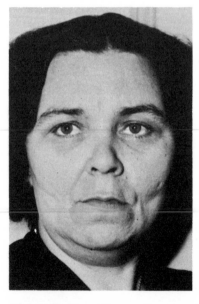

Marguerite Pitre. Why not blow up a taxi? *Toronto Star*

Part of the wreckage of the DC 3 in the Guay case. The doll is a reminder that three small children were on board   *Toronto Star*

emulate Guay, all except one of them abortive. In 1955 a United Airlines plane exploded in mid air near Denver, Colorado, and F.B.I. men investigating the crash found that the mother of John Gilbert Graham, who had a criminal record, had travelled on the plane. Graham had taken out a travel insurance on her life and was her sole beneficiary. His bomb was also made from an alarm clock and dynamite, but he had no accomplices. Graham died in the gas chamber in 1957.

John Gilbert Graham in court at Denver   *UPI*

District Attorney Bert Keating points to a model of the United Airlines DC 68 plane in which 44 people died   *UPI*

Mad and Sunday bombers

For some years New York was subject to occasional bomb scares and explosions, ascribed to a character called by the press 'the Mad Bomber'. There seemed to be no purpose in his operations, and not all the bombs went off. Nevertheless, he was undetected until Alice Kelly, a worker at Consolidated Edison, found a letter in their compensation files from one George Metesky, in which she recognized immediately the very same characteristics as those in a letter written by the 'Mad Bomber' to a New York newspaper. Metesky, a 53-year old toolmaker from Waterbury, Connecticut, was found by psychiatrists to be incapable of standing trial, and sent to a mental home.

The exploits of the 'Sunday Bomber' in 1960 were much more serious than those of Metesky. On five Sundays out of six he exploded bombs in public places where they were likely to injure people and to do the maximum amount of damage. The most serious of these incidents was that in which a bomb went off inside a subway car, but the bomb exploded on the Staten Island ferry might well have caused even more casualties. It is likely that the 'Bomber' was on the ferry, but police examined and questioned passengers without result. Did the Sunday Bomber's operations express a hatred of Sundays, of authority, of people? They stopped suddenly and he was never identified.

Unexploded bomb wrapped in a steel envelope, in the centre aisle of New York's Paramount Theatre, 28 December 1956 *UPI*

Alice Kelly, 25-year old assistant at Consolidated Edison, who identified the 'Mad Bomber' through a letter *UPI*

George Metesky, the 'Mad Bomber', after his arrest in January 1957 *UPI*

270   One of Metesky's home made bombs, 10 inches long. He had planted 32 of them over a period of 16 years *UPI*

First exploit of the 'Sunday Bomber', 2 October 1960. A bomb rocks Times Square, injuring six people *UPI*

Sunday Bomb No. 2, which exploded in front of New York Public Library, 9 October 1960 *UPI*

23 October 1960. A bomb on the Staten Island ferry *Knicker-bocker* blows a hole in a cabin and splinters several cross beams. No casualties *UPI*

6 November 1960. The fifth and worst of the Sunday bomb explosions. This one went off in a subway car, killing a woman and injuring twelve other people *UPI*

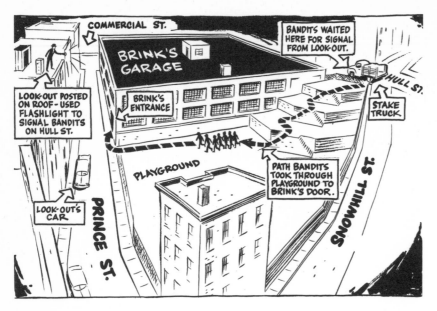

An artist's impression of the planning of the Brink's robbery in Boston. The bandits got away with nearly $ 1,250,000 *UPI*

Some of the money found by detectives in Faherty and Richardson's Boston apartment *UPI*

Brink's and the Early Bird

In 1950 Brink's North Terminal Garage in Boston was robbed of nearly $1,250,000 in one of the best-organized robberies in U.S. history. A great deal of money was kept at Brink's before being sent out in security trucks, and for eighteen months eleven professional criminals led by Anthony Pino studied the set-up meticulously, and made several 'dry runs' in preparation for the robbery. Under the noses of the lax Brink's watchmen Pino and his men padded about the whole place in stockinged feet. They learned just where the money was kept, which way every door swung. They removed the locks from the doors, made keys for them, and refitted the locks before leaving. They even broke into a burglar alarm company one night, so that they could study the details of Brink's alarm system.

When the time came everything worked smoothly. Seven of the bandits, wearing grotesque masks, gloves, and crepe-soled shoes, unlocked the doors, walked into the vault where five Brink's men were counting the cash, held them up with pistols, and took the money. Others kept watch, as shown in the drawing. The whole raid was over in twenty minutes.

The perfect robbery? Very nearly. Although F.B.I. agents and local police knew the names of most of the bandits, they had no proof against them until 'Specs' O'Keefe, who had taken part in the raid, resented being (as he said) gypped out of $63,000, and turned informer. Within days the rest of the

gang were arrested. At their trial they were sent down for long prison terms.

Eleven years after the Brink's robbery a branch of the Bank of Nova Scotia in Montreal was cleaned out of 377 safe deposit boxes, the contents of which totalled more than $4 millions. It was the biggest haul in the history of the North American continent. Three days later a warrant was issued for the arrest of a pudgy but athletic playboy named Georges LeMay, who although he had previously been suspected of a number of crimes had never served a prison sentence. Within a short time the police arrested some of LeMay's assistants, but the wanted man himself had vanished. He had been missing for more than two years when, in a test of the recently-launched Early Bird telecommunications satellite, Scotland Yard, the F.B.I. and the R.C.M.P. flashed pictures of wanted men on the screen in the hope that they might be recognized. Sure enough, a boatyard worker at Fort Lauderdale, Florida, identified the picture of LeMay as that of the owner of a sloop named the *Tirana*. The man called himself Rene Roy, but when the police took his prints they matched those of Georges LeMay.

Light-heartedly offering his sloop for sale at the bargain price of $25,000 because he wouldn't need it for a while, LeMay was removed to Dade County jail in Florida, and for maximum security put into

Six years later eight arrested men await trial on a total of 169 indictments. James Faherty and Thomas F. Richardson are second and third from left. Anthony Pino, the planner of the raid, is fifth from left *UPI*

an interior cell without windows. While the lengthy extradition proceedings went on he did his customary press ups – and then, what the Early Bird satellite had so notably achieved was undone by human frailty. Georges LeMay somehow got out of his cell (two guards were charged with helping him escape), rode in the elevator up to the seventh floor, tied a power and water cable to a radiator, slid ninety feet down it, dropped the remaining fifteen feet to the ground, and stepped into a waiting car. Neither the Early Bird nor ordinary police investigation has yet found him.

The 'Early Bird' satellite transmission, 2 May 1965, contained an exchange of 'Wanted' persons between Scotland Yard, the F.B.I. and the R.C.M.P., which led to the arrest of Georges LeMay *Wide World*

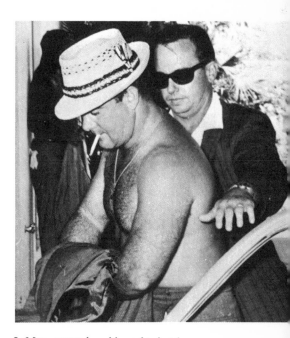

LeMay, arrested on his yacht, is taken in charge *Wide World*

President Kennedy, his wife Jacqueline and Governor Connally driving from Love Field, Dallas, before the assassination *AP*

A picture taken seconds after the shooting. The President has slumped forwards into his wife's arms *UPI*

A President dies

The death of President John F. Kennedy is in the tradition of meaningless assassination. Nothing was changed by it, neither U.S. foreign nor domestic policy, nor any of the ideas for which Kennedy stood. Simply, a man had died.

On 22 November 1963, President Kennedy's cavalcade, and the car in which he was riding with his wife and Governor Connally, went along the planned route from Love Field airport, greeted by cheering instead of the expected hostile crowds. It came down Main Street to the corner of Main and Houston, passing the city jail and the courthouse. The cavalcade turned to the right into Elm Street, with a little park on the left and a school book depository on the right. Three shots were fired. The President and Governor Connally were both hit, and although an operation was performed on the President it did not save him.

The overwhelming likelihood, in spite of books and articles written to the contrary, is that the killer was a neurotic chip-on-shoulder Communist named Lee Harvey Oswald, that he used the rifle found in the depository, and that he acted alone rather than with the aid of any political group or party. There are minor inconsistencies in the account of what happened issued by the Warren Commission's report, among them the speed and accuracy with which this indifferent marksman apparently fired, but on the whole it fits the facts. Some of the inconsistencies may have their origins in the confused stories told by the Dallas police, who seem to have acted with an ineptness crowned when, two days after Kennedy's death, Oswald was shot and killed

The window in the schoolbook depository from which the shots were fired *UPI*

Lee Harvey Oswald after his arrest *UPI*

The shooting of Oswald by Jack Ruby in the basement of Dallas Police Department. The figure beside Oswald is Dallas Police Captain Will Fritz, who had headed the investigation *UPI*

in the police headquarters by a man named Jack Ruby, while the police stood by. Oswald's death was watched on television by the biggest audience for any crime in history. It may well be that, as the Dallas police boasted, the case was already tied up, but Oswald had not spoken – about his reasons, his possible backers or even about his guilt – and he will never speak now.

The rifle found in the depository *UPI*

Robert Kennedy with Jacqueline Kennedy as the coffin containing the President's body is put into an ambulance on arrival at Washington *AP*

275

Bandits drove round perimeter road and out of disused gate to Staines-road

Bandit cars parked here before raid

Cars waited here and drove off down one-way street after the raid

Bandits got out of lift in foyer as money arrived

The robbery at London Airport, in November 1962, provided the cash used in the Great Train Robbery   *Mirrorpic*

The Great Train Robbery, part one

The train travelled regularly from Glasgow in Scotland to London. It had twelve mail coaches, and one of them always contained bags of money sent down to London East Central Post Office. In the early hours of 8 August 1963, the train was stopped by means of a false signal made by placing black paper over the green light and connecting a bulb and batteries permanently to the red. Thirty men jumped the train, hit the driver over the head – he was the only man seriously hurt – disconnected the first two coaches, and forced the driver and firemen to take the engine and these coaches forward half a mile. The raiders, wearing balaclavas that showed only their eyes, broke into the coach with money in it and took the mail bags. Their total haul was over £2,500,000.

That is the short story of the Great Train Robbery, the biggest and one of the best organized jobs of its kind, except for one disastrous piece of carelessness, in the history of crime. Up to the present time less than £500,000 of the money has been recovered. Of the four principals Bruce Reynolds and 'Buster' Edwards have not been caught, Charles Wilson made his escape from a maximum security prison where he was serving a 30 years' sentence, and Douglas Gordon Goody is serving a similar sentence. Most of the minor figures are in prison, although Ronald Biggs made a sensational prison escape in July 1965.

The Great Train Robbery was not only a planner's job. Money was spent on it in advance, in thousands rather than hundreds of pounds. The money came from a robbery at London Airport, which in its audacity exceeded even the train robbery. On 27 November 1962, a sum of £62,500 was brought into the Airport office, put on a trolley and wheeled to a lift to be taken up to the bank above. Three stockbroking types were standing near the lift when the security men pressed the button, wearing bowler hats, dark overcoats, and striped trousers, and carrying rolled umbrellas. When five men who had been waiting in the lavatory upstairs for the money to arrive stepped out of the lift wearing balaclavas and masks, they quickly overpowered the guards with the help of the apparent stockbrokers. Two stolen Jaguars swept up, the robbers got into them with the money, and the cars drove out of a disused exit, on which the chains had been snapped with a pair of bolt-cutters.

The lift in Comet House at London Airport from which the bandits pounced on the security guards. The stolen money was in boxes on the trolley   *Mirrorpic*

Bruce Reynolds, the chief planner of the robbery *Keystone*

Aerial view of the robbed mail train, showing the engine and two carriages standing in Cheddington Station *Keystone*

Wilson and Goody were tried and acquitted. Mickey Ball, who received a 5 years' sentence, said: 'You won't get me for the big job, anyway.'

Much of the money stolen from the airport went on getting specialists to work on the 'big job', and probably, though this was not proved, in bribery of Post Office and railway personnel. There was careful organization, and a high degree of co-operation and restraint was exercised. It did not, however, extend to the share-out. There was insistence that this should take place as nearly on the spot as possible. Leatherslade Farm, twenty miles from the robbery in Buckinghamshire, was bought to serve as a temporary hiding place where the money could be split up.

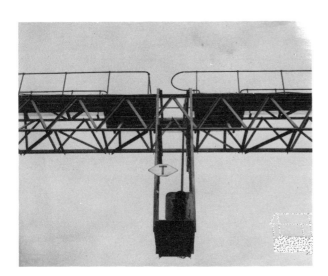

The signal and gantry where the raiders changed the lamps *Mirrorpic*

The Royal Mail van at Cheddington Station *Keystone*

An aerial view of Leatherslade farm, with the police searching the grounds *Mirrorpic*

The Great Train Robbery, part two

Leatherslade Farm was the downfall of the conspirators. It was a lonely property, and there were several routes by which it could be reached. In fact the robbers had no difficulty in getting there unobserved. So far, so good. But the stooge purchaser put up to buy it operated through the firm of solicitors which had defended the accused men in the London Airport case. That was foolish enough, but even more stupid was the neglect of discipline by which the strict injunction that everybody should wear gloves was ignored. The robbers, with the exception of Goody, neglected this precaution because they knew that one of them had arranged for somebody to come in, wipe away all prints, burn the mailbags, and remove all other traces of their presence. The length of time that they stayed at the farm after sharing out the money is still uncertain. It may have been as short as thirty-six hours, as long as five days. Their alarm seems to have been sudden, and they left in a hurry. But the conspirator they had relied on failed them. No clearing up was done at all. When the police arrived, tipped off by locals who had belatedly realized that something odd was going on, they found the mailbags intact and prints all over the place. Within days most of the robbers had been arrested and some of the money had been found – nearly £50,000 in a London telephone kiosk, over £100,000 in some woods near Dorking in Surrey, and £30,000 in a nearby caravan. Of the four leaders Reynolds got away after some hairbreadth escapes, and so did Edwards. Wilson was caught at his

Kitchen ware and camping equipment found at the farm. Fingerprints were left on many of the articles *Mirrorpic*

Some of the food stocks at the farm *Mirrorpic*

£30,000 was found hidden in this caravan near Box Hill, Surrey. Another £100,000 was discovered in the woods nearby   *Keystone*

Three of the minor conspirators being led into the magistrates' Court at Linslade, Bucks   *Keystone*

own house, and Goody was arrested while visiting a girl friend in Leicester.

They were tried at Aylesbury in Buckinghamshire, in January 1964, and because the number of the accused made it impossible to use the old Assize Court, the Rural District Council Offices were used to try the case. There was one sensational incident when John Thomas Daly, one of the accused, was acquitted. His fingerprints were on a Monopoly game found at the farm, but his counsel successfully argued that the set was not new and that the prints might have got on to it at some other time. Otherwise the only surprise was the severity of the sentences, which in the cases of several of the men was 30 years' imprisonment. If men were to receive such a sentence for a crime so

little marked by violence why, it was asked, should other robbers refrain from extreme violence on another occasion?

Since sentence was passed in March 1964, the case has been often in the headlines, first because of Wilson's escape, then because of the daring and carefully-planned escape of Biggs, most recently through the arrest of James White, one of the minor conspirators, who had been living quietly by the sea in Kent. There have been constant rumours of other escape plans, particularly for Goody. Some of the robbers still have plenty of money. The police are eager to find those who have consistently evaded capture. The last has certainly not been heard of the greatest train robbery of all time.

Charles Wilson   *Mirrorpic*
The scene of Wilson's escape, Winson Green Prison, Birmingham. A plank and ladder were found propped against the wall of the mental home nearby   *Mirrorpic*

How Ronald Biggs escaped from Wandsworth Jail, London. A rope ladder was thrown over the wall from the top of a pantechnicon, which had a trapdoor in its roof. Biggs and three other prisoners climbed the ladder, dropped through the roof, and ran to the getaway cars   *Mirrorpic*

Bibliography

Volumes of the Notable British Trials or Famous Trials series are devoted to many of the cases in this book, and these have not been listed. In relation to other cases I have generally listed only what seemed to me the most useful work. To take one example, there are many books dealing with the Tichborne Claimant, but Mr Douglas Woodruff's *The Claimant* is the most comprehensive of them.

Publication dates given are those of the first English edition, except in relation to books marked with an asterisk, which signify the first American edition.

H. L. Adam *Oriental Crime* 1908

H. L. Adam *The Police Encyclopaedia*, 8 vols 1920

H. L. Adam *Murder by Persons Unknown* 1931

M. S. Allen *Lady in Blue* 1936

Kenneth Allsop *The Bootleggers* 1961

Sir Robert Anderson *Criminals and Crime* 1907

H. Asbury *The Gangs of New York* 1928

H. Ashton-Wolfe *The Underworld* 1926

H. Ashton-Wolfe *The Thrill of Evil* 1929

T. B. L. Baker *War With Crime* 1889

J. Belin *My work at the Sûréte* 1950

James Berrett *When I was at Scotland Yard* 1932

William Bolitho *Murder for Profit* 1926

Douglas G. Browne and A. Brock *Fingerprints: 50 years of scientific crime detection* 1937

Douglas G. Browne and E. V. Tullett *Bernard Spilsbury, His Life and Cases* 1951

Wenzell Browne *Introduction to Murder* 1953

Thomas Byrnes *Professional Criminals* 1882*

Caryl Chessman *Cell 2455 Death Row* 1954

Caryl Chessman *Trial by Ordeal* 1956

Allen Churchill *Ivar Kreuger* 1960

Allen Churchill *A Pictorial History of American Crime 1849–1929* 1964*

C. Cook *Prisons of the World* 1891

Russell Crouse *Murder Won't Out* 1932*

P. Coremans *Van Meegeren's Faked Vermeers and de Hooghs* 1949

J. C. Curry *Indian Police* 1932

P. Curtin *Noted Murder Mysteries* 1914

C. R. M. Cuthbert *Science and the Detection of Crime* 1958

Harold R. Danforth and James D. Horan *The D.A.'s Man* 1958

George Dilnot *The Story of Scotland Yard* 1926

Louis Ducloux *From Blackmail to Treason* 1958

T. S. Duke *Celebrated Criminal Cases* 1910*

Henry Faulds *Guide to Fingerprint Identification* 1905

S. T. Felstead *Sir Richard Muir, Public Prosecutor* 1927

E. Ferri *Criminal Sociology* 1905

J. K. Ferrier *Crooks and Crime* 1928

J. B. Firth *A Scientist Turns to Crime* 1960

Peta Fordham *The Robbers' Tale* 1965

A. J. Forrest *Interpol* 1955

R. B. Fosdick *European Police Systems* 1915

R. B. Fosdick *Crime in America and the Police* 1920

Sir Francis Galton *Fingerprints* 1892

Sir Francis Galton *Memories of My Life* 1908

F. P. Geyer *The Holmes-Pitezel Case* 1896*

Frank Gibney *The Operators* 1960

Jean Giono *The Dominici Affair* 1956

S. S. Glueck *Crime and Justice* 1936

D. Graham and Hugh C. Gray *The Application of X-Ray Techniques in Forensic Investigation (in* X-Ray *Focus)* 1965

Arthur Griffiths *Mysteries of Police and Crime* 2 vols 1898

Hans Gross *Criminal Investigation* 1907

F. A. Hare *The Last of the Bushrangers* 1892

Richard Harrison *The C.I.D. and the F.B.I.* 1956

Sir Edward Henry *Classification and Uses of Fingerprints* 1900

W. J. Herschel *The Origin of Fingerprinting* 1916

Christopher Hibbert *The Roots of Evil* 1963

Paul Holmes *The Sheppard Murder Case* 1962

J. Edgar Hoover *Persons in Hiding* 1938

J. D. Horan and Howard Swiggett *The Pinkerton Story* 1950

J. E. Horwell *Horwell of the Yard* 1947

Christmas Humphreys *The Great Pearl Robbery of 1913* 1929

Sir Travers Humphreys *Criminal Days* 1946

Sir Travers Humphreys *A Book of Trials* 1953

H. Montgomery Hyde *Sir Patrick Hastings, His Life and Cases* 1960

H. B. Irving *Studies in Nineteenth Century Crime* 1901

H. B. Irving *The Book of Remarkable Criminals* 1918

H. B. Irving *Last Studies in Criminology* 1921

Joseph H. Jackson (editor) *San Francisco Murders* 1947*

Estes Kefauver *Crime in America* 1952

Ludovic Kennedy *Ten Rillington Place* 1961

Alister Kershaw *Murder in France* 1955

Charles Kingston *Dramatic Days at the Old Bailey* 1923

Charles Kingston *A Gallery of Rogues* 1924

Egon Larsen *The Deceivers* 1966

L. E. Lawes *20,000 Years in Sing Sing* 1932

W. L. M. Lee *A History of the Police in England* 2 vols 1901

Cesare Lombroso *Criminal Man* 1911

Cesare Lombroso *Crime: its Causes and Remedies* 1911

Donald McCormick *The Identity of Jack the Ripper* 1959

Sir Melville L. MacNaghten *Days of My Life* 1914

H. Mannheim (editor) *Pioneers in Criminology* 1961

Leonard Matters *The Mystery of Jack the Ripper* 1930

Norman C. Miller *The Great Salad Oil Scandal* 1966

C. A. Mitchell *Science and the Criminal* 1911

E. M. Morgan *The Legacy of Sacco and Vanzetti* 1954

F. D. Pasley *Al Capone* 1931

Michele Pantaleone *The Mafia and Politics* 1966

Edmund L. Pearson *Murder at Smutty Nose and other mysteries* 1927*

A. K. Perkons and R. E. Jarvis *Hair Individualization Studies* n.d.

A. K. Perkons and R. E. Jarvis *Trace Elements in Human Hair* 1966

M. W. Pinkerton *Murder in All Ages* 1898*

C. J. Polson *The Essentials of Forensic Medicine* 1955

R. F. Quinton *Crime and Criminals, 1876–1910* 1910

Edward Radin *Twelve Against the Law* 1950

Edward Radin *Lizzie Borden* 1961

Quentin Reynolds *Courtroom: the story of Samuel S. Leibowitz* 1950

H. T. F. Rhodes *Clues and Crime* 1933

H. T. F. Rhodes *In the Tracks of Crime* 1952

H. T. F. Rhodes *Alphonse Bertillon* 1956

H. de Rothschild *Pranzini* 1933

William Roughead *Classic Crimes* 1951

R. H. Rovere *Howe and Hummel* 1948

David Rowan *Famous European Crimes* 1956

Francis Russell *Tragedy in Dedham: the story of the Sacco-Vanzetti Case* 1963

Sir Harold Scott (editor) *The Concise Encyclopaedia of Crime and Criminals* 1961

E. Spencer Shew *A Companion to Murder* 1960

E. Spencer Shew *A Second Companion to Murder* 1961

E. H. Smith *Famous American Poison Mysteries* 1927

Sir Sydney Smith *Mostly Murder* 1959

Frederic Sondern *Brotherhood of Evil: the Mafia* 1959

V. Speer *Memoirs of a Great Detective: J. W. Murray* 1904

James Spenser *Limey* 1933

Philip J. Stead *Vidocq* 1953

Philip J. Stead *The Police of Paris* 1951

Irving Stone *Clarence Darrow for the Defence* 1941

Charles E. Still *Styles in Crime* 1938*

E. D. Sullivan *Look at Chicago* 1930

Julian Symons *Horatio Bottomley* 1955

Alfred Swaine Taylor *A Manual of Medical Jurisprudence, edited by Sir Sydney Smith and Keith Simpson* 2 vols 1956–7

Jurgen Thorwald *The Marks of Cain* 1965

Jurgen Thorwald *Dead Men Tell Tales* 1966

Tom Tullett *Portrait of a Bad Man* 1956

Tom Tullett *Dartmoor* 1966

John Toland *The Dillinger Days* 1963

Burton B. Turkus and S. Feder *Murder, Inc.* 1952

E. Villiers *Riddles of Crime* 1928

George Waller *Kidnap. The story of the Lindbergh Case* 1961

George W. Walling *Recollections of a New York Police Chief* 1887*

C. Walsh *Crime in India* 1929

F. P. Wensley *Detective Days* 1931

Frederic Wertham *The Dark Legend: a study in Murder* 1941

J. Wexley *The Judgment of Julius and Ethel Rosenberg* 1955

C. Whibley *The Book of Scoundrels* 1897

Henry A. White *Tales of Crime and Criminals in Australia* 1894

Don Whitehead *The F.B.I. Story* 1956

Colin Wilson and, Patricia Pitman *An Encyclopaedia of Murder* 1961

Sewell Peaslee Wright (editor) *Chicago Murders* 1945*

Douglas Woodruff *The Claimant* 1957

Horace Wyndham *Famous Trials Retold* 1925

Horace Wyndham *Crime on the Continent* 1928

Horace Wyndham *The Mayfair Calendar* 1925

Wayland Young *The Montesi Scandal* 1957

INDEX

Gautrat, Maître, 260, 261
Geissler, Gaston, 63
Gennas, the terrible, 137
Gentile, Nicola, 222
Germany, 211
    anthropometry in, 35
    capital punishment, 212, 213
    individual police forces, 16
    Köpenick hoax, 104-5
    police dogs, 26
    police methods, 188
    prisons, 93
    sex murderers, 240-41, 243
    teenage violence, 205
Ghent, 26
Ghiani, Raul, 210
Gibson, Eileen (Gay), 166-7
Gilchrist, Marion, 111
Giuliano, Salvatore, 222
Glasgow, 25, 51, 111, 186, 276
Glatman, Harvey, 245
Goddard, Calvin, 129, 174, 175
Goddard, Lord, 212
Goldman, Emma, 126
Gollin, John Lewis, 93
Goody, Douglas Gordon, 276,
    278, 279
Gordon, Aloysius 'Lucky', 254
Gordon-Baillie, Mrs, 69
Goron, Chef de la Sûreté, 62,
    63
Gouffé, 62, 63, 90
Graham, Daniel, 186, 187
Graham, John Gilbert, 269
Grant, General, 73
Gravelle, Philip, 174
Gray, Hugh, 186, 187
Gray, Judd, 8, 38, 132
Greenglass, David, 248
Griffiths, Peter, 184
Grizard, Cammie, 112
Grossmann, George Karl, 240
Guay, Albert, 268
Guichard, M., 126
Guiteau, Charles, 72-3
Guler, Cafer, 265
Gunness, Belle, 115, 126
Gusenberg, Frank and Pete, 139
Guthrie, Lord, 111
Guttentag, 63

Haarmann, Fritz, 240, 241
Haigh, John George, 243
Hall, Sir Edward Marshall, 123
Hamilton, Ontario, 160
Hammoude, Aly, 265

Harding, Warren, 140
Hastings, Sir Patrick, 123, 131
Hauptmann, Bruno Richard,
    236
Hay, Brecon, 125
Hayes, Susan, 259
Hays, Jacob, 18
Heath, Neville, 240, 243
Heidelberg, 64
Heirens, William, 234
Helle, Peippo Uolevi, 211
Hendon Police Training School,
    90
Henry, Sir Edward, 80, 81, 86
Henry, Major, 100
Herold, David, 70
Herschel, William John, 78, 79,
    184
Hesse-Darmstadt, 163
Heyer, Adam, 138
Hickman, William Herbert, 234,
    235
Hill, Mary E., 43
Hines, James J., 147
Hobbs, William Cooper, 107
Hoffa, Jimmy, 230, 231
Hoffert, Emily, 199
Hogue, Mrs, 264
Holland, 200, 212
Holloway Prison, 212, 219
Holmes, Harry Howard, 54
Hong Kong, 197, 198
Honoured Society, 220
Hooley, Ernest Terah, 108
Hoover, J. Edgar, 140, 144
Hope, Charles, 150-1
Hopewell, New Jersey, 236
Horsemonger Lane Gaol, 42
Howard, Frank, 239
Howard, Thomas, 48
Howe, 40
Howe, P.C., 267
Hulme, Juliet, 245
Hulten, Karl Gustav, 162
Hummel, 40
Humphreys, Mr Justice, 131
Hunter, Reginald, 267

Idsen, Teilmann, 86
Illinois State Penitentiary, 219
India, 88, 195
Interpol, 184, 196
Inzolia, Carlo, 210
Iraq Desert Patrol, 88
Isla da Pinos, 92, 93
Israeli Police, 190, 191

Italy:
    anthropometry in, 35
    capital punishment, 212
    carabinieri, 195
    drug smuggling, 196
    police, 188
    secret societies, 220, 221, 222
    teenage violence, 205
    vice, 207
Ivanov, Captain, 255
Izmir, Turkey, 265

Jaccoud, Pierre, 256-7
Jack the Ripper, 56-7, 243
Jacksonville, Florida, 97
James, Frank, 49
James, Jesse, 48, 49, 142
James, Robert, 8, 150
Japan, 78, 85, 183, 209
Jerome, William Travers, 103
Jervis, R. E., 178
Jess, Frank H., 246
Johannesburg, 54
Johnny the Bosch, 208
Johnson, Vice-President Andrew
    70
Jones, Charles T., 114
Jones, Elizabeth Maud, 162
Jones, James Hollis, 246
'Josef', 116
Joynson-Hicks, Sir William, 94

Kaleman, Petrus, 119
Kane, Detective Inspector, 110
Kansas, 60, 220
Karpis, Alvin, 142, 144
Kaser, Alfred, 239
Kay, 45
Keating, Bert, 269
Keeler, Christine, 254
Kefauver, 226
Kelly, Alice, 270
Kelly, Dan and Ned, 46-7, 48, 49
Kelly, Mary, 56
Kendall, Arthur James, 264
Kennedy, President John F., 7,
    274-5
Kennedy, Ludovic, 243
Kennedy, Robert, 230, 231, 275
Kerr, Francis M., 178
Ketchum, Edward, 67
Kiecorius, Edith, 239
Kinck, Jean, 55
King, James, 19
Koehler, Arthur, 236, 237
Koenigstein (Ravachol), 35